D0339920

Passport to Success

Passport to Success

The Essential Guide to Business Culture and Customs in America's Largest Trading Partners

JEANETTE S. MARTIN
LILLIAN H. CHANEY

Westport, Connecticut
London

Library of Congress Cataloging-in-Publication Data

Martin, Jeanette S.
Passport to success : the essential guide to business culture and customs in America's largest trading partners / Jeanette S. Martin and Lillian H. Chaney.
p. cm.
Includes bibliographical references and index.
ISBN 978–0–275–99716–8 (alk. paper)
1. Business etiquette. 2. Corporate culture. 3. Intercultural communication. 4. Industrial management–Social aspects. 5. United States–Commerce. I. Chaney, Lillian H. II. Title.
HF5389.M3753 2009
395.5'20973—dc22 2008028213

British Library Cataloguing in Publication Data is available.

Library of Congress Catalog Card Number: 2008028213
ISBN: 978-0-275-99716-8

First published in 2009

Praeger Publishers, 88 Post Road West, Westport, CT 06881
An imprint of Greenwood Publishing Group, Inc.
www.praeger.com

Printed in the United States of America

The paper used in this book complies with the Permanent Paper Standard issued by the National Information Standards Organization (Z39.48–1984).

10 9 8 7 6 5 4 3 2 1

Contents

Introduction

The globalization of business has made it imperative that companies conducting business abroad arm themselves with knowledge of the customs and manners of people of other countries, especially those with whom the United States conducts a majority of its international trade. Further, the composition of the U.S. workforce is becoming increasingly multiethnic, thus making it essential for workers in the United States to learn to understand people of other cultures to ensure that interactions with them are positive and productive. In addition, increased international travel has made knowledge of the culture and customs of people in other countries essential to avoid inadvertently offending them during cross-cultural encounters.[1]

When U.S. citizens go abroad, whether for business or pleasure, they understand that they are representatives of the United States and should, therefore, be concerned with behaving appropriately and using good manners to make a positive impression. The problem is that U.S. people naturally use their own norms as a guide to what is acceptable and appropriate in other countries. Unfortunately, using U.S. behavioral norms as a guide is a serious mistake. What is considered appropriate in one country could actually be offensive in another country; there is no international code for appropriate behavior.[2]

When interacting with people of other countries, making a *faux pas* when greeting and conversing with others, when exchanging business cards, when dining and exchanging gifts, or when gesturing can result in personal and professional embarrassment. Even what you wear may cause discomfort. In business situations the result may be the loss of a contract or may even be serious enough to close the door to future business relationships. Following are some examples of documented *faux pas* that have caused offense, resulted in embarrassment, or conveyed the impression that the person is insensitive, uncouth, or ignorant.

Greetings:

A well-known U.S. actor breached protocol by kissing the hand of Queen Elizabeth during a social function at the British Embassy in Washington, D.C.[3]

(Do not be the first to touch the Queen or any other member of the Royal Family.)

Conversational Customs:

During his first business trip to England, a U.S. businessman asked a man from Scotland about his wife and children. He was told it was none of his business.[4]

(Do not ask Scottish men personal questions.)

Business Cards:

A U.S. businessman used the business card of a Japanese person to dislodge food from between his teeth.[5]

(The Japanese treat business cards with respect; do not write on them, place them in your back pocket, or use them for a toothpick.)

Dining:

A frequent U.S. business traveler when dining at a restaurant during his first meeting in France initially drank red wine, then changed to white wine. The shocked expressions on the faces of others in the group spoke volumes.

(It is improper to drink a white wine after a red; the bouquet of the white cannot be enjoyed properly after having drunk a red wine.)[6]

Gift Giving:

When a U.S. person admired a valuable piece of folk art at the home of an Iranian friend, the Iranian insisted on giving it to her. The U.S. person, after initially refusing, accepted the gift.

(Do not express admiration of possessions of Middle Easterners, as many feel they must give them to you; continue to refuse when offered someone's possessions.)[7]

Gestures:

A U.S. office worker at a Japanese-owned company in the United States used a beckoning gesture (crooking the index finger) to indicate to her Japanese boss with limited English skills that she wished him to come to her desk to look at something. The office worker knew by the horrified expression on the boss's face that she had committed a serious *faux pas.*

(The office worker was humiliated to learn later that the gesture was obscene to the Japanese; her discomfort at inadvertently insulting her boss was so great that she eventually resigned.)[8]

Business Attire:

A columnist for the *New York Times*, while attending a business conference in Tokyo in July, wore a tan suit to a cocktail party. He said, "From the looks I got, I might as well have been wearing sandals, white socks, and a T-shirt with a beer company's logo."[9]

(Men visiting Tokyo do not wear anything but dark suits in business settings.)

Passport to Success: The Essential Guide to Business Culture and Customs in America's Largest Trading Partners contains information on the top 20 trading partners of the United States, according to U.S. export data provided by the U.S. Bureau of the Census. Based on 2007 data, the countries are Canada, Mexico, China, Japan, United Kingdom, Germany, South Korea, Netherlands, France, Taiwan, Singapore, Belgium, Brazil, Hong Kong, Australia, India, Switzerland, Italy, Israel, and Malaysia.[10] Following an introductory chapter and a chapter on the United States, a separate chapter for each of the 20 countries is presented. Countries are listed in alphabetical order, ending with a chapter on future U.S. trading partners.

Each of the country-specific chapters begins with data about U.S. exports to that country, followed by information divided into four major sections: country specifics, business and social customs, nonverbal communication, and travel tips.

Country Specifics:

Certain information about a country, specifically its location, topography, economy, population, ethnic groups, religions, time zones, and currency, is important to understanding the culture.

Business and Social Customs:

Knowledge of the business and social customs of a country can make the difference between building rapport with the host nationals and offending them. For each country the following topics are included: greetings, introductions, and business cards; business entertaining and seating customs; dining, toasting, and tipping customs; gift-giving customs; business meetings; dress and appearance; holidays; conversational customs; humor; attitude toward women in business; and public behavior.

Nonverbal Communication:

Successful intercultural interactions involve nonverbal communication. Such nonverbal behaviors as hand gestures may be positive in one country and insulting in another. Nonverbal topics covered for each country are gestures and posture, eye contact and facial expressions, space and touch, and punctuality and attitude toward time.

Travel Tips:

Travel tips include passport and visa requirements; tips for securing satisfactory hotel accommodations; suggestions for transportation in the destination country, including driving, public transportation, and taxis; emergency numbers to call when an ambulance, the police, or the fire department is needed; availability of public restrooms; and other guidelines for making your trip more pleasant, such as dates to avoid when scheduling trips and behaviors to avoid in order to make a positive impression.

References, including books, online sources, electronic media, and Web sites for international associations and consultants, are provided at the end of the book for individuals who are interested in additional information about these countries.

Passport to Success is a quick reference book for business professionals conducting business in the global marketplace; it is also useful for people traveling to the targeted countries for business or pleasure.

NOTES

1. Lillian H. Chaney and Jeanette S. Martin, *Intercultural Business Communication*, 4th ed. (Upper Saddle River, NJ: Pearson/Prentice Hall, 2007), ix.
2. Richard D. Lewis, *When Cultures Collide: Leading Across Cultures* (Boston: Nicholas Brealey International, 2006), 81–82.

3. Gary Stoller, "Doing Business Abroad? Simple Faux Pas Can Sink You," *USA Today*, August 24, 2007, B1.
4. Ibid.
5. Roger E. Axtell, *Gestures: The Do's and Taboos of Body Language Around the World* (New York: John Wiley & Sons, 1998), 24.
6. Stoller, *USA Today*, B2.
7. Norine Dresser, *Multicultural Manners: Essential Rules of Etiquette for the 21st Century* (Hoboken, NJ: John Wiley & Sons, 2005), 98.
8. Ibid., 20.
9. Joe Sharkey, "Avoiding Tan Suits and Other Travel Gaffes," *The New York Times*, May 2, 2006, C8.
10. U.S. Census Bureau Data, 2007, http://census.gov/foreign-trade/statistics, (accessed March 4, 2008).

CHAPTER 1
Global Business

Global business is here to stay. Whether companies become involved in global business generally has to do with the products or services they are selling.

INTERNATIONAL BUSINESS STATISTICS AND TRADE AGREEMENTS

Many sources are available for business statistics and trade agreements. Some of the more common ones are listed below.

Government information that is available includes *Background Notes* and daily press briefings at the U.S. Department of State Web site http: www.state.gov. The Overseas Security Advisory Council (OSAC) provides security information and regional news that could impact an individual or company abroad; its Web site is http://www.osac.gov. Information on export-related assistance and market information is available at http://www.export.gov. Information on economic, business, and international trade is available from STAT-USA/Internet at www.stat-usa.gov/. Its Web site provides current and historical trade-related releases, international market research, trade opportunities, and country analysis. The National Trade Data Bank is available at http://www.stat-usa.gov/tradtest.nsf.

GLOBAL U.S. COMPANIES

U.S. companies that are global tend to be companies that are trying to reduce their cost of production or the cost of their services. However, many companies are global because they are exporting the products they manufacture or are importing products or commodities to use or sell.

The largest global U.S. companies include Exxon Mobil, General Electric, Cisco Systems, Procter & Gamble, and Apple.[1] However, every year smaller companies are increasing their share of the global export market. Small companies account for 46 percent of the exports of the United States. Smaller companies help contribute to the economy by exporting and help replace some of the jobs that have been exported by larger organizations. Lower tariffs and free-trade agreements have been particularly helpful to these organizations. The decrease in the value of the dollar has also been helpful since it makes U.S. goods less expensive for importers in other countries to buy.[2]

TECHNOLOGY AND GLOBAL BUSINESS

The Internet and cell phones have made it much easier for small companies to sell overseas. Internet Web pages and e-mail have allowed smaller U.S. companies to obtain a "first-mover advantage" online. Examples of these success stories are Amazon.com, eToys, and eBay. Localizing Web sites helps to increase market share; however, U.S. companies are more reluctant to do this than European companies, which are more language sensitive. If companies will look at where their inquiries are coming from and then create a Web site for that country, they will see their revenues grow. Research has shown that when buyers are addressed in their own language they will stay on the site twice as long; research also shows that customer service costs drop when instructions are in the user's language.[3]

Another hurdle that companies face is being sure they can ship global orders in a timely manner. Some of their shipping problems include inaccurate addresses and not pricing delivery costs accurately. International order problems are generally accounted for by channel conflict and shipping issues. However, small firms can use companies such as Circle, Syntra, DHL, FedEx, Nexlinx, or other freight forwarders to help them with international shipping problems.[4]

RELATIONSHIP BUILDING

Learning about the culture of the country in which you wish to do business is important before your first meeting. Realizing that you are dealing with individuals who may or may not fit what you have learned about the culture is equally important. Stereotypes are very dangerous, as is being ethnocentric. While there are many differences between cultures in the world, there are also many similarities. The similarities may cause you to miss the differences that could destroy a business deal. Learning about cultural differences allows you to react with sensitivity when a new situation occurs. The more culturally and emotionally intelligent you are, the easier it will be for you to build relationships in a new culture.

Building relationships in another country includes being aware of the laws of that country. While you are in another country, you are subject to both the laws of your own country and the laws of the country you are visiting.

Building relationships in many cultures will take multiple visits. Communicating effectively is important because business opportunities may go to another company if your message is misunderstood. When you need an interpreter or translator, be sure to choose one that is fluent in both languages. Since many words do not exist in all languages, it is necessary to have someone who can accurately translate the concept that you are trying to convey.

ISSUES FACING WOMEN

Women must sometimes build business relationships in countries where there is inequality between the genders. When this occurs, the cultural norms of a country must be considered by a woman before traveling abroad. Generally, the higher the status of the woman in the organization, the fewer problems she will have when traveling to countries with gender inequality.[5]

Attitudes and actions that women will find effective when conducting business abroad include using a nurturing style, being compromising rather than domineering, showing sensitivity to others, being understanding and cooperative, using an inclusive leadership style, engaging in small talk, emphasizing harmony, and being direct in communications. In many cases where men in some countries have not dealt with women, they will find women a curiosity. This tends to work to a woman's advantage and may enable her to gain access to higher-level managers more easily.[6]

Many women who work abroad feel the major problems they have spring from within their own firms rather than from intercultural differences. Many foreign businessmen see women as more humane then men. Successful international women say that women need to be more confident and to believe they can survive and overcome difficult situations. They also need to realize that it is acceptable to do things differently and that they need to adopt an open management approach.[7] Women and men should be given equal consideration in global assignments; women are successful internationally and should be given an opportunity to prove their skill in the global arena.

LANGUAGE ISSUES

Part of cultural shock is hearing a new language being spoken or hearing your own language being spoken in a manner in which you are not accustomed. If it is your own language, the words may be used for different meanings, be spelled differently, or be pronounced differently. While English is considered the language of international business, the proficiency with which international businesspeople speak the language varies considerably. Because culture affects language, it is important to understand that language is a basis for building a relationship.

Learning about a host-country's language can help you build a relationship by understanding the five domains of rapport building: the act of speaking, the discourse content, the inclusion or exclusion of people present, the stylistic aspect, and the nonverbal domain.[8] Being able to speak the host-country language, even a little, allows you to have conversations with the people you encounter while working abroad. Speaking a language with native speakers allows you to learn the meaning of nonverbal cues and to interact socially.

Thought patterns are controlled by our native language and can be either linear or nonlinear. Linear language has a beginning and an end that is object oriented, and English is an example of a linear language that has a time continuum of present, past, and future. People who speak linear languages tend to practice short-range planning. Nonlinear language is circular, tradition oriented, and subjective. Cycles and patterns that repeat are common in nonlinear languages. Japanese and Chinese are examples of nonlinear languages. People who speak nonlinear languages tend to practice long-term business planning. Differences in our thought processes are embedded since birth and are difficult to change.[9] People who speak English as their first language must take the initiative to understand the other culture's language customs, particularly when the other culture is speaking English.

GENERAL TRAVEL INFORMATION

The U.S. Department of State suggests that U.S. citizens register via its Web site or at the nearest U.S. embassy or consulate when traveling abroad. This allows you to be contacted in an emergency. The URL is https://travelregistration.state.gov/ibrs/ui/. Emergency information about U.S. citizens traveling abroad may be obtained at 888-407-4747 or 202-501-4444.

U.S. passport information can be obtained at http://travel.state.gov/passport/passport_1738.html or by telephoning 877-487-2778.

Customer service is available Eastern Standard Time, Monday through Friday, 7:00 AM to 12:00 AM (EST), excluding federal holidays.

Health information, immunization requirements, and precautions on food and drinking water may be obtained from the Centers for Disease Control and Prevention's Web site at http://www.cdc.gov/travel/default.aspx. A hotline is available at 877-394-8747. "Health Information for International Travel" (CDC-95-8280) is available from the U.S. Government Printing Office, Washington, D.C. 20402, 202-512-1800.

NOTES

1. Paul Hickey and Justine Walters, "U.S. Companies Top List of Global Winners in Q3," Seeking Alpha: Bespoke Investment Group, October 2, 2007, http://www.seekingalpha.com/article/48749-u-s-companies-top-list-of-global-winners-in-q3 (accessed November 26, 2007).
2. Courtney Schlisserman, "Smaller Companies Are Grabbing a Bigger Share of U.S. Exports," *The Kansas City Star*, November 23, 2007, http://www.kansascity.com/business/v-print/story/374478.html (accessed November 26, 2007).
3. Bill Dunlap, The "First-Mover Advantage" in Foreign Markets, Global Reach, http://www.glreach.com/eng/ed/art/rep-eur19.html (accessed November 26, 2007).
4. Ibid.
5. Paula Caligiuri and Mila Lazarova, "A Model for the Influence of Social Interaction and Social Support on Female Expatriates' Cross-Cultural Adjustment," *The International Journal of Human Resource Management*, 13 (2002), 765.
6. Nancy K. Napier and Sully Taylor, "Experiences of Women Professionals Abroad: Comparisons Across Japan, China, and Turkey," *The International Journal of Human Resource Management*, 13 (2002), 843.
7. Philip R. Harris, Robert T. Moran, and Sarah V. Moran, *Managing Cultural Differences*, 6th ed. (Burlington, MA: Elsevier Butterworth-Heinemann, 2004), 233–245.
8. Helen Spencer-Oatey, "Rapport Management: A Framework for Analysis," in *Culturally Speaking: Managing Rapport Through Talk Across Cultures*, ed. H. Spencer-Oatey (London: Continuum, 2000), 20.
9. Yuji Tsunda, *Language Inequality and Distortion* (Philadelphia: John Benjamin, 1986), 116.

CHAPTER 2

United States

The United States of America, often shortened to U.S.A., United States, or U.S., has the largest and most technically advanced economy in the world. The country is a major world financial center; its economy has a significant impact on global markets and economic growth worldwide.

The United States is a world leader in high technology and industry. Exports include cars, capital and consumer goods, food, and machinery, in addition to pop culture, such as fashion, movies, music, sports, and television.[1]

The 20 countries that comprise America's largest trading partners, according to 2007 export statistics (in order, starting with the country to which the United States exports the most goods), are Canada, Mexico, China, Japan, United Kingdom, Germany, South Korea, Netherlands, France, Taiwan, Singapore, Belgium, Brazil, Hong Kong, Australia, India, Switzerland, Italy, Israel, and Malaysia.[2] The business culture and customs of these countries are examined in the following chapters; the countries are presented in alphabetical order.

COUNTRY SPECIFICS

A country's location, topography, economy, and population provide insight into understanding its culture. In addition, knowledge of ethnic groups, religions, time zones, and currency is helpful.

Location, Topography, and Land Mass

The United States, which covers the central part of North America, includes the contiguous 48 states as well as Alaska, which is northwest of Canada, and the Hawaiian Islands in the Pacific Ocean that lie south of

Alaska and about 2,400 miles west of the U.S. mainland. Washington, D.C. is the capital of the United States.

The topography is varied, including mountains, deserts, canyons, prairies, subtropical forests, and beaches on the mainland; Alaska has glaciers, valleys, and mountains; Hawaii has a volcanic topography that is green throughout the year.

With a land mass of 3,618,765 square miles (or 9,372,558 square kilometers), the United States is the fourth-largest country in the world.[3]

Economy

In addition to being the world's largest economy, the United States has the most diverse economy. The economic strengths are foreign investments, exports, and diversified service and industrial sectors.[4] The Gross Domestic Product (GDP) per capita is $45,660.[5]

The United States has been described as "first in volume of trade, first in industry, first in food output, and first in aid to others." In addition, people of the United States "own more cars, telephones, refrigerators, television sets, DVDs, dishwashers, microwave ovens, and cellular phones than any other people." U.S. Americans also lead the world in tourist spending; in addition, they enjoy the largest tourist receipts. (Income from tourism is twice the amount of France, which is in second place.) Unfortunately, people of the United States are also the world's largest polluters and have the highest rates of murder and divorce of any other country.[6]

Population, Languages Spoken, Ethnic Groups, and Religions

The population of the United States is approximately 301.1 million, making it the third-largest country in the world. Only China and India have larger populations. The U.S. macroculture, which comprises 74 percent of the population, is white. The largest microculture is Hispanic or Latino, which makes up 14.5 percent of the population. African Americans are the second largest microculture, making up 12 percent of the population. Other ethnic groups are Asians and Pacific Islanders, at 5 percent, and Native Americans, at 1 percent. With the intermingling of cultures, about 1.9 percent report more than one race.[7]

Although the United States does not have a federally mandated language, English is the predominate language and is used for federal court rulings, legislation, regulations, executive orders, and other official pronouncements. Over half of the states have passed legislation making English the official language; some states are officially bilingual.

Ethnic groups vary depending upon the region of the country. Larger numbers of Hispanics live in the west and southwest, while African Americans have large populations in the east and southeast. More than half of the people of Hawaii are Asians or Pacific Islanders.[8]

Although the United States does not have an official church, a majority of citizens (about 80 percent) are Christians. Over half of the population is Protestant; one-fourth is Roman Catholic. The largest Protestant groups are Baptists, Methodists, and Lutherans. Other religious groups are Jews, Muslims, and Buddhists. Since the government of the United States provides for the separation of church and state, religion has little impact on business.

Country Codes, Time Zones, and Currency

The country code for the United States is 1. When U.S. persons call someone in another country, they will dial the International Access Code, the country code, the city code, and the local telephone number. When calling from the United States to Buenos Aires, Argentina, for example, dial the International Access Code (011), followed by the country code (54), the city code (11), and the local telephone number.

The contiguous 48 states are divided into the following time zones: Eastern, Central, Mountain, and Pacific. The Eastern Time Zone (ET) is five hours behind Universal Time (UT), while Hawaii is 10 hours behind UT, and most of Alaska is nine hours behind UT. When placing a call from New York to Honolulu, for example, remember that when it is 8 PM in New York City it is 3 PM in Honolulu.[9] Alaska's two time zones are Alaska Standard Time (AKST) and Nome Standard Time; since Hawaii lies directly south of Alaska, it follows AKST. Because Alaska is so wide, it encompasses a third of the time zones of the world.[10] In addition, it is important to keep in mind that Daylight Saving Time (DST) is observed in most states. The effective dates for DST were extended in 2007 to begin in March and end in November (from previous beginning dates in April and ending dates in October).

The currency—the U.S. dollar (USD)—has been considered a major world currency. A currency converter is available at http://coinmill.com/AED_calculator.html that will convert any currency in the world to any other currency.

BUSINESS AND SOCIAL CUSTOMS

Greetings, Introductions, and Business Cards

The typical greeting in the United States is "Good morning, how are you?" This greeting is a ritual and should not be interpreted as an inquiry into the state of your health. The proper response is "Fine thanks, and how are you?" or "Great! And you?" While this ritualistic greeting may be confusing to people in some countries (especially in countries where people are sincerely interested in another person's well being when they make such an inquiry), it is merely a polite way to greet people in the United States. In office settings, superiors should remember to initiate the greeting to avoid being perceived as unfriendly and aloof. In some parts of the country, particularly the southern United States, women may hug each other when greeting. Men, however, do not typically hug each other. Variations in greeting behavior can be observed due to ethnic diversity; people who have emigrated from other countries to the United States often continue to greet each other as they did in their home culture.

Introductions are an important part of making a positive initial impression. When making introductions, you should mention first the name of the person with the highest rank, regardless of age or gender. When you introduce people of equal rank, it does not matter whose name is mentioned first. Regional differences exist; in the southern United States, a woman's name is often mentioned first when a man and woman are introduced. Address people to whom you are introduced by their titles and last names unless you are invited to use their first names. Typically, people in the United States who are about the same age and rank address each other by their first names. Sometimes additional information is provided during the introduction, such as, "Larry and I attended the Chicago conference last month."

When people (both men and women) are introduced in business situations, they are expected to rise, smile, and shake hands. U.S. handshakes are firm and last two or three seconds; eye contact is expected during the handshake. The typical handshake has one or two shakes with the hand held vertically. Shaking hands is expected when you first meet someone, when you welcome a person into your office, when you encounter a friend outside the office, and when you say goodbye. Although women are expected to shake hands in business situations, they may choose not to do so on social occasions.[11]

In the United States business cards are exchanged in business settings and are not distributed casually; they are exchanged only when there is some reason to contact the person later. No specific ritual for exchanging cards exists; sometimes people will simply place your business card into their pocket or purse without glancing at the information on the card. This apparent lack of interest in the other person's card may appear rude to people in some cultures, but U.S. persons do not intend to be socially insensitive by their behavior.

Business Entertaining and Seating Customs

Business entertaining is done in restaurants, at country clubs and golf courses, and at cocktail parties, cookouts, and buffet dinners in someone's home.

Restaurant entertaining is popular; the purpose is to discuss business, especially at breakfast or lunch meetings. Dinner is also a good time for restaurant entertaining, especially when interviewing applicants for important positions in an organization or when entertaining out-of-town visitors. Dinner entertaining is also an appropriate way to express appreciation for someone's contributions or to honor a special person. The host makes reservations, arrives early to arrange for seating, and pays for the meal. Guests arrive promptly and wait for the host to indicate where they are to sit and to initiate business discussions. Upon completion of the meal, guests should thank the host for the invitation, both in person and in writing.

Home entertaining is more personal than restaurant entertaining; it gives guests an opportunity to get to know each other on a more personal level than what is experienced in an office environment. Cookouts on the patio and Sunday morning brunches are excellent ways to entertain a group of colleagues or friends. During the holidays, some U.S. persons will host an open house, when guests stop by for a brief visit and help themselves to foods available on a buffet table. Guests should arrive within 15 minutes of the time specified on the invitation. When invited to someone's home, offering to bring something is polite; however, the host typically declines. Thank the host as you leave; write a thank-you note within a short period of time.[12]

At a restaurant, the host should make sure that guests have the preferred seats. Seating should be provided when entertaining at home, even though guests often stand when visiting with other guests. For seated meals, the hosts sit opposite each other, and the guest of honor is seated to the right of one of the hosts. Couples are usually seated separately.

Dining, Toasting, and Tipping Customs

The style of eating used by people of the United States is usually referred to as the American zigzag style. When using this style, hold the knife in the right hand and the fork in the left with the tines down. After you cut a piece of food, place the knife on the upper right edge of the plate with the cutting edge toward the center of the plate, then move the fork to the right hand and, with the fork tines up, place the piece of food into your mouth. To signal that you have finished eating, place the knife on the upper right edge of the plate at about the 11 o'clock and three o'clock position, with the blade toward the center of the plate and the fork aligned next to the knife, tines up.

People of the United States typically eat three meals a day; breakfast is around 7 AM to 9 AM, lunch from 11:30 AM to 1:30 PM, and dinner around 6 PM to 8 PM Breakfast may be rather light, consisting of cereal and juice; it may be more substantial, such as eggs, pancakes, or waffles served with bacon or sausage and toast or muffins. Some adults do not eat breakfast. Lunch is usually light, such as a salad or sandwich. Dinner is the largest meal of the day.

Table manners are important. You are expected to take something of everything that is offered. However, you are not expected to clean your plate. Leaving something on your plate indicates that you have had enough to eat. Place your napkin in your lap as soon as you sit down and leave it there until everyone is ready to leave the table. Pass food to others in a clockwise direction before you help yourself. Making noises during the meal, such as slurping or burping, is very rude. You are expected to chew with your mouth closed. Do not lean over your plate while eating, crush crackers in your soup, or put too much food on your plate. Never use toothpicks at the table or smoke without asking permission.[13]

Toasts may be made by either gender and are brief. The host proposes a welcoming toast at the beginning of the meal and another toast to honor the guest of honor. Customary U.S. toasts include "To your health," "Cheers," or "Bottoms up." The guest of honor then offers a toast honoring the host. Avoid reading a toast, clinking glasses, or drinking when you are being toasted. Guests who do not drink alcohol may toast with an empty wine glass or with another beverage, except perhaps water (sometimes viewed as disapproval of the toast).[14]

Tipping is expected in the United States. People who fail to tip or who leave a small tip are considered stingy. Tipping in U.S. restaurants ranges from the 15 percent considered appropriate in modest restaurants to the 20 percent expected in nice restaurants. In addition to the tip for your meal, in fine restaurants you are expected to tip the *maître d'hôtel* $10 if you were given a good table, the wine steward at least $5, attendants in the coat check room or ladies' room $1 to $2, and the person who brings your car around when you use valet parking at least $3.[15]

Gift-Giving Customs

Business gifts in the United States may not legally exceed $25. Occasions for giving office gifts include Secretaries' Day, observed with lunch or flowers, and Christmas, observed in various ways, including cash gifts to custodial workers or contributions to food banks or other charitable organizations. Group gifts are appropriate when an employee receives a promotion, is hospitalized, has a death in the family, or retires.

Gifts are also given on social occasions. These occasions include weddings, the birth of a baby, and when you are invited for dinner at someone's home. Additional occasions for giving gifts include Mother's Day, Father's Day, and Valentine's Day. House guests are expected to bring a gift; flowers, wine, or candy are good choices. When a friend has a death in the family, sending a card and flowers is appropriate. If the family has indicated a preference for donations to a specific charity, a contribution in the name of the deceased person is appreciated by the family.

Gifts given to people in other countries should be made in the United States, be unique to the United States, and be appropriately priced. The type of gift is important, as is the wrapping of the gift; knowing whether gifts are opened in front of the giver is also important. Appropriate gifts include U.S.-made sports equipment, local crafts, books featuring well-known U.S. landmarks, DVDs of U.S. movies, desk accessories, Native American art or jewelry, U.S.-made wines or spirits, or such food items as candy and nuts.

Guidelines for giving gifts include opening gifts in front of the giver and writing a note of appreciation. Red roses are inappropriate as a business or social gift as they are associated with romance in the United States.[16]

Business Meetings

Companies in the United States spend more time and money on meetings than do businesses in any other country. U.S. persons expect to receive an agenda in advance of the meeting and to know the purpose of the meeting. In formal meetings little interaction is expected, but in more informal meetings participation is encouraged.

In U.S. meetings, the leader is expected to start on time and end on time. The leader does not recognize latecomers, who are expected to enter as quietly and as inconspicuously as possible. The leader is also expected to follow parliamentary procedures. Issues are resolved by permitting participants to vote; the majority rules.

Participants are expected to listen attentively, to avoid carrying on side conversations with others, and to ask questions and make comments when appropriate. They may feel free to challenge the statements of others, as it is considered acceptable to openly disagree with others. Disagreeing publicly should, of course, be done in a civil manner. Participants who arrive late are expected to apologize to the leader at the end of the meeting and to offer a plausible reason for their late arrival.[17]

Dress and Appearance

Conservative business dress is expected in many firms; however, some companies permit their employees to dress casually. Because of the variations in what is considered appropriate work attire, a number of firms have developed their own dress codes to make sure employees understand what type of dress is expected in the office environment. Suits for men and skirted suits for women are viewed as the most appropriate professional business attire, according to U.S. researchers and image consultants. Dresses are also considered appropriate professional attire for women. While many women wear pantsuits, they do not have the credibility of skirted suits or dresses in most business settings. Color and fabric are also important attributes of professional dress. Dark colors are associated with wealth and are recommended for professional dress. In addition, neutral, basic colors are considered appropriate. Fabric is also a consideration; pure, natural fibers, such as cotton, linen, silk, and wool, convey higher status than such synthetic fibers as polyester. Business casual attire, now on the wane after its initial popularity in the 1990s, should be conservative and traditional, following the same guidelines in color and fabric as those recommended for professional attire.[18]

Holidays

The following are federal holidays in the United States; banks, government offices, and schools close, and mail is not delivered:

- New Year's Day (January 1)
- Martin Luther King Jr.'s Birthday (third Monday in January)
- Presidents' Day (third Monday in February)
- Memorial Day (last Monday in May)
- Independence Day (July 4)
- Columbus Day (second Monday in October)
- Veteran's Day (November 11)
- Thanksgiving Day (fourth Thursday in November)
- Christmas Day (December 25)

Other holidays are Valentine's Day on February 14 (celebrates love), Easter Sunday in March or April (a Christian holiday), and Halloween on October 31 (when children dress up in special costumes and go "trick-or-treating" to receive candy from their neighbors).

Conversational Customs

Small talk is an important U.S. conversational custom. Being an expert at small talk is very useful at social gatherings as well as in business settings. Topics appropriate for small talk include the weather, current events, travel experiences, sports, exhibits, or physical fitness. Do not ask questions about money matters (salaries, debts, taxes) or personal information (age, weight, sexual orientation, children), and do not bring up controversial subjects (religion, politics, abortion) or depressing topics (hurricanes, world hunger, terrorism).

When conversing with U.S. persons, stand about an arm's length away. Standing too close makes people of the United States uncomfortable.

Taking turns speaking is the preferred form of conversing. One speaker says a sentence or two, then glances away to signal that the other person may take a turn. Taking too long a turn is very irritating to U.S. persons and may result in interrupting, which is considered rude.

Although people in some cultures consider arguing an enjoyable pastime, U.S. persons try to avoid an argument because they think it may damage a relationship, and they will change the subject or excuse themselves to avoid arguing.

People of the United States are uncomfortable with silence; they will engage in small talk in social and business situations to avoid silence. Contrary to the saying that "silence is golden," U.S. Americans will initiate a conversation about the weather, books, travels, or movies to complete strangers they encounter while waiting in line at the supermarket, in department stores, or on public transportation to avoid silence.[19]

Humor

U.S. Americans appreciate humor during conversations and presentations in both business and social situations. U.S. humor is often self-deprecating; people will tell stories about dumb things they did. The ability to laugh at yourself is considered the mark of a self-confident person. U.S. persons do not appreciate humor that is laced with ethnic, sexual, or racial undertones, but they may not voice their disapproval; they simply do not laugh and remain silent.

The use of humor at the beginning of business presentations, including cartoons, jokes, or analogies, is intended to diffuse tension and to establish a relaxed atmosphere before getting down to business. Humor may be directed toward individuals; however, it should make them look good rather than diminish them.[20]

Attitude toward Women in Business

Despite significant salary differences between women and men (women earn about 76 percent of what their male counterparts earn), women are considered equal to men in the U.S. workplace. Women occupy positions of leadership and prestige in business, education, and government. Women have learned that they do not need to mimic the leadership style of men; they now realize that they can accomplish just as much as men using their own style. U.S. women are independent and do not expect any special considerations in their jobs, such as being allowed more time than men to do a specific job. Although women do not expect special considerations from men in the work environment, most appreciate such polite behavior from men as opening doors, rising when women enter or leave a room, and permitting women to precede them when entering a room or elevator.[21]

On the Human Development Index (HDI), the United States ranks 8 out of 177 nations.[22] The HDI is a measure of empowerment; it is based on life expectancy, literacy, infant mortality, and real GDP. The assumption is that societies that provide an opportunity for education, access to healthcare, and adequate wages are inclined to be more democratic and exhibit a respect for human rights.[23]

Public Behavior

People of the United States keep to the right when walking down halls or on sidewalks, in shopping malls, or any other place where people go in opposite directions.

U.S. persons also respect queues; they feel that people should wait their turn when in line at a bank or a special-events ticket office and do not expect any special consideration if they are elderly, disabled, or wealthy. Pushing ahead of others in line will be met with quick reminders of the location of the end of the line.

Although young people in some cultures are expected to give up their seats to the elderly, pregnant women, or others deserving of special respect when using public transportation, this behavior is not common in the United States.

U.S. people do not like to be touched in public; they will, in fact, avoid getting on a crowded elevator and will wait for an elevator that is less crowded. If you do inadvertently bump into someone, you are expected to apologize.

Smoking in many public places, including airports, grocery stores, theaters, restaurants, shopping malls, hospitals, and public buildings, is illegal in most U.S. cities and states. Many U.S. companies have established smoke-free environments in response to pressure from nonsmokers who insist on their right to breathe air that is free of carcinogens. Even in areas where smoking is permitted, visitors should be considerate of the wishes of the people around them to avoid being offensive.

Voice volume should be appropriate to the occasion and the situation. Visitors to the United States should not call attention to themselves negatively by speaking in a voice that is louder than people near them.

Other public behaviors that are viewed as offensive include using toothpicks in front of others, spitting on the street, chewing gum, eating or drinking while walking on the street, and demonstrating affection to members of the opposite gender.[24]

NONVERBAL COMMUNICATION

Gestures and Posture

People of the United States use moderate gesturing. They do not, however, gesture above shoulder level, except when waving to someone. The thumbs-up sign is used to indicate that everything is great; thumbs down shows disapproval. The "V" sign, which is made by using the index and middle fingers to form a V, means victory. The "OK" sign, with the thumb and forefinger joined to form a circle, is another positive U.S. gesture. These gestures should be used with caution around persons of other cultures as they may be insulting or even obscene in another culture. Avoid using the forearm jerk and the middle finger held up by itself; these two gestures are insulting and vulgar. Also avoid using a single finger to point at someone.

Posture while sitting, standing, or walking can send positive or negative nonverbal messages. Walking erect with assurance is associated with a self-confident person; conversely, standing and walking with stooped shoulders conveys a lack of confidence and assurance. The posture of U.S. Americans tends to be casual; they sit in a relaxed manner and often cross their legs—women at the ankle, men with ankle on the knee.[25]

Eye Contact and Facial Expressions

Direct eye contact is important in both business and social situations. Failing to give eye contact implies disinterest, lack of respect, or inattentiveness; it also suggests that you are trying to hide something. Winking has several meanings; it can mean flirtation, friendliness, or that the person is joking.

People of the United States smile more than people of many cultures; they even smile at complete strangers and expect people to return their smiles. U.S. people have been taught, "Smile and the world smiles with you; frown and you frown alone." U.S. service industries stress to their employees the importance of "Service with a smile!"[26] One fast-food restaurant, in trying to attract new employees, advertised: "We hire smiling faces."

Space and Touch

The preferred distance between two people when they are interacting is about an arm's length. Standing closer makes people uncomfortable; they will often step back when someone gets too close during conversations. Proper spacing also includes a person's possessions; thus, it is inadvisable to place something on a person's desk or to sit in the person's desk chair unless specifically invited by the owner to do so.[27]

The United States is a culture where little touching is the norm. Acceptable touching in business situations is limited to the handshake. Because of ethnic diversity in the United States, it is not uncommon to occasionally see people hugging or cheek-kissing when greeting each other. These behaviors are not, however, typical of the U.S. macroculture.[28]

Punctuality and Attitude toward Time

People of the United States are very conscious of time. They expect punctuality for business and social appointments. The United States is considered a five-minute culture when it comes to punctuality. That is, being five minutes late for a business appointment is acceptable; however, an apology is expected. Failure to be prompt sends numerous negative nonverbal messages, including disrespect for others or lack of organization.

The United States has been considered a monochronic culture; that is, people do only one thing at a time. For example, it is considered rude to accept a telephone call when a visitor is in the office. Some U.S. persons have been moving toward polychronic time (doing several things simultaneously), as the concept of multitasking is becoming popular. However, they refrain from engaging in this behavior when in the presence of others as doing so is considered rude.

A culture's view of time includes whether the people "work to live" or "live to work." The United States is a "live-to-work" culture; U.S. Americans work long hours and do not take long vacations compared with people of most other cultures.[29]

TRAVEL TIPS

- Passports are required for entry into the United States; they must be valid for at least six months from the date of entering the country; visas are required for longer visits.

- Do not bring the following into the United States, except with special permits: drugs, plants, meats and hides, gold, firearms and ammunition, and goods from specific countries. (Check with Foreign Assets Control, Washington, D.C., for a list of restricted countries.) Pets may be brought in provided they meet certain requirements. (Secure the booklet *So You Want to Import a Pet* from the U.S. consulate.)
- Hotel accommodations are spacious by European standards. Rooms have central air conditioning and private baths. Most rooms have other amenities, such as minibars, hair dryers, irons and ironing boards, and safes.
- Take precautions when walking, shopping, or using an Automatic Teller Machine (ATM). A shoulder bag should be kept closed and held in front of you. If you fear for your personal safety, you can call 911, the emergency telephone number in most areas of the United States.
- Public transportation is available in large cities, including taxicabs and buses. Rental cars are widely available. If you rent a car, keep your driver's license and vehicle registration with you. Always wear your seat belt as wearing a seat belt is mandatory in all states. While you are in the car, keep doors locked, windows up, and shopping purchases and other valuables in the trunk out of sight of potential thieves. Avoid driving after you have been drinking; driving intoxicated is a serious offense.
- Confirm that your medical insurance is in effect during your visit to the United States; if you need coverage, purchase a short-term policy.
- Speak English only when in hearing distance of U.S. persons; speaking another language is considered impolite.
- Although U.S. Americans are outwardly friendly—they often say "Hi" to complete strangers — they have few friends. It is advisable to proceed slowly when trying to develop a friendship with a U.S. person.
- U.S. Americans are serious about the importance of personal hygiene; personal odors, including body odor and bad breath, are offensive. Unkempt hair and nails are likewise offensive.
- Remember that U.S. persons value punctuality, hard work, independence, self-reliance, honesty, and freedom. They especially value their freedom of speech and feel free to criticize anything and everyone, including their political leaders. However, they resent having a visitor from another country criticize U.S. political, economic, social, or educational systems.

NOTES

1. *CultureGrams, North America, United States of America* (Ann Arbor, MI: ProQuest CSA, 2008), 764.
2. U.S. Census Bureau, 2007 Export of Goods, http://www.census.gov/foreign-trade/statistics (accessed March 4, 2008).
3. *CultureGrams, North America, United States of America,* 761.
4. Ibid., 764.

5. List of countries by GDP (nominal) per capita, http://en.wikipedia.org/wiki/List_of_countries_by_GDP_(nominal)_per_capita (accessed March 5, 2008). Figures (in U.S. dollars) are estimates for 2007 from *The World Factbook* provided by the Central Intelligence Agency (updated February 12, 2008). These figures do not take into account cost-of-living differences; using additional economic data is advisable when making country comparisons.

6. Richard D. Lewis, *When Cultures Collide: Leading Across Cultures*, 3rd ed. (Boston, MA: Nicholas Brealey International, 2006), 179.

7. *CultureGrams, North America, United States of America*, 758.

8. Ibid.

9. Terri Morrison and Wayne A. Conaway, *Kiss, Bow, or Shake Hands*, 2nd ed. (Avon, MA: Adams Media, 2007), 549.

10. Alison R. Lanier, *Living in the U.S.A.*, 5th ed. (Yarmouth, ME: Intercultural Press, 1996), 7.

11. William H. Bonner and Lillian H. Chaney, *Communicating Effectively in an Information Age*, 2nd ed. (Mason, OH: Thomson, 2004), 334–335.

12. Lillian H. Chaney and Jeanette S. Martin, *The Essential Guide to Business Etiquette* (Westport, CT: Praeger, 2007), 103.

13. Mary M. Bosrock, *Put Your Best Foot Forward: U.S.A.* (St. Paul, MN: International Education Systems, 1999), 169-–172; Jeanette S. Martin and Lillian H. Chaney, *Global Business Etiquette* (Westport, CT: Praeger, 2006), 109–110.

14. Martin and Chaney, *Global Business Etiquette*, 114–115.

15. Ibid., 119.

16. Bosrock, *Put Your Best Foot Forward: U.S.A.*, 193–200; Martin and Chaney, *Global Business Etiquette*, 40–41.

17. Gary Althen, *American Ways*, 2nd ed. (Yarmouth, ME: Intercultural Press, 2003), 254–255; Bonner and Chaney, *Communicating Effectively in an Information Age*, 99, 354–355.

18. Martin and Chaney, *Global Business Etiquette*, 75–79; Chaney and Martin, *The Essential Guide to Business Etiquette*, 18.

19. Lanier, *Living in the U.S.A.*, 15–16.

20. Ibid, 138.

21. Ibid., 44–45; Bosrock, *Put Your Best Foot Forward: U.S.A.*, 243–247.

22. *CultureGrams, North America, United States of America*, 764.

23. *CultureGrams, Concepts and Terminology*, (Ann Arbor, MI: ProQuest CSA, 2008), A-14.

24. Bosrock, *Put Your Best Foot Forward: U.S.A.*, 54.

25. Lillian H. Chaney and Jeanette S. Martin, *Intercultural Business Communication*, 4th ed. (Upper Saddle River, NJ: Pearson/Prentice Hall, 2007), 129.

26. Bosrock, *Put Your Best Foot Forward: U.S.A.*, 151.

27. Ibid, 149.

28. Roger E. Axtell, *Gestures: The Do's and Taboos of Body Language Around the World* (New York: John Wiley & Sons, 1998), 228–230.

29. Richard W. Brislin and Eugene S. Kim, "Cultural Diversity in People's Understanding and Uses of Time," *Applied Psychology: An International Review*, 52 (2003), 365–370.

CHAPTER 3
Australia

The Commonwealth of Australia, typically referred to as Australia and more informally as "The Land Down Under," is the fifteenth largest export market of the United States based on 2007 data.[1]

Major U.S. exports to Australia include agricultural products, chemicals, industrial supplies, machinery, electronics, automobiles, and pharmaceuticals.[2]

COUNTRY SPECIFICS

A country's location, topography, economy, and population provide insight into understanding its culture. In addition, knowledge of ethnic groups, religions, time zones, and currency is helpful.

Location, Topography, and Land Mass

Australia is located between the Indian Ocean and the South Pacific Ocean; it is west of New Zealand and southeast of Indonesia. The capital is Canberra.

The terrain of Australia is quite diverse. About one-third of the country comprises desert, while another third could be described as land of poor quality. Between the coast line and the Great Dividing Range—a long chain of mountains located along the Pacific coast—lies fertile farmland; the island state of Tasmania and the southwestern corner of Western Australia also have fertile farmland. The Australian Outback, which is not actually a defined area, refers to the country's remote and undeveloped regions. Life is difficult in the Outback, and those who live there are perceived to be tough and independent. The Great Barrier Reef is located along the northeast coast; it is the largest coral reef in the world, measuring 1,250 miles or 2,000 kilometers.[3]

Australia, the world's sixth-largest country, occupies a complete continent—the only country in the world with that distinction. The country is divided into six states (Queensland, New South Wales, South Australia, Tasmania, Victoria, and Western Australia) and two territories (the Northern Territory and the Australian Capital Territory). The area of Australia covers 2,967,892 square miles or 7,686,850 square kilometers, which is about the size of the 48 contiguous United States.[4]

Economy

Australia's Gross Domestic Product (GDP) per capita is $33,664.[5] The country's vast mineral deposits include bauxite, diamonds, coal, copper, gold, iron ore, and silver. In addition to exporting minerals, Australia is a world leader in exports of beef and wool. The country also exports agricultural products and has a large service sector. Over half of Australia's exports are to Asian and Pacific countries.[6]

Because of fluctuations in prices of Australia's mineral and agricultural exports, the country has experienced periods of restricted economic growth and recession.[7]

Population, Languages Spoken, Ethnic Groups, and Religions

The population of Australia is over 20.4 million; it is growing at almost 1 percent annually. More than one-third of Australians live in Sydney (the largest city) or Melbourne.[8] English is the national language. Australian English, although similar to British English, is a unique language; it has numerous colloquialisms and idioms, such as *prang* (fender bender), *bloke* (guy), and *spot on* (right on). In addition, Australians—often called "Aussies"—shorten words, such as *telly* (television), *uni* (university), and *footy* (football). Spelling is a mixture of American and British patterns. Visitors should speak standard English rather than try to use the expressions that are uniquely Australian.[9]

About 95 percent of Australian residents are Caucasian; 4 percent are Asian. The remaining residents are Aborigines, Australia's original inhabitants.[10]

About one-fourth of Australians are Anglican, one-fourth are Roman Catholic, and another one-fourth belong to other Christian denominations. The remaining quarter of residents is made up of nonreligious groups and other religions, including Buddhism, Hinduism, Islam, and Taoism.[11]

Country Codes, Time Zones, and Currency

Australia's country code is 61; city codes are 06 for Canberra, 03 for Melbourne, and 02 for Sydney. To place a call from the United States to Sydney, for example, dial first the International Access Code (011), followed by the country code (61), the city code (02), and the local telephone number.

The three time zones in Australia are the Western Australian Time (13 hours ahead of U.S. Eastern Standard Time (EST), Central Australian Time (14.5 hours ahead of U.S. EST), and Eastern Australian Time (15 hours ahead of U.S. EST). When it is 5:00 PM in New York, it is 8:00 AM the next day in Eastern Australia. In Universal Time (UT) the times would be written as 1700 and 0800, respectively. The country (except for Queensland and Western Australia) observes Daylight Saving Time (DST) between the last Sunday of October and the last Sunday in March. Travelers from the United States to Australia will lose a day when crossing the International Date Line.[12]

The country's currency is the Australian dollar (AUD) and, like the currency in the United States, is based on 100 cents as being equal to $1. Since both Australia and the United States use dollars as their currency, "A" or "US" is placed before the dollar sign to differentiate the two currencies.[13] A currency converter is available at http://coinmill.com/AED_calculator.html that will convert any currency in the world into any other currency.

BUSINESS AND SOCIAL CUSTOMS

Greetings, Introductions, and Business Cards

When Australians greet each other, they usually say "Hi" or "G'day" (good day) to their friends; "Hello" or "How are you?" are used for more formal greetings. Visitors should not mimic the Australian greeting of "G'day, mate" (meaning "Good morning" or "Hello"), as it is viewed as patronizing by businesspeople.[14] The greeting is accompanied by a handshake. The main difference between the U.S. and Australian handshake is that the Australian handshake does not last as long. Women do not usually shake hands with each other. When saying goodbye, Australians usually say "All the best."[15]

During introductions, use a person's title and last name. Since Australians are informal, you can expect to be addressed by your first name rather quickly. You would respond by using first names with your Australian colleagues. However, it is customary to address people of higher rank or those who are your elders by their title (Mr., Mrs., Ms.) and last name.

Introducing yourself when no one introduces you in social situations is acceptable.[16]

While it is advisable to be prepared for exchanging business cards, the practice is less important than in many other countries. You should, however, be prepared to exchange business cards during introductions.[17]

Business Entertaining and Seating Customs

Business entertaining is typically conducted at restaurants, not private homes. Lunch is more popular for conducting business; dinner invitations are typically for socializing. You may be invited to someone's home for drinks at what is typically considered the dinner hour, only to find that no meal is served. This practice is quite common. If you are invited to tea, the invitation is actually for dinner, which is served between 6:00 PM and 8:00 PM. (Afternoon tea is served around 3 PM and consists of light refreshments.) Remember that the person who issues an invitation pays for the meal. When you are hosting a business dinner, you are expected to bring alcoholic beverages since most restaurants do not have a license to serve alcoholic drinks.[18]

Seating etiquette in Australia is similar to that in many other countries; the guest of honor is seated to the right of the host.

Dining, Toasting, and Tipping Customs

Australians use the Continental style of eating, with the fork remaining in the left hand and the knife in the right. Although elbows should not be placed on the table, wrists lean against the edge of the table. Hands are not placed in your lap. Everyone is expected to remain at the table until all have finished eating. Using a toothpick at the table is impolite. Beer is usually served with meals; however, wine is becoming more popular. [19]

When toasting in Australia, "cheers" is probably used most frequently; "bottoms up" and "to your health" are also common.

The Australian attitude toward tipping has been linked in the past to the country's egalitarian views; tipping was perceived as a show of social superiority over the person being tipped. Since most Australians are acquainted with U.S. tipping customs, however, those in service positions are appreciative of tips from tourists. Although tipping in restaurants is not expected, adding 10 percent to the bill when the service is good is appropriate. Tipping in other situations is likewise optional, but giving a small tip to taxi drivers and hotel personnel who have been especially helpful is appreciated.[20]

Gift-Giving Customs

Giving business gifts is not customary in Australia. If you are invited to dinner at an Australian's home, however, bring a small gift. Chocolates, flowers, or wine are appropriate; a book featuring your country or city also makes a good gift.[21]

Business Meetings

Make appointments with your Australian business colleagues at least a month in advance. Avoid planning a business trip during their vacation months, December through February. Being on time for business appointments is important.

Business presentations should be simple, accurate, direct, and to the point; they should emphasize the equality of the two negotiation teams. Even when you make an effective presentation, your Australian colleagues will not usually compliment you on doing a good job.[22]

During business discussions, be prepared for the competitive nature of Australians. Be prepared to bargain and to give up something when necessary. Treat your Australian colleagues as equals; since they believe that "no man is a servant, and no man is a master." Friendship plays no role in business transactions; decisions are based on policy and facts. The decision-making process can be quite lengthy because of the number of people typically involved in the process. Be patient; high-pressure tactics are ineffective.[23]

Dress and Appearance

When traveling to Australia, you will want to remember that the country is in the Southern Hemisphere and seasons are the opposite of those in the United States, which is located in the Northern Hemisphere. Check the weather in the area of Australia you plan to visit before deciding which clothing to pack.

Business dress for visitors should be conservative, with men wearing dark suits and tie and businesswomen wearing professional suits or dresses. In some cities, women wear pantsuits. However, Australian businesswomen wear pantsuits much less frequently than do U.S. businesswomen.

Gold chains and other ostentatious jewelry should not be worn. Even when dressing casually, Australians do not wear sloppy or tattered clothing in public. They do wear shorts in a solid color with high socks and a short-sleeved shirt in warm weather. Because of rapidly changing weather, it is wise to be prepared to add or remove layers of clothing. Bringing along a raincoat and comfortable walking shoes is also recommended. You can expect to wear professional attire when dining in nice restaurants. Since variations exist in what is considered appropriate business attire, however, check with your Australian colleagues on the attire appropriate for special events and occasions.[24]

Holidays

Australians celebrate the following national holidays. Since most businesses close on these holidays, attempting to schedule meetings on these dates is not advised.

- New Year's Day (January 1)
- Australia Day (January 26)
- Labor Day (first or second Monday of March)
- Easter (Good Friday through the following Monday or Tuesday of April)
- Anzac Day—national memorial day (April 25)
- Queen's Birthday (second Monday of June)
- Melbourne's Cup Day (first Tuesday of November)
- Remembrance Day to commemorate the end of World War II (November 11)
- Christmas Day (December 25)
- Boxing Day (not observed in South Australia) (December 26)

In addition to the preceding holidays, Wattle Day is celebrated in many areas on August 1 or September 1. The Wattle, a large acacia tree, is Australia's national floral emblem.[25]

Conversational Customs

Australians are friendly, relaxed, and positive. They often start conversations with strangers in the local pub or in other public places. Conversations with Australians are always lively; they enjoy a good debate. Since their conversations can take unexpected turns, you should be prepared for wherever the conversation goes. Remember that Australians have strong opinions and are quite direct in their conversations. They tend to be cynical of people in positions of wealth or power and applaud the underdog. When talking to Australians, always keep in mind their belief in egalitarianism, which espouses the view that theirs is a classless society. Thus, everyone—regardless of background, educational level, or wealth—should be treated equally. Australians do not like people who think they are better than others. The "tall poppy syndrome" is associated with Australians; this syndrome suggests that poppies that grow taller than their surroundings usually get picked first.[26]

Most topics seem to be appropriate for conversations, including politics. Australians enjoy discussing sports, especially cricket and rugby, and are happy to explain these sports to you if you have never seen a game. Be complimentary of the country and its beauty. However, resist the temptation to talk about convicts or Crocodile Dundee. Australians have become weary of these subjects; bringing up these topics will label you a *galah*, which means a stupid native bird.[27]

In conversations with Australians, avoid praising them too enthusiastically; they become suspicious of people who are lavish with praise. In addition, avoid bragging or boasting. Egalitarianism prevails in Australia, and self-promotion is frowned upon. Also avoid discussions of race relations, control of the kangaroo population, labor disputes, and treatment of the Aborigines. While it is acceptable to ask about a person's occupation, it is inappropriate to ask personal questions about salary and religion.[28]

Humor

Australians enjoy humor but do not use it very much during business meetings; they are more concerned about getting down to business quickly.[29]

Australian humor is often self-deprecating; it has an abundance of sarcasm, irony, and satire and can be barbed and provocative. Australians appreciate people who can laugh when the joke is on them. They enjoy teasing, so visitors should learn to laugh it off or even to return the teasing.[30]

Attitude toward Women in Business

Women in Australia, like those in the United States and Canada, hold positions at the highest level in both business and government; however, the proportion of women to men in such positions is smaller than in the United States and Canada. Australian women expect to be treated equally to men in business situations.[31] Women from North America conducting business in Australia may experience some discomfort from Australian men because male chauvinism is still quite strong. Some Australian men are uncomfortable with women in positions of authority. However, Australians overall are accepting of businesswomen from other countries.[32]

On the Human Development Index (HDI), Australia ranks 3 out of 177 nations.[33] The HDI is a measure of empowerment; it is based on life expectancy, literacy, infant mortality, and real GDP. The assumption is that societies that provide an opportunity for education, access to healthcare, and adequate wages are inclined to be more democratic and exhibit a respect for human rights.[34]

Public Behavior

Visitors to Australia should avoid eating, drinking, or smoking in shops and public buildings, as well as when using public transportation. Never cut in line at special events or other places where people await their turn; simply get in line and wait your turn. In addition, blowing your nose in public is offensive; this should be done in private.

Do not litter; Australians value a clean environment and expect visitors to maintain their high standards of cleanliness. Fines are quite high for those found guilty of littering.[35]

NONVERBAL COMMUNICATION

Gestures and Posture

The "thumbs up" gesture is rude and should be avoided; it means "up yours." The V for Victory or peace gesture, with the forefinger and middle finger in the shape of a V with the palm faced outward, is widely understood. However, when the palm faces inward, the meaning is very rude; it means "Up yours!" Use your entire hand when pointing to someone; using only your index finger to point is offensive.[36]

An erect posture and moderate gesturing is important when speaking before audiences.

Eye Contact and Facial Expressions

Eye contact is important, especially during business meetings. Eye contact suggests honesty when communicating. Winking at a woman should be avoided as it is considered rude.[37]

Space and Touch

Australians prefer to have about two feet of space between them and those with whom they interact. They are uncomfortable when someone stands too close when conversing. Since Australian men do not engage in physical demonstrations of affection, refrain from placing your arm around the shoulders of your Australian male colleague.[38]

Punctuality and Attitude toward Time

Punctuality is very important to Australians. Always be on time for business appointments; in fact, being a little early is recommended.[39]

TRAVEL TIPS

- A passport is required when traveling to Australia; it must be valid for at least three months beyond the intended stay. A visa is also required.
- Avoid packing fruits, food, seeds, plants, or leather skins to take into Australia; their discovery will result in a large fine and, of course, the confiscation of the items.[40]
- When making hotel reservations, you will want to confirm amenities, such as air conditioning, TV, and refrigerator. You may wish to consider renting serviced flats of one to three rooms, which have kitchens for preparing your own meals. Flats, which are less expensive than hotels, are a good choice for families. Private hotels are not the same as those in the United States; they may not provide washcloths, sell liquor, or serve meals. Since the word "hotel" is used to mean a pub as well as a place that accepts guests, it is advisable to check accommodations carefully.[41]
- Public transportation in Australia includes buses, trains, and taxis; Melbourne has trams that are very popular. Bus fare is based on distance traveled; the driver will tell you the amount you owe. Train tickets are purchased from a station attendant or at automatic ticket machines. You may wish to buy an *Austrailpass* if you plan to do a lot of train travel.
- Taxis may be hailed on the streets or at downtown hotels; you may also call for a taxi. A custom not usually practiced in other countries is that a man traveling alone will sit in the front seat beside the driver (another indication of the concern Australians have for equality); women traveling alone, however, would occupy a seat in the back of the vehicle.[42]
- Women should avoid walking alone on the streets at night; they would be wise to take a taxi.
- If you wish to drive in Australia, you may use your U.S. driver's license for short visits. Before renting a car, take into consideration that Australians drive on the left. Seat belts are required. Avoid drinking and driving. If you wish to drive to the Outback, car-rental firms will probably require you to rent a four-wheel-drive vehicle because the unpaved roads would make it impractical to drive any other type of vehicle.[43]
- When shopping, it is acceptable to bargain for a lower price. In some stores, particularly in discount stores, the price is lower when you pay cash; ask about the store's policy.[44]
- Public restrooms are widely available. Use the term "toilet" when requesting the location of a restroom.

- The number to call for medical emergencies or when you need the services of the police or the fire department is 000.
- Water is reported to be safe to drink; however, people who travel frequently will probably continue to take bottled water with them to be on the safe side.
- Initiating a conversation with a stranger is acceptable; feel free to chat with people you do not know in the local pubs and to stop strangers on the street to ask for directions.[45]
- When invited to join Australians for a drink at the local pub, keep in mind that Australian beer has a higher alcoholic content than U.S. beers; it is also important to observe the drinking customs there, which involve buying a round of drinks when it is your "shout," meaning your turn to buy. You should probably be aware of a custom in some Australian pubs; i.e., turning your glass upside down after finishing your drink signals that you can drink more than anyone else there.[46]
- Even though Australians speak English, visitors should be aware that certain words have different meanings from the English spoken in other English-speaking countries. For example, if you say "I'm stuffed" following a large meal, you have just announced that you are pregnant. Because of the numerous language differences, visitors may wish to purchase a book of Australian words and phrases before they travel.[47]
- Additional information about travel to Australia is available from the Embassy of Australia, 1601 Massachusetts Avenue NW, Washington, D.C. 20036, (202-797-3000), or from the Australian Tourist Commission, 6100 Center Drive, Suite 1150, Los Angeles, CA 90045, (310-695-3200).

NOTES

1. U.S. Census Bureau Data, 2006, http://www.census.gov/foreign-trade/statistics (accessed April 25, 2007).
2. U.S. Census Bureau Data, 2007, http://www.census.gov/foreign-trade/statistics (accessed March 4, 2008).
3. *CultureGrams, Oceania, Australia* (Ann Arbor, MI: ProQuest CSA, 2008), 37.
4. Ibid.; Ann Marie Sabath, *International Business Etiquette: Asia and the Pacific Rim* (New York: ASJA Press, 2002), 18.
5. List of countries by GDP (nominal) per capita, http://en.wikipedia.org/wiki/List_of_countries_by_GDP_(nominal)_per_capita (accessed March 5, 2008). Figures (in U.S. dollars) are estimates for 2007 from *The World Factbook* provided by the Central Intelligence Agency (updated February 12, 2008). These figures do not take into account cost-of-living differences; using additional economic data is advisable when making country comparisons.
6. *CultureGrams, Oceania, Australia*, 38.
7. Ibid., 40.
8. Ibid., 38.
9. Ibid.; Philip R. Harris, Robert T. Moran, and Sarah V. Moran, *Managing Cultural Differences*, 6th ed. (Burlington, MA: Elsevier Butterworth-Heinemann, 2004), 359.

10. *CultureGrams, Oceania, Australia*, 38.
11. Ibid.
12. Carol Turkington, *The Complete Idiot's Guide to Cultural Etiquette* (Indianapolis, IN: Alpha Books, 1999), 294.
13. Sabath, *International Business Etiquette: Asia and the Pacific Rim*, 19–20.
14. Peggy Post and Peter Post, *Emily Post's The Etiquette Advantage in Business* (New York: HarperCollins Publishers, 1999), 524–525.
15. Roger E. Axtell, Tami Briggs, Margaret Corcoran, and Mary Beth Lamb, *Do's and Taboos Around the World for Women in Business* (New York: John Wiley & Sons, 1997), 116.
16. Nan Leaptrott, *Rules of the Game: Global Business Protocol* (Cincinnati, OH: Thomson Executive Press, 1996), 196; Terri Morrison and Wayne A. Conaway, *Kiss, Bow, or Shake Hands*, 2nd ed. (Avon, MA: Adams Media, 2006), 26.
17. Roger E. Axtell, *Gestures: The Do's and Taboos of Body Language Around the World* (New York: John Wiley & Sons, 1998), 175.
18. Sabath, *International Business Etiquette: Asia and the Pacific Rim*, 23.
19. *CultureGrams, Oceania, Australia*, 38.
20. Sabath, *International Business Etiquette: Asia and the Pacific Rim*, 27.
21. Morrison and Conaway, *Kiss, Bow, or Shake Hands*, 26.
22. Sabath, *International Business Etiquette: Asia and the Pacific Rim*, 26.
23. Leaptrott, *Rules of the Game: Global Business Protocol*, 195–196.
24. *CultureGrams, Oceania, Australia*, 38.
25. Sabath, *International Business Etiquette: Asia and the Pacific Rim*, 21.
26. Richard D. Lewis, *When Cultures Collide: Leading Across Cultures* (Boston: Nicholas Brealey International, 2006), 208; Jeanette S. Martin and Lillian H. Chaney, *Global Business Etiquette: A Guide to International Communication and Customs* (Westport, CT: Praeger, 2006), 130; Michael Powell, *Behave Yourself! The Essential Guide to International Etiquette* (Guilford, CT: The Globe Pequot Press, 2005), 8.
27. Elizabeth Devine and Nancy L. Braganti, *The Travelers' Guide to Asian Customs and Manners* (New York: St. Martin's Griffin, 1998), 327; Powell, *Behave Yourself! The Essential Guide to International Etiquette*, 9.
28. Ibid.; Axtell, Briggs, Corcoran, and Lamb, *Do's and Taboos Around the World for Women in Business*, 115.
29. Post and Post, *Emily Post's The Etiquette Advantage in Business*, 524.
30. *CultureGrams, Oceania, Australia*, 37; Lewis, *When Cultures Collide: Managing Successfully Across Cultures*, 14.
31. Post and Post, *Emily Post's The Etiquette Advantage in Business*, 524.
32. Axtell, Briggs, Corcoran, and Lamb, *Do's and Taboos Around the World for Women in Business*, 114.
33. *CultureGrams, Oceania, Australia*, 49.
34. *CultureGrams, Concepts and Terminology* (Ann Arbor, MI: ProQuest CSA, 2008), A-14.
35. Powell, *Behave Yourself! The Essential Guide to International Etiquette*, 10.
36. Axtell, Briggs, Corcoran, and Lamb, *Do's and Taboos Around the World for Women in Business*, 115.
37. Axtell, *Gestures: The Do's and Taboos of Body Language Around the World*, 175.
38. Morrison and Conaway, *Kiss, Bow, or Shake Hands*, 26.
39. Turkington, *The Complete Idiot's Guide to Cultural Etiquette*, 294.

40. Devine and Braganti, *The Travelers' Guide to Asian Customs and Manners*, 339.
41. Ibid., 333.
42. Ibid., 337–338; Powell, *Behave Yourself! The Essential Guide to International Etiquette*, 10.
43. Devine and Braganti, *The Travelers' Guide to Asian Customs and Manners*, 338.
44. Ibid., 339.
45. Turkington, *The Complete Idiot's Guide to Cultural Etiquette*, 298.
46. Axtell, Briggs, Corcoran, and Lamb, *Do's and Taboos Around the World for Women in Business*, 116.
47. Ibid., 115.

CHAPTER 4
Belgium

The Kingdom of Belgium, typically referred to as Belgium, is the twelfth largest export market of the United States.[1]

Major U. S. exports to Belgium are agricultural products, plastics, chemicals, synthetic rubber, industrial supplies, electrical apparatus, machinery, engines, electronics, medical equipment, pharmaceuticals, and gems.[2]

Understanding that Belgium is actually made up of three cultures—French, Flemish, and German—is important to understanding the cultural values of its residents.

COUNTRY SPECIFICS

A country's location, topography, economy, and population provide insight into understanding its culture. In addition, knowledge of ethnic groups, religions, time zones, and currency is helpful.

Location, Topography, and Land Mass

Belgium is located in Western Europe, bounded on the east by the Netherlands and Germany, on the southeast by Luxembourg, and on the south and southwest by France. The North Sea is on Belgium's northern border.

The three geographical areas of the country are the Ardennes tableland in the southeast, the western section known as Lower Belgium, and the central plain in the center of the country. Brussels is the capital of Belgium and is also headquarters for the North Atlantic Treaty Organization (NATO) and the European Union (EU).[3]

Most of the country is flat, with the exception of hilly terrain near the Ardennes forest. Forests cover approximately one-fifth of the country.

The major rivers in Belgium are the *Schelde* and the *Meuse*. Belgium covers an area of 11,780 square miles, or 30,510 square kilometers.[4]

Economy

The economy of Belgium is the 19th largest economy in the world; it is highly industrialized and is also diversified. The country enjoys a highly skilled workforce. Belgium's Gross Domestic Product (GDP) per capita is $37,374.[5]

Belgium is the largest exporter of chocolate and medicines in the world. In addition, 90 percent of the world's raw diamonds are handled in Antwerp.[6] Although steel is Belgium's main export, exports of steel have been declining in recent years. However, exports of goods associated with other industries (biotechnology, chemicals, food processing, and engineering) have increased. The country is one of the world's largest exporters of meats, wool, and beer (they reportedly make more than 800 kinds of beer). Other exports include automobiles, crystal, and glass. Factors in Belgium's success as a major exporter include the large seaport in Antwerp and the country's central location among members of the European Union, with whom they conduct a majority of trade.[7]

Although only a small percentage of the population is involved in agriculture, they produce a sufficient amount of food to be self-sustaining. About three-fourths of the residents are employed in service industries.

Population, Languages Spoken, Ethnic Groups, and Religions

The population of Belgium is almost 10.4 million people;[8] the population is growing at about 0.13 percent. The primary official languages of the country are Dutch (Flemish) and French. The language of the population that spoke French was formerly called Walloon; however, the term now is used to describe the culture of the French-speaking population. French is the main language spoken in the southern part of Belgium and in Brussels, the capital. Dutch is the main language in the north. Although German is also an official language, only one percent of the residents speak German.[9]

The primary ethnic groups have different patterns of behavior as well as different cultural values. The French and Flemish, for example, value interpersonal relationships more than do the Germans, who tend to have abstract opinions about right and wrong behavior and follow a strict code of behavior.[10]

About three-fourths of the population is Roman Catholic. The remaining one-fourth is made up of Protestants and other religious groups.

Although only a small percentage of the population regularly attend church, religion does have an impact on the personal lives of the residents, such as when celebrating births, marriages, and deaths.[11]

Country Codes, Time Zones, and Currency

The country code for Belgium is 32. City codes are 3 for Antwerp, 50 for Bruges, 2 for Brussels, 9 for Ghent, 4 for Liege, and 65 for Mons. When calling from the United States to Antwerp, for example, dial the International Access Code (011), followed by the country code (32), the city code (3), and the local telephone number.

Belgium is six hours ahead of U.S. Eastern Standard Time (EST).[12] When it is 5 PM in New York, it is 11 PM in Belgium; in Universal Time (UT) the times would be written as 1700 and 2200, respectively. The European Union (EU) in 1996 standardized its version of Daylight Saving Time (DST), which is observed from the last Sunday in March to the last Sunday in October. Since Belgium is a member of the EU, it observes DST.

The *euro* is now the currency of Belgium; it replaced the *Belgian franc* in 2002. A currency converter is available at http://coinmill.com/AED_calculator.html that will convert any currency in the world to any other currency.

BUSINESS AND SOCIAL CUSTOMS

Greetings, Introductions, and Business Cards

A brief handshake when meeting someone is the common greeting in Belgium. People also shake hands when leaving. Women who wish to shake hands will initiate the handshake. Close friends may exchange light kisses on the cheek. The cheek-kissing ritual involves kissing on one cheek, then the other, and then back to the first cheek.[13]

During business introductions use the person's title and last name since first names are used only between close friends. Always keep in mind the primary language of the person you are meeting when deciding which title to use. English titles (Mr., Mrs., Miss, or Ms.) may be used with people who speak English or German; *Monsieur* (Mr.), *Madame* (Mrs.), and *Mademoiselle* (Miss) are used with those who speak French. *Meneer* (Mr.), *Mevrouw* (Mrs.), and *Juffrouw* (Miss) are used for those who speak Flemish.[14]

Exchanging business cards is common in Belgium. Information on the card should be printed in English on one side and in the language of the people with whom you conduct the most business (usually French,

Flemish, or German) on the other side. When presenting your card, position it so that your colleague can read the information.[15]

Business Entertaining and Seating Customs

Belgians prefer to do their business entertaining at lunch in a restaurant since they like to spend evenings with their families. Business lunches usually last about two hours, typically from 1 PM to 3 PM. Wine is generally served with the meal. Should you decide to invite your Belgian colleague to dinner at a restaurant, invite your colleague's spouse as well. If you are invited to dinner at a Belgian home, you would not expect to discuss business.

Wait for your host to indicate where you should sit in meetings and restaurants. When you are the host at a meal function, take the position at the head of the table. Your spouse, when he or she accompanies you, sits opposite you. The highest-ranking female guest will sit to the host's right; the highest-ranking male guest sits to the right of the hostess.[16]

Dining, Toasting, and Tipping Customs

Belgians use the Continental style of eating, which involves leaving the knife in the right hand and the fork in the left. Wrists should be kept on the edge of the table, not in the lap, during the meal. Resting your utensils between bites involves placing them in the center of the plate in an "X" position, with the tines of the fork on top of the knife. To indicate that you are finished, place the knife and fork at approximately the 10 o'clock and 4 o'clock position, fork tines up.[17]

Some dining customs to be aware of include the serving of salad after the main course, not before it. Bread lovers may wonder why they are not offered bread when dining in northern Belgium. Their custom is to serve a maximum of one starch at each meal. Thus, if potatoes will be on the menu, no bread is served. Do not request it. In southern Belgium, on the other hand, bread is typically served at each meal. You may not be served butter, however. If butter is not offered, do not ask for it. In addition to the wine that is served with the meal, you may wish to order coffee or hot tea. Just ask for it after the entrée. Since Belgium is a country where you are expected to clean your plate, take small portions.[18]

Smokers should follow the host's lead on smoking etiquette. Offering cigarettes to others at the table before you light your own cigarette is customary. Smoking is acceptable only before the first course is served and after the last course has been removed.[19]

Toasting is especially festive in Belgium, a country famous for excellent beers. Always wait to drink until your host makes the first toast. The toasting custom among the Flemish is a bit different from the rest of the country. You will raise your glass initially during the host's verbal toast but will not drink; you then exchange glances and lift your glass a second time before drinking.[20] When proposing a toast, the Dutch-speaking segment of the population will say *Op uw gezondheid* ("a toast to"); the French-speaking segment of the population will say *Á votre santé* ("to your health"), which is the same toast used in France.

Tipping customs in Belgium are similar to other European countries. A tip of 15 percent is usually included in the bill in restaurants; it is not necessary to leave an extra amount. Of course, rewarding exemplary service by leaving an additional tip is always appreciated. Tipping the wine steward (*sommelier*) is not customary. Tipping hotel personnel and washroom attendants is expected. Tip the hotel shuttle driver 15 percent of what you would have paid a taxi driver—more when the driver helps you with your luggage. Do not tip taxi drivers, as the fare includes a tip.[21]

Gift-Giving Customs

Your Belgian associates will not expect gifts from you; however, it is acceptable to present a small gift to a business colleague with whom you have developed a close relationship. A gift containing your company's logo, however, is inappropriate. In addition, do not include your business card with your gift.

If you are invited to someone's home, be sure to bring a gift for the hostess. Chocolates are welcomed, as are flowers provided they are not chrysanthemums (considered funereal), red roses (associated with romance), or 13 of any type of flower (believed to be unlucky). The gift should be presented before the meal rather than after it.

The proper procedure when being presented a gift is to open it in front of the giver and express your appreciation. Your Belgian colleague will likewise open his or her gift from you in your presence.[22]

Business Meetings

Make business appointments with your Belgian colleagues at least a week in advance. Avoid trying to schedule Saturday appointments. In addition, avoid trying to schedule Monday meetings in Antwerp and Wednesday meetings in Brussels, as Belgian businesspeople in these cities typically have lunch with their business colleagues on these days.

Upon arrival at the meeting, shake hands with everyone. Business meetings in Belgium usually begin with a period of small talk before discussing business. Actually, your first meeting may be spent simply getting to know each other. You should follow the lead of your Belgian associate in moving from small talk to business discussions.

Agendas are appreciated, as they provide structure to the meeting. Make copies of the agenda and handouts of supporting documentation for your presentation to distribute to each person in attendance. Avoid interruptions and try to keep the meeting running smoothly without distractions. Since developing trust is important to Belgians, be patient. Present your proposal assertively but not aggressively. Being too pushy could cost you a good business deal. At the conclusion of the meeting, shake hands with everyone before leaving.[23]

Dress and Appearance

Business dress in Belgium is conservative and follows European fashions. People dress well in public and typically wear casual attire only in the home. In keeping with their preference for conservative, tasteful attire, Belgians keep their shoes well polished; men do not wear loafers or other slip-on shoes, unless their travel plans include passing through security checkpoints in airports. People of Belgium wear their best clothing on Sundays, regardless of whether or not their plans include attending special events or visiting friends.[24]

Attire for business meetings and for formal restaurants includes suits for men and dresses or skirted suits for women. Proper dress for concerts and the theater consists of dark suits and ties for men and cocktail dresses for women unless, of course, formal attire is specified on the invitation. In that event, men wear either tuxedos or dark suits and women wear cocktail dresses.[25]

Holidays

Belgium celebrates the following public holidays and religious celebrations:

- New Year's Day (January 1)
- Easter (March/April)
- Ascension Day (five weeks after Easter, May/June)
- Whit Monday (eight weeks after Easter, May/June)
- Corpus Christi (60 days after Easter, June/July)
- Independence Day (July 21)

- Assumption (August 15)
- All Saints' Day (November 1)
- Armistice Day (November 11)
- Christmas (December 25/26)

Conversational Customs

Belgians are somewhat reserved when meeting someone for the first time. During conversations keep your voice low and controlled, and avoid showing excitement. Tact and diplomacy are important to Belgians; being totally honest is perceived as rude.

Belgians often start conversations by discussing the weather or some aspect of the world's economy. They also like to talk about sports, especially bicycle racing and soccer. Other good topics of conversation include special tourist attractions and Belgian history. Thus, it is important to read about Belgian culture and history so that you can be prepared to ask questions and make appropriate comments about the country.

Topics to avoid include Belgian religion and politics. In addition, do not criticize the monarchy. Be sensitive to language differences in Belgium and avoid making negative comments about either the French or the Flemish. Do not speak French in the Flemish or German areas. Avoid asking personal questions. Even asking about a person's family or occupation is viewed as too intrusive.[26]

Humor

Belgian humor leans toward irony and wit; it is usually at the expense of someone else. Unlike people of some European countries, Belgians are able to laugh at themselves. In some countries, including Belgium, residents have a penchant for targeting special nationalities for their barbs. People of Belgium, for example, like to make jokes about the ignorance of the Dutch. Likewise, the Dutch make jokes about their slow-witted neighbors, the Belgians. In addition, Belgians do not like to be compared to their other neighbor, the French, and even make rude jokes about them. As in other countries, the best advice when you commit a gaffe in Belgium is to laugh it off. In most cultures, being able to laugh at yourself is a quality that people admire. People in all cultures enjoy a good laugh; however, we must remember that we do not all laugh at the same things.[27]

Attitude toward Women in Business

Although women have made progress in the Belgian work environment in the past several decades, they continue to hold primarily support staff positions. With the exception of businesses that are family owned, few women professional managers are found in Belgian companies.[28]

On the Human Development Index (HDI), Belgium ranks 13 out of 177 nations.[29] The HDI is a measure of empowerment; it is based on life expectancy, literacy, infant mortality, and real GDP. The assumption is that societies that provide an opportunity for education, access to healthcare, and adequate wages are inclined to be more democratic and exhibit a respect for human rights.[30]

U.S. businesswomen need to be aware that Belgian businessmen do not typically permit women to pay for entertainment. Thus, when they entertain Belgian businessmen, U.S. businesswomen should arrange for payment prior to the event and should say that entertainment expenses are borne by their company.[31]

Public Behavior

Men open doors for women and permit them to precede them when boarding buses, entering rooms, and so forth. Women are treated with respect; men stand when women enter a room.

Using a toothpick in public is rude. Other rude behavior includes blowing your nose or scratching in public. In addition, do not keep your hands in your pockets during conversations as this is considered rude.

NONVERBAL COMMUNICATION

Gestures and Posture

Belgians are restrained in their hand movements, so it is advisable to refrain from gesturing during visits to this country. Pointing with your index finger is rude; use the entire hand for pointing. Another gesture to be avoided is snapping the fingers on both hands; this gesture is considered obscene.[32]

Maintain good posture while standing and sitting as good posture is important to Belgians. Also avoid placing your feet on chairs and tables.[33]

Eye Contact and Facial Expressions

People of Belgium value eye contact. Maintain steady eye contact when shaking hands; do not glance away. Yawning is viewed as rude by Belgians; therefore, make a strong effort to avoid it.

Space and Touch

Space is important in Belgium. Keep an arm's length away during interactions; moving closer is viewed as an invasion of personal space. Do not pat another person on the back. Belgians do not typically touch each other during interactions.[34]

Punctuality and Attitude toward Time

Belgians are punctual and expect others to be prompt as well. Thus, being on time for meetings and appointments is essential to successful business negotiations.

TRAVEL TIPS

- Travel to Belgium requires a passport that is valid for at least 90 days beyond the expected return date. No visa is required for visits of up to three months.
- If you wish to drive in Belgium, you will not need an International Driver's License. Seat belts are mandatory. Traffic laws are strictly enforced for all drivers, including those from other countries. If you are stopped for a violation, do not argue with the police officer.
- Since penalties for driving while intoxicated are severe, including losing your driver's license and spending a year in jail, do not drink and drive. The legal drinking age is 18.[35]
- If you decide to use public transportation, you may buy tickets for a bus or streetcar when you board. When using the subway (Metro), purchase a ticket at the ticket window. You will have a choice of first- and second-class accommodations. Always keep your ticket, as it will be checked as you exit. Trains are another option for public transportation. Again, you will have a choice of first- and second-class accommodations, in addition to a choice between smoking and nonsmoking cars. Purchase your ticket before boarding if time permits; if not, mention to a conductor as you board that you will need to purchase a ticket. Boarding without a ticket and without reporting this fact to a conductor will result in your being fined.[36]
- Taxis, which are quite expensive, are available at taxi stands; they may not be hailed on the street. You can, of course, telephone for a taxi.[37]
- If you need to call the police, dial 101 or 112; if you have a medical emergency or need the help of the fire department, call 100 or 112.
- Public restrooms, which are usually available in cafes, bars, restaurants, and hotels, will be marked with *Dames* or *Damen* for women and *Messieurs* or *Herren* for men. They may also be marked OO or W.C., indicating use by both genders.[38]
- Since Belgians do not like braggarts, do not brag about your accomplishments, your personal possessions, or your family. Avoid displays of wealth, such as flashing large sums of money or wearing expensive jewelry.[39]
- Avoid scheduling business trips during the period between Christmas and New Year's; also avoid the months of July and August.

- Learn about the language and cultural differences in Belgium. Cultural values are different for the people of the three ethnic backgrounds—French, Flemish, and German—and are very important to conducting business in this country.
- Additional information about Belgium is available from the Embassy of Belgium, 3330 Garfield Street NW, Washington, D.C. 20008, (202-333-6900), or from the Belgian Tourist Office, 220 East 42 Street, Suite 3402, New York, N.Y. 10017, (212-758-8130).

NOTES

1. U.S. Census Bureau Data, 2007, http://www.census.gov/foreign-trade/statistics (accessed March 4, 2008).
2. U.S. Census Bureau Data, 2006, http://www.census.gov/foreign-trade/statistics (accessed June 17, 2007).
3. Terri Morrison and Wayne A. Conaway, *Kiss, Bow, or Shake Hands*, 2nd ed. (Avon, MA: Adams Media, 2006), 40.
4. *CultureGrams, Europe, Belgium* (Ann Arbor, MI: ProQuest CSA, 2008), 69.
5. Ibid., 72; Richard D. Lewis, *When Cultures Collide: Leading Across Cultures*, 3rd ed. (Boston: Nicholas Brealey International, 2006), 252; List of countries by GDP (nominal) per capita, http://en.wikipedia.org/wiki/List_of_countries_by_GDP_(nominal)_per_capita (accessed March 5, 2008). Figures (in U.S. dollars) are estimates for 2007 from *The World Factbook* provided by the Central Intelligence Agency (updated February 12, 2008). These figures do not take into account cost-of-living differences; using additional economic data is advisable when making country comparisons.
6. Elaine Sciolino, "Belgium: Two Nations United in Ire," *The Commercial Appeal* (September 23, 2007): A6.
7. Ibid.
8. U.S. Census Bureau, "*IDB: Countries and Areas Ranked by Population*," as of 2007, http://www.census.gov/cgi-bin/ipc/idbrank.pl (accessed January 16, 2008).
9. Ibid., 70; Terri Morrison and Wayne A. Conaway, *The International Traveler's Guide to Doing Business in the European Union* (New York: Macmillan Spectrum, 1997), 44.
10. Carol Turkington, *The Complete Idiot's Guide to Cultural Etiquette* (Indianapolis, IN: Alpha Books, 1999), 75.
11. *CultureGrams, Europe, Belgium*, 70.
12. Ann Marie Sabath, *International Business Etiquette: Europe* (Franklin Lakes, NJ: Career Press, 1999), 34.
13. Roger E. Axtell, *Gestures: The Do's and Taboos of Body Language Around the World* (New York: John Wiley & Sons, 1998), 132.
14. Michael Powell, *Behave Yourself! The Essential Guide to International Etiquette* (Guilford, CT: The Globe Pequot Press, 2005), 15; Turkington, *The Complete Idiot's Guide to Cultural Etiquette*, 80.
15. Morrison and Conaway, *Kiss, Bow, or Shake Hands*, 43.
16. Sabath, *International Business Etiquette: Europe*, 40.
17. Ibid., 38
18. Ibid.

19. Ibid.; Powell, *Behave Yourself! The Essential Guide to International Etiquette*, 15.
20. Turkington, *The Complete Idiot's Guide to Cultural Etiquette*, 83.
21. Sabath, *International Business Etiquette: Europe*, 42.
22. Ibid., 40; Turkington, *The Complete Idiot's Guide to Cultural Etiquette*, 81–82.
23. Nancy L. Braganti and Elizabeth Devine, *European Customs and Manners* (New York: Meadowbrook Press, 1992), 25–26; Turkington, *The Complete Idiot's Guide to Cultural Etiquette*, 78.
24. Sabath, *International Business Etiquette: Europe*, 45; Turkington, *The Complete Idiot's Guide to Cultural Etiquette*, 81.
25. Braganti and Devine, *European Customs and Manners*, 21.
26. Ibid., 19–20; Lewis, *When Cultures Collide: Leading Across Cultures*, 254.
27. Roger E. Axtell, *Do's and Taboos of Humor Around the World* (New York: John Wiley & Sons, 1999), 88–89; John Mole, *Mind Your Manners* (London: Nicholas Brealey Publishing, 1998), 116.
28. Roger E. Axtell, Tami Briggs, Margaret Corcoran, and Mary Beth Lamb, *Do's and Taboos Around the World for Women in Business* (New York: John Wiley & Sons, 1997), 85.
29. *CultureGrams, Europe, Belgium*, 72.
30. *CultureGrams, Concepts and Terminology* (Ann Arbor, MI: ProQuest CSA, 2008), A-14.
31. Braganti and Devine, *European Customs and Manners*, 26.
32. Sabath, *International Business Etiquette: Europe*, 39.
33. Powell, *Behave Yourself! The Essential Guide to International Etiquette*, 15.
34. Braganti and Devine, *European Customs and Manners*, 26.
35. Ibid., 28.
36. Ibid., 27.
37. Ibid.
38. Ibid., 21.
39. Turkington, *The Complete Idiot's Guide to Cultural Etiquette*, 79.

CHAPTER 5

Brazil

The Federative Republic of Brazil, commonly referred to as Brazil, is the thirteenth largest export market of the United States.[1]

Major U.S. exports to Brazil are agricultural, coal, and petroleum products; plastics; chemicals; industrial supplies; oilfield equipment; industrial engines and machines; electrical apparatus; electronics; medical equipment; aircraft; automotive; pharmaceutical; and records, tapes, and disks.[2]

COUNTRY SPECIFICS

A country's location, topography, economy, and population provide insight into understanding its culture. In addition, knowledge of ethnic groups, religions, time zones, and currency is helpful.

Location, Topography, and Land Mass

Brazil is the largest country in South America; in fact, it comprises half of South America. The country borders all other South American countries except for Chile and Ecuador. The eastern part of the country extends to the Atlantic Ocean. São Paulo and Rio de Janeiro are the largest cities. The capital of Brazil is Brasília.

The five regions of Brazil are north, northeast, southeast, south, and central-west. The Amazon River and the largest tropical rain forest in the world run along northern Brazil; the Amazon is the longest river in South America. The Pantanal, which is the world's largest wetlands, is also located in Brazil. In the southern part of the country, known for agriculture and manufacturing, is located one of the largest hydroelectric dams in the world. The southeast region, which has the largest population of the five regions, enjoys an abundance of minerals and natural resources.[3] The area of Brazil is 3,286,488 square miles, or 8,511,965 square kilometers.[4]

Economy

Brazil's economy is the largest in South America and the eighth largest worldwide. Brazil sustains itself in the areas of consumer goods and food production. The Gross Domestic Product (GDP) per capita is $6,679.[5] The country produces bananas, coffee, and oranges. The sugarcane it produces is used in ethyl alcohol production, which is used in about one-third of the cars in Brazil. The country exports automobiles and parts, metals, minerals, and textiles. Major imports include oil and natural gas.[6]

The economy of Brazil has remained quite stable, despite the problems with inflation during the 1980s and early 1990s. The country survived its economic crisis by initiating cuts in government spending, increasing taxes, and implementing additional emergency measures. Unemployment ranges from high in such cities as São Paulo to moderate in other areas.[7]

Population, Languages Spoken, Ethnic Groups, and Religions

With a population of just over 190 million people, Brazil's population is the fifth largest in the world.[8] The official language of Brazil is Portuguese; it is the only Portuguese-speaking country in South America. The most popular second languages are English and French. Spanish is spoken in some areas, no doubt due to increased trade with its South American neighbors. German and Italian are also spoken in some of the southern cities where descendants of European immigrants reside.[9]

About 55 percent of the population of Brazil is white; they are primarily of German, Portuguese, Italian, Polish, and Spanish descent; about 38 percent of Brazilian residents are of mixed heritage. Ethnic communities are located in southern Brazil, comprising immigrants from Japan, Germany, Italy, and Lebanon, .

About 70 percent of the population is Roman Catholic; approximately 20 percent is Protestant.[10]

Country Codes, Time Zones, and Currency

The country code for Brazil is 55. City codes include 11 for São Paulo and 61 for Brasília.[11] When calling from the United States to Brasília, for example, dial the International Access Code (011), followed by the country code (55), the city code (61), and the local telephone number.

Since Brazil is so large, slightly larger than the 48 contiguous United States, it is divided into two time zones. Most of the country is two hours ahead of U.S. Eastern Standard Time (EST). The western part of Brazil is one hour ahead of U.S. EST.[12] Thus, when it is 5 PM in New York, it is 7 PM in Brasília. In Universal Time (UT) the times would be written as 1700 and 1900, respectively. With the exception of equatorial Brazil, Daylight Saving Time (DST) is usually observed starting the first Sunday in October and ending the third Sunday in February. (The dates may vary.)

Brazil's new currency, which was introduced in 1994, is the *real* (BRL); it has been effective in curbing inflation.[13] A currency converter is available at http://coinmill.com/AED_calculator.html that will convert any currency in the world to any other currency.

BUSINESS AND SOCIAL CUSTOMS

Greetings, Introductions, and Business Cards

The handshake is the proper greeting between people in business. However, more personal greetings, especially between women, include one or two kisses on the cheeks—three kisses when a woman is unmarried to wish her luck in finding a mate. While men often kiss women on the cheeks, men do not typically kiss each other; they do pat each other on the back during the handshake. Greeting and saying goodbye to each person is expected; the group greeting of "Hello, everybody!" often used by U.S. persons is viewed as impersonal by Brazilians and should be avoided.[14]

Although many Brazilians are not as formal as residents of other countries in Latin America, it is a good idea to use appropriate titles until you get to know your Brazilian acquaintances. Often the title *Doutor* or *Doutora* (Doctor) is used even when the person is neither an M.D. nor a Ph.D.; it is used as a sign of respect, especially with older people. Another custom is the use of a title with a person's first name; in fact, some people introduce themselves in this manner. When in doubt, ask people how they wish to be addressed. The number of names people use may be somewhat confusing to visitors; a person's full name may, in fact, contain five or six names. A Brazilian will have two surnames; the mother's surname followed by the father's surname. People are usually addressed by the father's surname. While women take their husband's surname when they marry, in business situations they typically use their father's surname.[15]

Business card exchange is important in Brazil. Having your business cards printed in English on one side and in Portuguese on the reverse side is recommended.[16]

Business Entertaining and Seating Customs

Business entertaining is usually done in restaurants. Although it is acceptable to be late to business meetings, punctuality is expected for business meals. Business lunches and dinners are common; business breakfasts are not. These meals may be lengthy; lunches often last two hours and dinners last as long as three hours. Always wait for your Brazilian host to initiate business discussions. Do not appear anxious to discuss business, as Brazilians prefer to concentrate on the food rather than on discussing business.

When you entertain your Brazilian host, select a prestigious restaurant. Image is important to Brazilians. Using proper table manners is also important, so be sure to observe the rules of dining etiquette.[17]

Your Brazilian host will usually sit at the head of the table; you will probably be offered the seat to the host's right. When you are hosting a business meal, offer the seat at the head of the table to the highest-ranking Brazilian.[18]

Dining, Toasting, and Tipping Customs

Brazilians use the Continental style of eating, with the fork remaining in the left hand and the knife in the right. When not in use, the tip of the knife rests on the edge of your plate; the knife handle rests on the table. You are expected to keep your hands on the table during the meal rather than in your lap. Other dining guidelines include using a knife for cutting food rather than the side of your fork, not touching food with your hands (including sandwiches and fruit), and never drinking from a can or bottle—always drink from a glass. [19]

When someone offers a toast, simply raise your glass, say *saude* ("health!") or *viva* ("hurrah!"), and take a sip of your wine. When you wish to make a toast, avoid getting people's attention by tapping the glass with silverware; this is impolite.

Tipping in restaurants is usually 10 percent, which is typically included in the bill. Leaving an additional 5-percent tip when the service is good is customary. Tips for taxi drivers are 10 percent in Rio, but they are not expected in other parts of Brazil. Since taxis have set prices, you will want to ask the price to your destination before departing. Porters are usually tipped the equivalent of $1 per bag.[20]

Gift-Giving Customs

Giving business gifts in Brazil is not required; however, Brazilians appreciate receiving gifts as they view their business relationships as personal relationships. At the initial meeting, however, paying for a meal is more appropriate than giving a gift.

Appropriate gifts to give at subsequent meetings include small electronic gadgets, including iPods or CD players. Other appropriate gifts include wine, good-quality whiskey, name-brand pens, chocolate (especially Copenhagen chocolate, a high-quality candy made in Brazil), DVDs of U.S. movies, or mementos of your country or city, such as illustrated coffee-table books. Wrap gifts attractively. When you are presented a gift, open it in the presence of the giver.[21]

Gifts or gift wrappings should not be purple or black, as these colors have funereal connotations. Handkerchiefs are inappropriate as well as they suggest grief. Do not give gifts with sharp edges, such as knives and scissors, which are interpreted as a desire to sever the relationship.[22]

Business Meetings

Business appointments should be made at least two weeks in advance. Avoid making business trips during Brazil's summer vacation period, which is mid-December to the end of February. Also avoid July, which is a school holiday month.

Meetings typically start with small talk, with topics ranging from the weather to current events. Topics that could be controversial are to be avoided. A period of getting to know their potential business partners is important to Brazilians; they like to establish a personal relationship with people before conducting business with them. You can expect meetings to be a bit chaotic as participants stray from agenda items. People from other countries should be aware of the tendency of Brazilians to stretch the truth since they are more concerned with telling people what they wish to hear rather than with being completely candid. Another business custom that foreign visitors need to know is that the initial enthusiasm Brazilians show for a new project may wane; thus, it may be necessary to monitor commitments to make sure they are seen to completion. In addition, it is important to know that Brazilians are indirect, avoid confrontations, and practice saving face in their business relationships. Therefore, you can expect meetings to be lengthy. Do not leave when the meeting ends; this behavior would be impolite and would imply that you have somewhere else to go that is more important.[23]

Use the same people throughout negotiations because Brazilians place great importance on building a personal relationship prior to doing business. Be prepared to make several visits before signing a contract. Agreements are often made with a handshake; the written contract will be prepared and signed later. Unlike in the United States and in many other cultures, a signed contract is still subject to modifications.[24]

Dress and Appearance

Brazilians are well known for the importance they place on being fashionably and stylishly dressed; they are also concerned with keeping in good physical condition, which includes running and working out in fitness clubs. They tend to favor European fashions. Their business attire consists of stylish suits in black and neutral colors. Visitors should be especially careful not to wear clothing containing green and yellow together as these are the colors of the Brazilian flag. Shorts or tennis shoes should not be worn in public.[25]

Women who wish to do business in Brazil should dress conservatively, yet elegantly. They should avoid suggestive attire or expensive jewelry, even though they may observe Brazilian businesswomen wearing attire that would often be considered either very casual (sundresses) or too dressy (low-cut, spaghetti strap dresses). Wearing matching purses and shoes is important to Brazilian women. In addition, women who wish to be taken seriously in business should avoid being flirtatious and should behave in a professional, businesslike manner at all times.

Grooming is important to both men and women; Brazilians keep their shoes polished and their nails neatly manicured. Cleanliness is extremely important; Brazilians often take two showers a day in hot weather. Keeping their teeth clean is likewise important to Brazilians; they are often observed brushing their teeth in company or restaurant restrooms. Because of the value that Brazilians place on dress and appearance, people of other cultures who wish to do business in Brazil would be wise to give special attention to their grooming and attire.[26]

Holidays

When planning your business trip, avoid the following holidays:

- New Year's Day (January 1)
- St. Sebastian Day—Rio only (January 20)
- Foundation of the City—São Paulo only (January 25)
- Carnival Celebration (February/March)
- Good Friday and Easter (March/April)
- Tiradentes Day (April 21)
- Labor Day (May 1)

- Corpus Christi (June—date varies)
- Independence Day (September 7)
- Day of the Patroness of Brazil (October 12)
- All Souls' Day (November 2)
- Proclamation of the Republic (November 15)
- Christmas (December 25)[27]

Conversational Customs

The Brazilian style of communication is animated and expressive; speech is rapid with few pauses between words. Even though the dialogue may seem to bystanders to be a heated argument, it is usually a friendly exchange. The Brazilian habit of constantly repeating what has already been stated causes people of many cultures to conclude that they are disorganized in their oral communication.[28]

Constant interruptions when conversing with others are to be expected. Interrupting, regarded as rude in many cultures, is a sign of enthusiasm to Brazilians. Silence during conversations is uncommon.[29]

Appropriate topics for small talk include soccer (*futebol*) and other sports, such as fishing, skiing, basketball, and volleyball; the beautiful beaches; food; tourist attractions; Brazilian dances; and the importance of the family.[30]

Subjects to avoid during conversations include politics, destruction of the rain forest, AIDS, poverty, and religion. Do not ask personal questions, including age, marital status, or salary; however, Brazilians may ask you personal questions, even your political persuasion and religion.[31]

Humor

Although using humorous anecdotes is intended to be a way of establishing a relaxed atmosphere before beginning serious business discussions in international meetings, Brazilians do not typically use humor during business meetings. Perhaps, as has been suggested, Brazilians do not feel it necessary to use humor to "break the ice" since their gossipy conversation style often provides sufficient humor for putting meeting participants at ease.[32] While Brazilians enjoy humor, it is advisable to refrain from participating in the ethnic jokes Brazilians tell about the Portuguese.

Attitude toward Women in Business

Many Brazilian women work outside the home, especially in large cities. Although more women are holding upper-management positions, women rarely hold the top positions in large companies. Women are well accepted in medicine, education, and journalism; they also hold political positions. In addition, women are holding governmental positions as cabinet members and as members of Brazil's Supreme Court.[33]

Women from other countries should encounter no difficulties conducting business in Brazil. They will need to become accustomed to having men stare at them in public and make comments to them as they pass them on the street as this behavior is not viewed as rude in Brazil.[34]

On the Human Development Index (HDI), Brazil ranks 69 out of 177 nations.[35] The HDI is a measure of empowerment; it is based on life expectancy, literacy, infant mortality, and real GDP. The assumption is that societies that provide an opportunity for education, access to healthcare, and adequate wages are inclined to be more democratic and exhibit a respect for human rights. [36]

Public Behavior

Do not yawn or stretch in public as this is considered rude. Avoid pushing others when in a crowd. Do not eat on the street or in public places. (Brazilians prefer to enjoy their meals and eat slowly rather than eating "on the run.") Eating food purchased from street vendors is not recommended.

Visitors should be aware that smoking is not permitted in many public places.[37] Visitors should also be aware that items they carry while walking on the streets should be wrapped in paper or carried in a bag.

Brazilians do not seem to be averse to littering; it is not uncommon to see cigarette butts, paper cups, and other types of trash on the ground. Since the streets are cleaned daily, this littering habit does not become a major problem.[38]

NONVERBAL COMMUNICATION

Because nonverbal elements are often more important than verbal expressions, it is important to study the nonverbal communication patterns of Brazilians.

Gestures and Posture

Brazilians use a lot of gestures, some of which you may not have encountered. Ask for an interpretation if you are uncertain about the meaning of any gesture.

Some gestures commonly used by Brazilians include the "fig," formed by tucking the thumb between the index and middle finger (good luck); the "thumbs up" gesture (approval); finger snap (do it quickly); and wiping hands together (it does not matter). When Brazilians brush the back of their fingers beneath the chin and move them outward, they are indicating that they do not know. Pinching the earlobe between the thumb and forefinger signals appreciation. When the gesture is used at the conclusion of a meal, for example, it signals enjoyment of the food. Another gesture used by Brazilian men to express appreciation for a pretty girl is the telescope — cupping both hands together and looking through them as if they were a telescope.[39]

Gestures to avoid include the "O.K." sign, pointing the middle finger up, and punching your fist into your open palm; all are vulgar gestures.[40]

Eye Contact and Facial Expressions

Brazilians maintain eye contact when conversing, especially with others of equal status. Little eye contact exists between those of different ages or status. When conversing with someone who is younger or of a lower status, it is customary for the younger person or the one of lower status to look down to show respect. Brazilians often stare at others in public places; this behavior can cause discomfort for people of many other cultures.[41]

Space and Touch

During conversations, Brazilians tend to stand close to each other. Stepping back should be avoided since you may be perceived as aloof. You can also expect to be touched during conversations as Brazilians are very tactile people. Hugging and touching each other signifies friendship.

Punctuality and Attitude toward Time

In the workplace, punctuality is important. However, it is not unusual for meetings to begin late—10 to 30 minutes late, in fact—because of the heavy traffic in the larger cities. Appointments generally run longer than had been scheduled as Brazilians are generous when it comes to giving their time. This lack of staying on schedule causes subsequent appointments during the day to also run late.[42]

In social situations, it is customary to arrive about 15 minutes later than the time stated on the invitation. Hosts do not expect you to be early or even on time.[43]

Brazil is a polychronic culture; they do several things simultaneously.

TRAVEL TIPS

- A passport is required for traveling to Brazil; it should be valid for six months from the date of entry. A visa is also required.
- Before you travel to Brazil, check for recommended immunizations, including cholera, typhoid, and yellow fever, especially if you plan to travel outside urban areas.
- When making hotel reservations, check the hotel's rating, which will range from one to five stars. Since accommodations vary, be sure to confirm whether the hotel is equipped with air conditioning, TV, refrigerator, and other amenities. If you plan to visit during Carnival, you will need to make reservations at the better hotels a year in advance. Avoid motels; they are frequented by lovers and often rented by the hour.[44]
- You will probably wish to take a taxi from the airport to your hotel. At your destination airport, you may purchase a voucher at the taxi stand, which covers your fare, except for a tip. When you take a taxi at other times, either make sure that the meter is turned on or that you agree to the fare in advance. City buses should be avoided; however, buses that travel between cities have bathrooms and air conditioning and are quite comfortable. You may wish to take the subway in the larger cities. Trains between São Paulo and Rio de Janeiro are inexpensive and comfortable; they include food service.[45]
- Drink bottled water only; do not request ice in your beverages. Avoid eating fruits or vegetables that have not been peeled or cooked.[46]
- Since pickpockets and thieves are problems, take proper precautions to avoid being victimized. Avoid places known to be dangerous, do not walk after dark, and do not wear jewelry when you leave your hotel. Before leaving your valuables in the hotel safe, make sure the hotel has insurance against theft. Be especially cautious at the beach.[47]
- Be careful crossing streets; traffic is fast, and drivers are not inclined to watch out for pedestrians. In fact, pedestrians do not have the right of way; drivers do.
- Driving in Brazil is not recommended. If you do decide to drive, you should have an International Driver's License. You should also be able to speak Portuguese since you will probably have to ask for directions. Seat belts are mandatory. When you park your car, take advantage of the services offered by numerous children who will guard your car for a small fee while you shop.[48]
- Check the local phone book (listed under *Bombeiros* or *Policia Civil*) for the emergency phone numbers should you need to call a police officer, an ambulance, or the fire department since they are different for each city. The emergency numbers to call in Rio, for example, are 190 for police and 193 for an ambulance or for the fire department.[49]

- Do not take photographs at religious ceremonies. When you visit museums and churches, you will be asked to leave your camera with an attendant at the entrance. Always ask permission before photographing people.[50]
- Public restrooms are not plentiful; they are available at hotels and restaurants. The public restroom accommodations found at airports and train and bus stations require a fee to enter. Restrooms for women will be labeled *mulher*, and those for men will be labeled *senhor*.[51]
- When shopping in markets, you may be successful in bargaining for a lower price, especially if you can speak Portuguese.
- Additional information about Brazil is available from the Embassy of Brazil, 3006 Massachusetts Avenue NW, Washington, D.C. 20008, (202-238-2700), or from the Brazilian Tourism Office, 2141 Wisconsin Avenue NW, Suite E-2, Washington, D.C. 20007, (800-727-2945).

NOTES

1. U.S. Census Bureau Data, 2007, http://census.gov/foreign-trade/statistics (accessed March 4, 2008).
2. U.S. Census Bureau Data, 2006, http://www.census.gov/foreign-trade/statistics (accessed June 17, 2007).
3. *CultureGrams, South America, Brazil* (Ann Arbor, MI: ProQuest CSA, 2008), 97.
4. Ibid.
5. List of countries by GDP (nominal) per capita, http://en.wikipedia.org/wiki/List_of_countries_by_GDP_(nominal)_per_capita (accessed March 5, 2008). Figures (in U.S. dollars) are estimates for 2007 from *The World Factbook* provided by the Central Intelligence Agency (updated February 12, 2008). These figures do not take into account cost-of-living differences; using additional economic data is advisable when making country comparisons.
6. Ibid., 100.
7. Ibid.
8. U.S. Census Bureau, "*IDB: Countries and Areas Ranked by Population*," as of 2007, http://www.census.gov/cgi-bin/ipc/idbrank.pl (accessed January 16, 2008).
9. *CultureGrams, South America, Brazil*, 98.
10. Ibid.
11. Ann Marie Sabath, *International Business Etiquette: Latin America* (Franklin Lakes, NJ: Career Press, 2000), 50.
12. Ibid., 52.
13. *CultureGrams, South America, Brazil*, 100.
14. Philip R. Harris, Robert T. Moran, and Sarah V. Moran, *Managing Cultural Differences*, 6th ed. (Burlington, MA: Elsevier Butterworth-Heinemann, 2004), 335.
15. Ibid., 335–336; Sabath, *International Business Etiquette: Latin America*, 58.
16. Sabath, *International Business Etiquette: Latin America*, 53.
17. Ibid., 54; Mary M. Bosrock, *Put Your Best Foot Forward: South America* (St. Paul, MN: International Education Systems, 1997), 220.
18. Sabath, *International Business Etiquette: Latin America*, 61.
19. Ibid., 54.

20. Ibid., 20.

21. Harris, Moran, and Moran, *Managing Cultural Differences*, 337; Terri Morrison and Wayne A. Conaway, *Kiss, Bow, or Shake Hands: Latin America* (Avon, MA: Adams Media, 2007), 49.

22. Michael Powell, *Behave Yourself! The Essential Guide to International Etiquette* (Guilford, CT: The Globe Pequot Press, 2005), 18.

23. Richard D. Lewis, *When Cultures Collide: Leading Across Cultures*, 3rd ed. (Boston:Nicholas Brealey International, 2006), 543.

24. Bosrock, *Put Your Best Foot Forward: South America*, 218–219; Sabath, *International Business Etiquette: Latin America*, 59–60.

25. Sabath, *International Business Etiquette: Latin America*, 53.

26. Harris, Moran, and Moran, *Managing Cultural Differences*, 336–337.

27. Sabath, *International Business Etiquette: Latin America*, 51.

28. Harris, Moran, and Moran, *Managing Cultural Differences*, 339.

29. Lewis, *When Cultures Collide: Leading Across Cultures*, 543.

30. Sabath, *International Business Etiquette: Latin America*, 55.

31. Bosrock, *Put Your Best Foot Forward: South America*, 207.

32. Lewis, *When Cultures Collide: Leading Across Cultures*, 14.

33. Harris, Moran, and Moran, *Managing Cultural Differences*, 340–341.

34. Bosrock, *Put Your Best Foot Forward: South America*, 222.

35. *CultureGrams, Europe, Brazil*, 100.

36. *CultureGrams, Concepts and Terminology* (Ann Arbor, MI: ProQuest CSA, 2008), A-14.

37. Powell, *Behave Yourself! The Essential Guide to International Etiquette*,18.

38. Roger E. Axtell, *Gestures: The Do's and Taboos of Body Language Around the World* (New York: John Wiley & Sons, 1998), 213.

39. Ibid., 212; Bosrock, *Put Your Best Foot Forward: South America*, 206–207.

40. Axtell, *Gestures: The Do's and Taboos of Body Language Around the World*, 212; Jeanette S. Martin and Lillian H. Chaney, *Global Business Etiquette: A Guide to International Communication and Customs* (Westport, CT: Praeger, 2006), 52–53.

41. Harris, Moran, and Moran, *Managing Cultural Differences*, 339.

42. Lewis, *When Cultures Collide: Leading Across Cultures*, 542.

43. Harris, Moran, and Moran, *Managing Cultural Differences*, 338.

44. Elizabeth Devine and Nancy L. Braganti, *The Travelers' Guide to Latin American Customs and Manners* (New York: St. Martin's Griffin, 2000), 67.

45. Ibid., 74–75.

46. Bosrock, *Put Your Best Foot Forward: South America*, 223.

47. Ibid., 224; Devine and Braganti, *The Travelers' Guide to Latin American Customs and Manners*, 76.

48. Ibid., 75.

49. Ibid., 60.

50. Ibid., 61.

51. Ibid.

CHAPTER 6
Canada

Canada is the largest export market of the United States.[1] Major U.S. exports to Canada include agricultural and wood products, coal, petroleum, natural gas, electricity, metals, newsprint, plastics, chemicals, cloth, industrial supplies, generators, machinery, industrial equipment, electronics, engines, passenger cars, books, toiletries, toys, and records/tapes/disks.[2]

COUNTRY SPECIFICS

A country's location, topography, economy, and population provide insight into understanding its culture. In addition, knowledge of ethnic groups, religions, time zones, and currency is helpful.

Location, Topography, and Land Mass

Canada is located north of the United States and south of Greenland. The Atlantic Ocean is on the east, and the Pacific Ocean is on the west. The capital is Ottawa.

With its large land mass, Canada has a variety of terrains, including wet climates, desert climates, prairies, forests, and tundra. A large portion of northern Canada is not inhabited due to the very cold climate and land that is permanently frozen. Forests cover much of the Canadian Shield, the U-shaped area that surrounds Hudson Bay. A majority of Québec's mining, timber, and hydroelectric wealth is located in this area.[3]

Canada is the second-largest country in the world, after Russia, with a total area of 3,850,000 square miles, or 9,970,000 square kilometers.[4]

Economy

The economy of Canada is one of the strongest in the world; the Gross Domestic Product (GDP) per capita is $34,262.[5]

Canada produces agricultural and wood products, copper, gold, silver, uranium, oil, and natural gas. With the signing of the North American Free Trade Agreement (NAFTA) in 1994, Canada now has a large market for numerous goods from Mexico and the United States, the other members of NAFTA. Even though most Canadians enjoy economic prosperity, 14 percent of Canadian residents live in poverty.[6]

Population, Languages Spoken, Ethnic Groups, and Religions

The population of Canada is 33.4 million;[7] its population growth rate is 0.9 percent annually. Cities with the largest populations are Toronto (4.7 million), Montreal (3.4 million), Vancouver (2 million), and Ottawa (1 million). About four-fifths of residents of Canada live within 100 miles of the U.S. border.[8]

The official languages of Canada are English and French. English is spoken by 60 percent of the population; 24 percent speak French. French is the primary language spoken in Québec; the remainder of the country is primarily English-speaking. Differences exist between Canadian English and U.S. English. The English spoken by Canadians is articulate and easier to listen to than some U.S. accents that are very nasal.[9] The only province in which there is no dominant language is New Brunswick. Chinese has now become the third most common language because of the large numbers of people from China who have immigrated to Canada.[10]

Canada, with its high immigration rate, has become culturally diverse. In addition to people of British and French descent, Canada has large numbers of people who are Chinese, Italian, German, Portuguese, and Polish. Indigenous people, who include Métis and Inuit, make up about 2 percent of the population.[11]

The two primary religions in Canada are Roman Catholic (46 percent) and Protestant (41 percent). Jews and Eastern Orthodox each comprise less than 2 percent of the population.

Country Codes, Time Zones, and Currency

The country telephone code for Canada is 1, the same as the United States.

Canada spans six time zones. In addition to the four time zones corresponding to the time zones of the contiguous 48 United States (Eastern Standard Time, Central Standard Time, Mountain Standard Time, and Pacific Standard Time), two additional time zones in Canada are Atlantic Standard Time, one hour ahead of Eastern Standard Time, and Newfoundland Standard Time (observed only on Newfoundland Island), which is 30 minutes ahead of Atlantic Time.[12] Daylight Saving Time (DST) is observed in most of Canada between March and November. (In both Canada and the United States, the dates for DST changed in 2007 to March to November from April to October.)

The currency in Canada is the Canadian dollar (CAD). The one-dollar coin is called the *loonie*; the two-dollar coin is called the *twoonie*.[13] A currency converter is available at http://coinmill.com/AED_calculator.html that will convert any currency in the world to any other currency.

BUSINESS AND SOCIAL CUSTOMS

Greetings, Introductions, and Business Cards

Businesspeople should remember that province differences are important when it comes to Canadian greeting customs. Specifically, in Québec male or female friends may embrace lightly when greeting each other; females will include a light kiss to the cheek. French greetings include *bonjour* (good day) and *ça va?* (how's it going?).

In the western and Atlantic provinces, the greeting is a handshake for men, along with the question, "How are you?" (This question is just a ritual, as in the United States, and is not an inquiry into the state of a person's health.) The appropriate response is, "Fine, thanks, and how are you?" Handshakes are firm, accompanied by direct eye contact. Women may choose to shake hands or not; they may simply say "hello" and nod their heads. In casual situations, people often say "Hi" and raise their hand in greeting.[14]

When making introductions in most provinces of Canada, use the title and last name until your Canadian hosts suggest that you use their first names. In most of Canada, you would use the same titles as those used in the United States: Mr., Ms., Miss, Mrs., or Dr. In Québec, use *Monsieur* (Mr.), *Madame* (Mrs.) or *Mademoiselle* (Miss) without including the surname. (While *Madame* is correctly used for all women over the age of 18, food servers are always addressed as *Mademoiselle*.)[15]

Business cards should be printed in English on one side and in French on the other side when doing business with French-Canadians.

Business Entertaining and Seating Customs

Business entertaining is usually done over lunch or dinner; conducting business over breakfast is less common than in the United States. Dinners tend to be more social than business events. Wait for your Canadian host to initiate business discussions. While invitations to Canadian homes are infrequent, in the western provinces you may be invited to enjoy an outdoor event, such as a barbeque, at the home of one of your Canadian colleagues.[16]

Dining, Toasting, and Tipping Customs

The majority of Canadians use the Continental style of eating; some use the American zigzag style. Both styles of eating are acceptable. Unlike in the United States, refusing food offered is acceptable. Polite behavior dictates that when passing food to others, you serve yourself last. Diners are expected to keep both hands above the table while eating.

Toasting customs in Canada are similar to those in the United States. People typically say "Cheers;" in Québec, however, people say *A votre sante* ("To your health").

Tipping in restaurants is usually 15 percent to 20 percent, which is in addition to the 7 percent Goods and Services Tax (GST) that has been added to the bill. Tipping is usually expected in bars, too, even if you buy only one drink.[17]

Gift-Giving Customs

Canadians typically give business gifts at the conclusion of negotiations after the contract has been signed. Business gifts are typically exchanged at Christmas; gifts should be modest and could be wine, liquor, an office-related item, or dinner at a nice restaurant. Gifts from your home country are appreciated. The custom in Canada, as is true in the United States, is to open the gift in the presence of the giver and to show it to those in attendance. If you are invited to a Canadian home, it is customary to bring a gift of wine, candy, or flowers, except white lilies (funereal) or red roses (romance).[18]

Business Meetings

When conducting business with Canadians, remember to appreciate their unique identity; do not consider the country as an extension of the United States. It is important to recognize the two dominant cultural groups—the English Canadians and the French Canadians (dominant in Québec)—and how they are similar as well as how they are different. Both groups, for example, appreciate punctuality; being 5 or 10 minutes late for an appointment would be interpreted as a personal affront. Starting and ending meetings on time is appreciated. Both groups are conscientious in meeting deadlines and in adhering to schedules. While each has its own negotiation style, you will find all Canadians easy to deal with, reasonable, calm, and tolerant of the views of others. Both groups confront conflict and work through the areas of disagreement. French Canadians, however, are more inclined to focus on building a relationship, whereas English Canadians focus on getting the job done. Another difference between the two groups that must be considered in business meetings is that English Canadians (like U.S. persons) are low-context communicators (i.e., the words convey the intended message) while French Canadians are high-context communicators (i.e., the nonverbal aspect of what is being communicated is important). Another area of difference between English and French Canadians relates to trust. French Canadians are more likely to distrust information than are English Canadians. When making presentations to French Canadians, remember to have all materials written in both French and English.[19]

Dress and Appearance

Dress in Canada is conservative. Men typically wear a suit and tie, and women wear conservative suits or dresses. Women may also wear well-tailored pantsuits with appropriate accessories in many areas of Canada. Dress varies somewhat by region; in Vancouver you will see more casual attire, but in Toronto more formal attire is worn. Generally speaking, Canadians do not wear casual attire to the extent that people in the United States do.[20]

Visitors should be aware that Canadians do not typically wear scented products, such as perfume or aftershave lotion, for business. Because scented products can actually be a health hazard for people who have asthma, wearing scented products in healthcare facilities is forbidden in many Canadian jurisdictions.

Holidays

Canada celebrates the following official holidays:

- New Year's Holidays (January 1–2)
- Easter Sunday and Monday (dates vary)
- Labor Day (May 1)
- Victoria Day (third Monday in May)
- Canada Day (July 1)
- Thanksgiving Day (second Monday in October)
- Remembrance Day (November 11)
- Christmas (December 25)
- Boxing Day (December 26)

Holidays celebrated in Québec only include New Year's (January 3), the *Carnaval de Québec* (February), and St. Jean-Baptiste Day (June 24).[21]

Conversational Customs

Canadians prefer speaking in a calm, composed manner, except for French-Canadians, who are a bit more animated. People of Canada are polite listeners; they rarely interrupt others. Canadians, though, consider it acceptable to challenge the ideas of others and to engage in friendly debate.[22]

Both English-speaking and French-speaking Canadians excel at small talk and discuss with ease such nonsubstantive topics as sports, movies, television programs, restaurants, and the day's news. In conversations with Canadians, however, do not boast about your accomplishments or possessions; ostentatious behavior is considered inappropriate. In addition, avoid using the term "Native Americans" when conversing as Canadians find this offensive; the preferred usage in Canada is "people of the First Nation."[23]

Humor

Humor, like hockey, is a widely shared value by Canadians. Some humor comes from differences between English-speaking Canadians and French-speaking Canadians. Other Canadian humor stems from political situations and decisions; humor also stems from family-centered sitcoms. Evidence of Canada's appreciation of humor is the Just-for-Laughs festival and the Just-for-Laughs Museum in Montreal. In addition, Humber College in Toronto has the only national post-secondary program in comedy.

Attitude toward Women in Business

Canadians share the U.S. attitude that women are equal to men in the business world. Almost half of the workforce comprises women, and Canada has a large number of women in executive positions. While women's salaries are still a little lower than those of men, which is also true in the United States, more women are receiving college degrees and are perceived in some area as being more literate than men.

On the Human Development Index (HDI)), Canada ranks 6 out of 177 nations.[24] The HDI is a measure of empowerment; it is based on life expectancy, literacy, infant mortality, and real GDP. The assumption is that societies that provide an opportunity for education, access to healthcare, and adequate wages are inclined to be more democratic and exhibit a respect for human rights.[25]

Public Behavior

Avoid displaying rude behavior in public. Evidence of Canadians' disdain for public displays of rude behavior is the passage of a law in Calgary, Alberta, which bans public displays of rudeness. Examples of rude behavior that should be avoided include yawning and scratching oneself in public and using toothpicks or combs. Sneezing or blowing your nose should be done discretely; excusing yourself and leaving the room is considered polite behavior. Also, do not eat while walking on the street; food purchased from street vendors or fast-food establishments should be eaten while seated or standing.

When conversing with others, it is polite to remove your hat and sunglasses to permit eye contact during interactions. Also remove your hat when entering a public building. Proper public behavior includes refraining from speaking in a foreign language when in the presence of other people. In addition, Canadians do not engage in public displays of emotion; they are tactful and do not argue or cause a scene in public. Another rule of proper behavior in public is that men are expected to rise when a woman enters or leaves a room.[26]

NONVERBAL COMMUNICATION

Gestures and Posture

Most U.S. gestures are recognized by Canadians. The beckoning gesture, though, is a little different: The palm of the hand faces inward, fingers up; the fingers are used to motion toward the body. Do not, however, use this gesture to summon a waiter. Beckoning a server in a restaurant is done by raising the hand above the head. Avoid pointing with a single finger, as this is considered rude; instead, use the entire hand for pointing. Also, do not use the thumbs-down gesture, which is considered offensive. French Canadians will use more gestures than other Canadians during conversations.[27]

Good posture is important in business situations. Correct seated posture for men includes crossing the legs at the knees or ankles or sitting with an ankle crossed on the opposite knee. Do not sit with your legs apart or place your feet on tables or chairs. In casual settings, posture is more relaxed and may include placing feet on furniture.[28]

Eye Contact and Facial Expressions

Eye contact is very important to Canadians; it helps establish credibility and convey sincerity. However, it is not uncommon for people belonging to some of the minority groups in Canada to avoid eye contact to convey respect. Although direct eye contact is important to members of the macroculture, it should not be so intense that it exceeds the comfort level of the other person. Eye contact is especially important when greeting and shaking hands with others.[29]

Space and Touch

Canadians value their personal space and prefer to keep about four feet or 1.2 meters between them and the people with whom they interact. Atlantic Canadians prefer more personal distance when interacting than U.S. persons require. Avoid touching people during greetings and when conversing with Canadians. However, touching between close friends and relatives is customary.[30]

Punctuality and Attitude toward Time

Punctuality is important to Canadians, especially in business situations. For social events, it is acceptable to arrive about a half hour late.[31]

TRAVEL TIPS

- Passports are required; visas are not needed for visits of up to 180 days. U.S. citizens traveling to and from Canada by air need a valid passport to enter the United States. A driver's license is no longer considered sufficient identification to enter Canada.
- Hotel accommodations in the major cities are Western style; you will not need to bring voltage connectors or plug adaptors.[32]
- Public transportation systems are well developed in larger cities; subways and buses are widely available. Ferries are popular for traveling between islands in the Atlantic provinces. Domestic air transportation and trains are common forms of transportation throughout Canada.[33]
- If you plan to drive in Canada, you will not need an International Driver's License; your U.S. driver's license is acceptable. Most U.S. automobile insurance is valid for driving in Canada; however, it would be wise to check with your insurance carrier before you leave. Remember that Canadians use the metric system (one U.S. gallon is equal to 3.78 liters, and the speed limit on rural highways is 100 kilometers per hour (about 60 miles per hour). Also remember that radar detectors are illegal—the fine is about $1,000—and that bicycles and pedestrians have the right-of-way. You should also be aware that driving while intoxicated is a serious offense; if caught, you may be asked to leave the country and may be prevented from reentering Canada. Seat belts are mandatory.[34]

- The water is reported to be safe to drink.
- In some Canadian cities, people feel safe walking on the streets of their cities after dark because of the low level of crime activity. In other areas, however, visitors have been targeted and have had their possessions stolen, especially from parked vehicles. (Visitors should be aware that in Montreal and in some other cities, you can be fined for leaving your car unlocked or for leaving valuables in sight.) Do not carry Mace; it is illegal.
- The underground cities make for enjoyable shopping, regardless of the weather. The underground city in Montreal is considered the most famous in the world and has the largest underground network, with 2,000 shops that cover in excess of 41 city blocks and 32 kilometers of tunnel. The underground shopping complex in Toronto is also impressive; it has 1,200 shops and 27 kilometers of walkways. Access to office buildings, banks, cinemas, train stations, and other public places can be made from these underground cities. Vancouver and Winnipeg also have underground shopping areas.
- Waiting in line at theaters, stores, and other places where people wait to be served is customary. Canadians, like U.S. persons, feel that people should be accommodated on a "first-come, first-served basis," without consideration for age, status, or physical impairments. Canadians do not appreciate it when others push ahead of them in line and may issue tactful reminders of the location of the end of the line.
- Smokers should be aware that smoking is not permitted in most public places. However, smoking/nonsmoking sections are available in a majority of restaurants.
- You will want to save your receipts for all purchases. You can receive a refund of Canada's federal Goods and Services Tax (GST)—similar to the European VAT—as well as the additional Provincial Sales Tax (PST) that many provinces charge.[35]
- The number to call for emergencies throughout Canada is 911.
- Although U.S. dollars are accepted in Canadian restaurants and stores, it is wise to pay in Canadian dollars. By purchasing Canadian dollars at a bank, the exchange rate will be more advantageous than paying in U.S. dollars.[36]
- Before traveling to Canada, do some research about the country's culture and history. Be aware of the regional differences that exist in Canada. Never make comparisons between Canada and the United States and never take sides in discussions about national issues. Since Canadians are more polite and reserved than U.S. persons and take etiquette more seriously, U.S. visitors should be on their best behavior and mind their manners to be well received by Canadians.[37]
- Additional information about Canada is available from the Embassy of Canada, 501 Pennsylvania Avenue NW, Washington, D.C. 20001, (202-682-1740), or from the Canadian Consulate General, 1251 Avenue of the Americas, New York, NY 10020, (212-596-1628).

NOTES

1. U.S. Census Bureau Data, 2007, http://www.census.gov/foreign-trade/statistics (accessed March 4, 2008).
2. U.S. Census Bureau Data, 2006, http://www.census.gov/foreign-trade/statistics (accessed June 17, 2007).
3. *CultureGrams, North America, Canada* (Ann Arbor, MI: ProQuest CSA, 2008), 125.
4. Richard D. Lewis, *When Cultures Collide: Leading Across Cultures,* 3rd ed. (Boston: Nicholas Brealey International, 2006), 189.
5. List of countries by GDP (nominal per capita, http://en.wikipedia.org/wiki/List_of_countries_by_GDP_(nominal)_per_capita (accessed March 5, 2008). Figures (in U.S. dollars) are estimates for 2007 from *The World Factbook* provided by the Central Intelligence Agency (updated February 12, 2008). These figures do not take into account cost-of-living differences; using additional economic data is advisable when making country comparisons.
6. *CultureGrams, North America, Canada,* 128.
7. U.S. Census Bureau, "*IDB: Countries and Areas Ranked by Population,*" as of 2007, http://www.census.gov/cgi-bin/ipc/idbrank.pl (accessed January 16, 2008).
8. Ibid., 126
9. Lewis, *When Cultures Collide: Leading Across Cultures,* 190.
10. Terri Morrison and Wayne A. Conaway, *Kiss, Bow, or Shake Hands,* 2nd ed. (Avon, MA: Adams Media, 2006), 73.
11. *CultureGrams, North America, Canada,* 126.
12. Terri Morrison, Wayne A. Conaway, and Joseph J. Douress, *Dun & Bradstreet's Guide to Doing Business Around the World* (Paramus, NJ: Prentice Hall, 1997), 46–47; Carol Turkington, *The Complete Idiot's Guide to Cultural Etiquette* (Indianapolis, IN: Alpha Books, 1999), 48.
13. *CultureGrams, North America, Canada,* 128.
14. Roger E. Axtell, *Gestures: The Do's and Taboos of Body Language Around the World* (New York: John Wiley & Sons, 1998), 111–112; Michael Powell, *Behave Yourself! The Essential Guide to International Etiquette* (Guilford, CT: The Globe Pequot Press, 2005), 22.
15. Mary M. Bosrock, *Put Your Best Foot Forward: Mexico and Canada* (St. Paul, MN: International Education Systems, 1995), 162–163.
16. Morrison and Conaway, *Kiss, Bow, or Shake Hands,* 77.
17. Powell, *Behave Yourself! The Essential Guide to International Etiquette,* 23.
18. Morrison, Conaway, and Douress, *Dun & Bradstreet's Guide to Doing Business Around the World,* 49.
19. Philip R. Harris, Robert T. Moran, and Sarah V. Moran, *Managing Cultural Differences* (Burlington,MA: Elsevier Butterworth-Heinemann, 2004), 293–295; Lewis, *When Cultures Collide: Leading Across Cultures,* 190–192.
20. Jeanette S. Martin and Lillian H. Chaney, *Global Business Etiquette* (Westport, CT: Praeger, 2006), 85.
21. Lillian H. Chaney and Jeanette S. Martin, *Intercultural Business Communication,* 4th ed. (Upper Saddle River, NJ: Pearson/Prentice Hall, 2007), 193.
22. Lewis, *When Cultures Collide: Leading Across Cultures,* 190.

23. Martin and Chaney, *Global Business Etiquette*, 129; Powell, *Behave Yourself! The Essential Guide to International Etiquette*, 23.
24. *CultureGrams, North America, Canada*, 128.
25. *CultureGrams, Concepts and Terminology* (Ann Arbor, MI: ProQuest CSA, 2008), A-14.
26. Bosrock, *Put Your Best Foot Forward: Mexico and Canada*, 174—175; Martin and Chaney, *Global Business Etiquette*, 103.
27. Ibid., 66.
28. Morrison and Conaway, *Kiss, Bow, or Shake Hands*, 79.
29. Ibid.
30. Lewis, *When Cultures Collide: Leading Across Cultures*, 190.
31. Powell, *Behave Yourself! The Essential Guide to International Etiquette*, 22.
32. Martin and Chaney, *Global Business Etiquette*, 17.
33. *CultureGrams, North America, Canada*, 128.
34. Ibid.
35. Bosrock, *Put Your Best Foot Forward: Mexico and Canada*, 174.
36. Ibid., 173–174.
37. Ibid., 173.

CHAPTER 7

China

The People's Republic of China, typically referred to as China, is the third largest export market of the United States.[1]

Major U.S. exports to China include agricultural and wood products, metals, chemicals, control instruments, industrial machinery, electronics, and aircraft.[2]

COUNTRY SPECIFICS

A country's location, topography, economy, and population provide insight into understanding its culture. In addition, knowledge of ethnic groups, religions, time zones, and currency is helpful.

Location, Topography, and Land Mass

China is located in Eastern Asia; its area is about 3,705,820 square miles, or 9,598,032 square kilometers, which is larger than the United States. The capital of China is Beijing. Most of the Chinese population lives in eastern China, where the plains and rivers are conducive to agriculture; western China is primarily mountains or deserts. China has a number of well-known geographic features, including the Qinghai-Tibet Plateau, the Himalaya Mountains, and the Great Wall of China, which covers 4,470 miles or 7,200 kilometers. China is also known for having some of the longest rivers in the world, including the Yangtze River, which is 3,900 miles, or 6,300 kilometers, long.[3]

Economy

China's economy experienced rapid growth in the 1990s; expectations are that the growth will continue. About half of China's population is employed in agriculture. China leads the world in the production of barley, corn, peanuts, soybeans, rice, and tobacco; it produces numerous manufactured goods, including coal, oil, minerals, and steel. The real Gross Domestic Product (GDP) per capita is $2,178.[4] China's economic problems include rising unemployment, crime, corruption, and pollution.[5] In 2007, China experienced problems with certain exports to the United States, including toys and pet food, that had to be recalled.

Population, Languages Spoken, Ethnic Groups, and Religions

China has a population of over 1.3 billion people, the largest of any other country in the world.[6] The largest cities are Shanghai, with 13 million people, and Beijing, with 12.2 million people. The government is attempting to control population growth by offering incentives to families who have only one child and by penalizing those who have more than one. The incentives and penalties have resulted in lowering the population growth rate.[7]

The national language is Standard Chinese (*Putonghua*) or Mandarin. Many people speak dialects of their particular region, including *Yue* (Cantonese), *Kejia*, *Min*, and *Wu*. Although verbal communication problems may occur between people of different regions, people are able to communicate in writing because the various language variations share a common set of characters.[8] China modernized the cuneiforms for written Mandarin; as a result, older and younger people now have a problem reading each other's writing. English is being taught in schools as the second major language of the country.

China has 55 minority groups, the largest of which are the Zhuang, Mongolian, Hui, Tibetan, Uygur, Miao, Yi, Buyi, Korean, Manchu, Dong, Yao, Bai, Tujia, and Hani.

About 70 million Chinese practice some religion; however, atheism is officially encouraged by the government. Religions practiced include Buddhism, Taoism, Christianity, and Islam, which has about 20 million followers. Confucianism, a philosophy and a way of life, is practiced by a majority of Chinese. Some Chinese practice Islam, Catholicism, and Protestantism. Public worship is not encouraged; participating in unauthorized religious activities may result in punishment, including imprisonment.[9]

Country Codes, Time Zones, and Currency

China's country code is 86; when calling within China, dial the 7-digit telephone number preceded by 01 for Beijing, 020 for Guangzhou

(Canton), or 021 for Shanghai. When calling someone in one of the three regions from outside of China, dial the area codes, omitting the initial 0.

China is 13 hours ahead of U.S. Eastern Standard Time. The entire country is in one time zone. Therefore, when it is 5 PM in New York, it is 6 AM the next day in China as you lose a day when you cross the International Date Line. In Universal Time the times would be written as 1700 and 0600, respectively. Although China observed Daylight Saving Time from 1986 to 1991, the country does not observe it now.

The currency is the *renminbi* (RMB). The *yuan* (¥) is the standard unit of currency; each *yuan* (frequently referred to as *kuai* and pronounced kooaye), is made up of 100 *fen*. Chinese coins are 1, 2, and 5 *fen*. Since some shops may not have a working credit card machine, it is advisable to carry a sufficient supply of cash with you.[10] The rate of exchange is controlled by the government, so you pay the same exchange rate everywhere. A currency converter is available at http://coinmill.com/AED_calculator.html that will convert any currency in the world into any other currency.

BUSINESS AND SOCIAL CUSTOMS

The customs of a country vary from greetings and introductions to dining and tipping customs. Becoming knowledgeable about a country's business and social customs is important to successful interactions with the people of the country.

Greetings, Introductions, and Business Cards

The Chinese often greet someone with "Have you eaten?" This greeting is the U.S. equivalent of "How are you?" Regardless of whether you have eaten or not, your response would always be "yes."[11] When greeting people of China, remember that they customarily greet the most senior person first; the Chinese are very conscious of rank. In addition, the surname is spoken first, followed by the first name. Titles are used with the name.[12]

The Chinese bow or nod when being introduced, but usually they will offer a gentle handshake to Westerners. The Chinese do not typically smile during introductions. Business introductions are generally made by agents.[13]

Business cards are exchanged frequently; have your cards printed in English on one side and Mandarin Chinese on the reverse side. Since titles are important to the Chinese, emphasize your title, especially if you hold a position of authority. Use black ink printed on white card stock. Present your card with both hands to show respect; receive another person's card in the same way. Take a few moments to study the information on the card and make a comment about the person's position or some other information. When you receive the card in a meeting, place it on the table where you can view it; otherwise, place it in your business card case.[14]

Business Entertaining and Seating Customs

Business entertaining, an important part of doing business in China, is usually conducted in restaurants at lunch or dinner; you can expect dinners to be early, usually beginning at 6 PM to 7 PM. You can also expect to be invited to an evening banquet and should invite your Chinese colleagues to a banquet of equal monetary value in return. As a guest, you should be on time, wait to begin eating or drinking until the host starts, and refrain from discussing business during the meal.

At banquets and dinners, the main beverage will be beer rather than the wine commonly served in other countries. In China the three glasses at your place setting are for your beverage choice—usually beer or bottled water, wine, and a third glass for small shots of *maotai*, a sorghum-based liquor that is often used for toasting. The following section contains guidelines for dining and toasting.

Since seating etiquette is important in this country, wait for the Chinese host to indicate where you are to sit. The primary host will take a seat facing the door, with the secondary host sitting at the other end of the table across from the primary host. Guests with the highest status will sit to the right or left of the primary host; other guests will sit in order of their rank, with those of lower rank seated next to the secondary host.[15]

Dining, Toasting, and Tipping Customs

Dining is an important aspect of business entertaining and requires knowledge of the nuances of Chinese dining etiquette. Many dining practices, including eating with chopsticks and making noises during meals, are uncommon to Westerners.

The Chinese use chopsticks for eating, so knowledge of customs associated with their use is important. Bring your bowl of food to your mouth and use the chopsticks to push food into your mouth. Do not place chopsticks upright in your rice or drop your chopsticks; this use of chopsticks is associated with bad luck. Place your chopsticks across your dish when you finish eating.

You will want to follow the Chinese custom of sampling all dishes presented and leaving something on the plate to indicate satisfaction with the food. Do not refuse food offered, even if shark's-fin or bird's-nest soup does not sound very appetizing.

Slurping soup and belching during the meal are acceptable noises; this indicates enjoyment of the food. Toothpicks that will be offered at the conclusion of the meal may be used for dislodging food between your teeth; just be sure to cover your mouth. Do not use your fingers to remove food from your teeth, as the Chinese find putting your fingers in your mouth distasteful.

Sometimes tea is served after food that requires use of the hands; rather than drinking the tea, you are expected to dip your fingers into it. When dining in someone's home, the host signals that it is time for guests to leave by offering hot towels or fruit.[16]

Toasting is common in China. In many countries wine is the principal banquet beverage and is used for toasting; however, in China shots of *mao-tai* are used. When toasts are proposed, simply raise your glass, say *Gan bei*, meaning "bottoms up," and finish the contents of the small glass in one swallow. After the meal, the host will rise and toast the guests; this ritual signals the end of the evening.[17]

While tipping is not a usual practice in China, foreigners are expected to tip. When tipping taxicab drivers or servers in restaurants, giving them a handful of change is a usual practice. Acceptable substitutes for a monetary reward include books, DVDs, or U.S.-made cigarettes that are appreciated by tour guides and others who have performed special services for you.[18]

Gift-Giving Customs

Gift-giving is common in China, except at the first meeting. Having an appropriate gift in one's briefcase is advisable in case a gift is offered. Gifts may be given to an individual or to the company. Individual gifts are given in rank order beginning with the person of highest rank; a group gift would be presented to the group's leader. Gifts should be modest so that the Chinese host does not feel obligated to respond in kind. The Chinese lunar New Year is an important date to remember in gift giving.

Gifts are typically wrapped in red as red is considered a lucky color; avoid white wrapping paper as it is viewed as funereal. Do not include bows on your gifts, but do include an appropriate card. While red paper is appropriate for wrapping a gift, using red ink when writing a note or addressing the envelope is not. Red ink indicates a desire to sever a relationship forever.

Recommended gifts include a paperweight or pens of good quality, imported whiskey or chocolates, desk items, illustrated books about your city or region, and music. A gift of a clock is to be avoided as are white flowers and handkerchiefs since they are associated with death. Knives and other cutlery should also be avoided as they suggest a desire to sever ties. Avoid gifts of cheese as many Chinese citizens are lactose intolerant and do not include cheese in their diet. Avoid a gift of a green cap as it implies adultery by a family member. Gifts of fruit or other foods imply poverty and should be avoided. Gifts should not be given in fours as the number four is considered bad luck. However, eight is seen as a lucky number so giving eight of any item is recommended.

Gifts are opened in private rather than in front of the giver. When conducting business in China, bring gifts to all who participated in the negotiations. Remember that the Chinese traditionally refuse a gift several times before finally accepting it; visitors should be prepared for this custom and should follow the same ritual.[19]

Business Meetings

Before meeting with the Chinese, send a list of the people in your group in rank order, together with information on the agenda items. You may wish to make arrangements for your own interpreter, although the Chinese often provide one. The Chinese value punctuality, so show respect for the occasion by being on time or even a little early.

The top-ranking person from the Chinese delegation enters the meeting room first and introduces members of the Chinese team, who distribute their business cards. If you are the top-ranking person on your team, you would do the same and instruct others on your team to present their cards. You would also instruct members of your team to refrain from speaking unless called upon to provide certain information; when asked for information, they should speak quietly, slowly, and without emotion. It is important to resist the temptation to try to speed up the tempo; be patient and expect periods of silence.[20]

Do not expect to start discussing business right away. Prior to getting down to business, the Chinese will begin with a short period of conversation, often over tea. This is a good time for you to demonstrate that you have studied their culture and history; showing an interest in their country is appreciated.

Meetings with the Chinese will be successful if you simply follow the lead of your Chinese host in initiating greetings, seating, and meeting procedures. When meeting your Chinese hosts, bow your head slightly and shake hands; avoid direct eye contact to show respect. Remember to include titles or positions before your Chinese counterparts' last names when addressing them. Seating, which was described earlier, is just as important in business meetings as it is when dining. You may be offered the seat in the middle of the table facing the door, with your host directly across from you. Others will be seated according to rank. Be prepared for the numerous and lengthy meetings that may be necessary to build a strong relationship before getting a signed contract. The Chinese prefer to deal with people with whom they have a good relationship, and relationship-building takes time. Be prepared for slow negotiations and for the Chinese to try to renegotiate the deal after the contract has been signed since they do not view the contract as a binding legal document. Remember that if your negotiations are unsuccessful, you should attempt to save face. Do not make critical comments about the Chinese team since you never know what the future holds; you may wish to conduct business with them at a later time.[21]

To indicate that the meeting is coming to a close, the Chinese host will again offer tea. You are expected to decline with the comment that you will be leaving shortly. You are expected to leave before the Chinese delegation.[22]

Dress and Appearance

When conducting business in China, business professional attire is expected on most occasions. Appropriate business attire for men includes a dark suit with a light shirt and conservative tie. In some areas men may wear sport coats and ties. During the summer men may wear open-necked shirts and slacks without a jacket or tie for business meetings.

Attire for women includes a skirted suit or business dress in a conservative length and in neutral colors. Blouses and dresses should have a high neckline, and shoes should have low heels to avoid appearing taller than the hosts. Women should avoid expensive jewelry or jewelry that dangles; they should not wear heavy makeup. Business casual attire is inappropriate for business meetings in China.[23]

Holidays

China celebrates the following official holidays:

- New Year's Day (January 1)
- Chinese New Year and Spring Festival (a three-day celebration in January or February, as determined by the Chinese lunar calendar)
- International Working Woman's Day (March 8)
- Labor Day (May 1)

- Youth Day (May 4)
- Children's Day (June 1)
- Founding of Communist Party of China (July 1)
- People's Liberation Army Day (August 1)
- National Day (October 1)
- In addition to public holidays, the Chinese celebrate festivals throughout the year, such as the Lantern Festival on the 15th of the first lunar month and the Dragon Boat Festival on the fifth of the fifth lunar month. The Chinese time for giving thanks is the Moon Festival in the fall.[24]

Conversational Customs

During conversations, it is important to remember to speak softly, as speaking in a loud voice is considered rude. Boasting is also rude; be modest about your accomplishments. While conversing, avoid showing emotion; use neutral facial expressions. When conversing with the Chinese, you may expect to be asked where you are from, your age, your marital status, and your salary. In addition to these personal questions, good topics of conversation include the Chinese culture and favorite sights and shops. Avoid criticizing anything or anyone. Remember to refer to the country correctly as "People's Republic of China" or "China;" do not say "Mainland China" or "Communist China."

Silence is valued highly in China. Remaining silent when someone else is speaking is equated with polite behavior; it also indicates contemplation. Interrupting someone is viewed as quite rude.

Humor

While humor does not cross cultural boundaries easily, certain types of humor seem to have universal appeal. For example, humorous stories about husband-wife relationships, youth and old age, restaurant jokes, and stories about golfers are appreciated by people in China as well as by those in the United States and other countries. Attempts at humor related to sex, government leaders, or politics are inappropriate and should be avoided. The people of China use proverbs and parables to convey humor; they often use Confucian aphorisms to make a humorous point. Avoid humor when making business presentations to the Chinese; the chances are good that what you thought would be humorous will be incomprehensible to your Chinese business partners.[25]

Attitude toward Women in Business

Chinese women are currently found in few positions in management. The reason for this can be traced in part to the place Chinese women held in society in years past; they were subordinated since the fifth century B.C. Chinese women did not have equal access to education, their literacy rate was low, and their marriages were often arranged. Life for women in China has improved considerably in recent years; the literacy rates for women have increased, more women are enrolled in higher education, and women are allowed to select the husbands they wish and to divorce them if they choose to do so. Over half of Chinese women are in the workforce; they hold about one-third of official jobs and one-fifth of parliamentary deputy positions.[26]

Women of other cultures who wish to conduct business in China will be treated politely but would be advised to remember certain rules. Rank is important, so you will want to make sure the Chinese men with whom you do business are aware of your credentials and position. In addition, spend time building relationships and obtain the services of an intermediary to introduce you to potential clients. Remember that saving face is important; conducting business with a woman of higher rank results in gaining face for the Chinese man, but dealing with a woman of the same rank results in losing face. Age is another important consideration; with age comes respect and status. Further, women must remember to show patience and humility, to be soft-spoken and adaptable, and to avoid displaying anger and impatience. In addition, women should dress conservatively and wear little jewelry. They should drink alcohol in moderation and should be especially cautious of toasts with *mao tai*, the national drink, which is quite potent.[27]

On the Human Development Index (HDI), China ranks 81 out of 177 nations.[28] The HDI is a measure of empowerment; it is based on life expectancy, literacy, infant mortality, and real GDP. The assumption is that societies that provide an opportunity for education, access to healthcare, and adequate wages are inclined to be more democratic and exhibit a respect for human rights.[29]

Public Behavior

A social custom that is common in China but uncommon in the United States and in many other countries is spitting on the street and blowing your nose with no handkerchief. These practices are viewed as acceptable ways of getting rid of bodily waste.

The Chinese enjoy applauding, so you may be greeted with group applause. The polite response to this group clapping is to return their applause.[30]

Smokers should ask permission of others near them before they smoke. If others have asked permission to smoke and you are allergic to smoke, just explain the situation to your host. The Chinese do not typically designate certain areas as smoking or nonsmoking. Smoking on public transportation and in stores and theaters is inappropriate.

Show respect for the elderly; permit them to precede you through doors and offer them your seat on public transportation.[31]

NONVERBAL COMMUNICATION

Nonverbal communication can reinforce or negate what is said. In some cases, nonverbal communication is used instead of oral communication. Major sources of nonverbal communication are gestures and posture, facial expressions and eye contact, space and touch, punctuality and attitude toward time, and other nonverbal communicators, such as silence.

Gestures and Posture

Gesturing is limited in China. In China the thumbs-up gesture means everything is fine. When pointing, the entire hand is used rather than a single finger. While many U.S. gestures are understood by the Chinese, the "OK" sign should be avoided as it is not widely understood. To beckon someone, the downward facing palm is used with the fingers making a scratching motion. Pulling on your earlobe with your thumb and index finger indicates excellence. When the Chinese shake their head from side to side without speaking, the meaning being conveyed is that whatever is being requested may be difficult for them to do. Another behavior that indicates a problem with a proposal is noisily sucking in air through the teeth and lips. Since the Chinese have a problem saying "no," it is a good idea to change your request when you observe these behaviors.[32]

Posture is very important; do not place your feet on chairs or slouch while seated. Do not use your feet to move articles or to gesture.[33]

Eye Contact and Facial Expressions

Direct eye contact is to be avoided in public; staring and making eye contact are uncommon in large cities; in smaller towns, you can expect to be stared at, especially if your hair is blond or red. Smiling is uncommon during introductions. In fact, the Chinese typically do not reveal their emotions by their facial expressions.[34]

Space and Touch

Standing close during conversations is common; the Chinese are accustomed to being in a crowd. Since China is not a touch-oriented culture, it is inappropriate to pat someone on the head, back, or shoulder. Embracing and kissing are not customary greeting behaviors. Showing affection in public is unacceptable, even between people who are married. Chinese youth, however, are beginning to display affection in public; seeing schoolchildren with their arms around each other is becoming common.[35]

Punctuality and Attitude toward Time

Punctuality is important to the people of China. Arriving early when invited to dinner or when arriving for a business meeting is recommended; punctuality is viewed as a sign of respect.[36]

TRAVEL TIPS

- Passports and visas are required; passports should be effective for at least six months beyond the expected duration of the visit.
- Travelers to China need Hepatitis A, typhoid, chicken pox, and tetanus vaccinations.
- Confirm hotel amenities when making reservations; check such amenities as air conditioning and private bath, as accommodations may not be Western style.
- Women should not go out at night, especially in large cities, because of street crime.
- Emergency numbers include 110 for Police, 120 for medical assistance, and 119 for the fire department. Call 122 to report a traffic accident.
- Be aware of the way dates are written in China; the year comes first, then the month, and the day. For example, June 10, 2011 is written 11.06:10.
- Exercise caution when eating and drinking; do not drink tap water or eat unpeeled fruits or vegetables; do not purchase ice cream or popsicles from street vendors; bring along a small cup to use when buying tea from street vendors.
- While bicycles are the main method of transportation, there are many cars in the larger cities; public transportation systems are widely available, including a subway system, buses, taxis, and railroads.

- Do not expect to be able to rent a car; you may rent a bicycle, however, by leaving a deposit or your passport. Bicycle parking lots are available, which require you to pay an attendant.
- Smoking is not permitted on buses and subways as well as in stores and theaters.
- Ask permission before photographing local residents; do not photograph airports, police stations, military institutions, railroads, bridges, or situations that depict poverty.
- Expect people to push and shove without offering an apology in stores or when boarding public transportation.
- Do not be upset when Chinese people stare at you or follow you around as you shop; they are just curious and do not mean to be rude.
- Bring along toilet paper and tissues; they are often unavailable in China. Also bring a supply of prescription drugs and nonprescription medicines that you commonly use.
- If you intend to do business in China, plan to make several trips there to establish a relationship; schedule meetings well in advance.
- Do not exchange your currency for Chinese currency ahead of time and attempt to bring it into China or to take it with you when you leave; remember that it is illegal to purchase anything with foreign currency.
- Be aware of the dangers of pickpockets, especially on buses and in stations.
- Do not try to get emergency medical treatment in China; call your embassy for advice when medical care is needed.[37]
- Additional information about China is available from the Embassy of China, 2300 Connecticut Avenue NW, Washington, D.C. 20008, (202-328-2500), or from the China National Tourist Office, 350 Fifth Avenue, Suite 6413, New York, NY 10118, (888-760-8218).

NOTES

1. U.S. Census Bureau Data, 2007, http://www.census.gov/foreign-trade/statistics (accessed March 4, 2008).
2. U.S. Census Bureau Data, 2006, http://www.census.gov/foreign-trade/statistics (accessed June 17, 2007).
3. *CultureGrams, Asia, China* (Ann Arbor, MI: ProQuest CSA, 2008), 145.
4. List of countries by GDP (nominal) per capita, http://en.wikipedia.org/wiki/List_of_countries_by_GDP_(nominal)_per_capita (accessed March 5, 2008). Figures (in U.S. dollars) are estimates for 2007 from *The World Factbook* provided by the Central Intelligence Agency (updated February 12, 2008). These figures do not take into account cost-of-living differences; using additional economic data is advisable when making country comparisons.
5. *CultureGrams, Asia, China* (Ann Arbor, MI: ProQuest CSA, 2008), 148.
6. U.S. Census Bureau, "*IDB: Countries and Areas Ranked by Population,*" as of 2007, http://www.census.gov/cgi-bin/ipc/idbrank.pl (accessed January 16, 2008).

7. Ibid., 146.
8. Ibid.
9. Ibid.; Fred E. Jandt, *An Introduction to Intercultural Communication*, 4th ed. (Thousand Oaks, CA: Sage Publications, 2004), 204.
10. Sabath, *International Business Etiquette: Asia and the Pacific Rim*, 31.
11. Michael Powell, *Behave Yourself! The Essential Guide to International Etiquette* (Guilford, CT: The Globe Pequot Press, 2005), 26.
12. Ibid., 34
13. Larry A. Samovar and Richard E. Porter, *Communication between Cultures*, 5th ed. (Belmont, CA: Wadsworth/Thomson Learning, 2004), 216.
14. Sabath, *International Business Etiquette: Asia and the Pacific Rim*, 34.
15. Roger E. Axtell, *Gestures: The Do's and Taboos of Body Language Around the World* (New York: John Wiley & Sons, 1998), 179; Terri Morrison and Wayne A. Conaway, *Kiss, Bow, or Shake Hands: Asia* (Avon, MA: Adams Media, 2007), 10–11.
16. Jeanette S. Martin and Lillian H. Chaney, *Global Business Etiquette: A Guide to International Communication and Customs* (Westport, CT: Praeger, 2006), 122; Sabath, *International Business Etiquette: Asia and the Pacific Rim*, 34–35.
17. Powell, *Behave Yourself! The Essential Guide to International Etiquette*, 27.
18. Lillian H. Chaney and Jeanette S. Martin, *Intercultural Business Communication*, 4th ed. (Upper Saddle River, NJ: Prentice Hall, 2007), 175; Devine and Braganti, *The Traveler's Guide to Asian Customs and Manners*, 19, 27.
19. Mary Murray Bosrock, *Put Your Best Foot Forward: Asia* (St. Paul, MN: International Education Systems, 1997), 201–203; Elizabeth Devine and Nancy L. Braganti, *The Traveler's Guide to Asian Customs and Manners* (New York: St. Martin's Griffin, 1998), 14; Sabath, *International Business Etiquette: Asia and the Pacific Rim*, 37.
20. Peggy Post and Peter Post, *Emily Post's The Etiquette Advantage in Business* (New York: HarperResource, 1999), 510.
21. Morrison and Conaway, *Kiss, Bow, or Shake Hands: Asia*, 10; Sabath, *International Business Etiquette: Asia and the Pacific Rim*, 38–39.
22. Morrison and Conaway, *Kiss, Bow, or Shake Hands: Asia*, 10.
23. Martin and Chaney, *Global Business Etiquette*, 85.
24. *CultureGrams, Asia, China*, 148.
25. Roger E. Axtell, *Do's and Taboos of Humor Around the World* (New York: John Wiley & Sons, 1999), 77–78; Richard D. Lewis, *When Cultures Collide: Leading Across Cultures*, 3rd ed. (Boston, MA: Nicholas Brealey International, 2006), 12–13.
26. Jandt, *An Introduction to Intercultural Communication*, 269.
27. Roger E. Axtell, Tami Briggs, Margaret Corcoran, and Mary Beth Lamb, *Do's and Taboos Around the World for Women in Business* (New York: John Wiley & Sons, 1997), 104–107.
28. *CultureGrams, Asia, China*, 148.
29. *CultureGrams, Concepts and Terminology* (Ann Arbor, MI: ProQuest CSA, 2008), A-14.
30. Martin and Chaney, *Global Business Etiquette*, 141, 103; Axtell, *Gestures: The Do's and Taboos of Body Language Around the World*, 179.
31. Axtell, *Gestures: The Do's and Taboos of Body Language Around the World*, 179.
32. Ibid., 178; Chaney and Martin, *Intercultural Business Communication*, 67.
33. Ibid., 132.

34. Martin and Chaney, *Global Business Etiquette*, 66–67.
35. Ibid.
36. Chaney and Martin, *Intercultural Business Communication*, 132.
37. Bosrock, *Put Your Best Foot Forward: Asia*, 203–205; Devine and Braganti, *The Traveler's Guide to Asian Customs and Manners*, 36–38.

CHAPTER 8

France

France, officially the French Republic, is the ninth largest export market of the United States.[1]

U.S. exports to France include agricultural, petroleum, and wood products; metals; chemicals; industrial machines; electronics; aircraft; medical equipment; laboratory instruments; pharmaceuticals; and art.[2]

COUNTRY SPECIFICS

A country's location, topography, economy, and population provide insight into understanding its culture. In addition, knowledge of ethnic groups, religions, time zones, and currency is helpful.

Location, Topography, and Land Mass

France is located in Western Europe; the Atlantic Ocean and English Channel are on the west and northwest, and on the south is the Mediterranean Sea. Spain and Andorra lie to the south and west; Italy, Switzerland, and Germany lie to the east; and Belgium and Luxembourg are located on the northeast. The Mediterranean island of Corsica is also part of France. The capital is Paris, located on the Seine River in northern France.[3]

The terrain includes mountains along France's borders with Italy, Spain, and Switzerland. Mont Blanc, one of the highest peaks in Europe at 15,771 feet (4,807 meters), is located on France's eastern coast. The Rhine River, which divides France and Germany, is also located along the eastern coast. In the northern area is a flat plain with rolling hills. In addition, forests and farmlands are part of the topography of France.[4]

France, the largest west European country, covers approximately 211, 208 square miles (about 547,030 square kilometers).

Economy

France ranks sixth in economies worldwide; its Gross Domestic Product (GDP) per capita is $35,218.[5] France is one of Europe's leading producers of agricultural products, which include wine, butter, barley, cheese, milk, and wheat. In addition to agricultural products, France exports iron and steel products, machinery and transportation equipment, plastics, pharmaceutical products, and beverages. Tourism is also a major industry; in fact, more tourists visit France than any other country.[6] France has the lowest poverty rate of the major world economies and enjoys some of the strongest social services (i.e., education, healthcare, and retirement systems) as well as strong public service sectors. France does have some economic problems, however, that include the unemployment rate and budget deficits.[7]

Population, Languages Spoken, Ethnic Groups, and Religions

The population of France is slightly more than 63.7 million;[8] the population is growing at the rate of 0.58 percent annually. Three-fourths of residents live in urban areas. Paris, the capital, has the largest population at almost 11 million people.[9]

In spite of the numerous nationalities in France, almost everyone in the country speaks French. English is the next most popular language, followed by Spanish and German.[10]

The ethnic makeup of the country consists of the French, Algerians, and groups who have immigrated from Portugal, Italy, Spain, North and West Africa, the Caribbean, and Southeast Asia.[11]

A majority (approximately 85 percent) of the population is Roman Catholic; the second-largest religion is Islam. Smaller percentages (1 percent to 2 percent) are Protestant, Jewish, or Buddhist. Approximately 6 percent claim no religious affiliation.[12]

Country Codes, Time Zones, and Currency

The country code for France is 33. The city code for Paris is 1; other city codes include 556 for Bordeaux, 491 for Marseilles, and 388 for Strasborg.[13]

France is six hours ahead of U.S. Eastern Standard Time. This means when it is 5 PM in New York, it is 11 PM in France. In Universal Time the times would be written as 1700 and 2300, respectively. The European Union (EU) in 1996 determined that all members would observe Daylight Saving Time (DST) between the last Sunday in March and the last Sunday in October. Since France is a member of the EU, it observes DST.

The currency of France is the *euro*, which replaced the *French franc* in 2002. One *euro* is equal to 100 *eurocent*. A currency converter is available at http://coinmill.com/AED_calculator.html that will convert any currency in the world into any other currency.

BUSINESS AND SOCIAL CUSTOMS

Greetings, Introductions, and Business Cards

When greeting others, the French shake hands using a single shake, which is light and quick. The French shake hands frequently; those of higher rank should initiate the handshake. French women are expected to extend their hands first, unless they are shaking hands with a man of higher status. When greeting good friends or family members, the French kiss each other on alternating cheeks. Rather than actually kissing the cheeks, they kiss the air and simply touch the cheeks from one to four times, depending upon the region of the country.[14]

During introductions, use a person's title; e.g., *Monsieur le professeur* rather than *Monsieur Tixier*. When you become better acquainted, your French colleagues will probably suggest that you use their first names. Women over the age of 18 can expect to be addressed as *Madame*, including those who are single.[15]

Business cards are exchanged frequently; have yours printed in English on one side and in French on the other. Be sure to include your academic credentials, particularly on the side printed in French. Remember to present your card first to the person of higher rank. Thank the person who gives you a card before placing it in your card carrier.[16]

Business Entertaining and Seating Customs

Since the French keep their professional and personal lives separate, business entertaining in France is usually conducted in restaurants, either at lunch or dinner. Although conducting business over breakfast is becoming more accepted, business lunches remain the most popular meal for entertaining business clients. You can expect your first lunch meeting with your French host to be lavish and long. Wait for your French host to initiate business discussions, which may be at any time during the meal or at the end when coffee is served. Formal meals may have as many as 8 to 12 courses, starting with an appetizer and ending with dessert.

When you are the host, make reservations at a restaurant (preferably a French one) well in advance; ask your guests for food and wine suggestions (or let the *sommelier* or wine steward select the wine). When you are a guest, always ask the host for food suggestions. You can be sure that the food will be excellent; the French are known for their wonderful sauces, wide variety of cheeses, and fresh breads. Be generous in your praise of the food. Your dining experiences will probably be some of the highlights of your visit to France.[17]

Guests at formal dinners should wait for the hosts to indicate where they are to sit. The host will usually sit at the center of the table, with the hostess sitting opposite him. Guests are usually seated next to the host and hostess, with the female guest of honor seated next to the host and the male guest of honor seated next to the hostess.[18]

Dining, Toasting, and Tipping Customs

Proper dining etiquette is important to the French. They use the Continental eating style; the knife remains in the right hand and the fork in the left. Wrists should rest on the edge of the table rather than in the lap. Customary dining practices include peeling fruit with a knife and eating it with a fork (not the hands), folding lettuce into small pieces (not cutting it) before eating it with a fork, and breaking bread, eating it with the fingers, and placing the remainder on the tablecloth since bread-and-butter plates are uncommon. Another French dining custom is eating food considered finger food in the United States (e.g., French fries and sandwiches) with a knife and fork; they do not usually eat with their fingers. You are expected to sample everything you are offered and to clean your plate, as leaving food is viewed as rude and wasteful. When you are served cheese, remember to slice the wedge vertically; do not cut off the point. Using bread to enjoy the sauces is acceptable provided your host initiates the practice. Wine is typically served with lunch and dinner. At the end of the meal, the knife and fork are placed parallel across the right side of the plate. According to French custom, the person who issues the meal invitation pays the bill.[19]

Guests should wait for the host to offer the first toast; the host will offer a toast after wine has been served to everyone. An appropriate toast is *Á votre santé*, which means "To your health." To show appreciation to the host, guests (either male or female) offer a toast later during the meal.[20]

In most French restaurants, a 15 percent tip is usually included in the bill; an additional tip for good service is appreciated. When the tip has not been included, the bill will state *service non compris;* you should then leave a tip of 10 percent to 15 percent. Tips for taxi drivers and hairdressers are typically 10 percent. Small amounts are given to hotel maids, washroom attendants, and airport or hotel porters.[21]

Gift-Giving Customs

Business gifts are not presented at the first meeting with your French contact; wait until you have developed a business relationship. Gifts should be in good taste and wrapped elegantly; they should be neither too extravagant nor too inexpensive. Appropriate gifts include books (especially U.S. bestsellers), DVDs, gourmet foods, or music. Gifts that are recommended when invited to dinner at a French home include candy, cookies, or flowers; flowers should not be given in odd numbers, especially 13. In addition, avoid flowers that convey inappropriate messages, such as chrysanthemums (funereal), carnations (bad luck), or red roses (romance). Avoid a gift of a bottle of wine, as fine wines are specialties of the French; also avoid giving anything containing your company's logo. Include with your gift a personal note rather than enclosing your business card.[22]

Business Meetings

The French consider business meetings formal occasions; their attire will be formal to reflect this attitude. Introductions will also be formal, and seating will be in order of rank. To maintain this attitude of formality, do not remove your jacket or discuss personal matters, including details of your family life or your job.

The French will use logic when making their presentations and during discussions. Because of their lengthy analysis of items being discussed, meetings tend to be long. During business meetings, the French do not put all their cards on the table, as is common in U.S. meetings. Rather, the French attempt to determine the other team's goals at the outset and reveal their own demands toward the end of negotiations. People who conduct business with the French should be aware that they do not ordinarily make important decisions during the meeting, since the person responsible for making decisions is not usually in attendance. Despite their argumentative and opinionated style during negotiations (which has led to charges of arrogance during international meetings), the French think clearly and logically. They simply feel that their perspective on the situation is correct. Their opinions and viewpoints should be considered carefully as the French arrive at meetings well prepared.[23]

Dress and Appearance

The French are world leaders in fashion; many of the world's foremost fashion designers live in Paris. Parisians tend to dress more formally than people in other French cities. The French in all parts of the country are known for dressing well, whether for professional or social events. Those who wish to conduct business with the French would be wise to wear high-quality clothing and accessories.

Recommended professional attire for men includes dark suits with white shirts and complementary ties; women should wear suits or dresses that are conservative, yet feminine, with elegant accessories. Remember that suit coats are not removed in restaurants and offices. When invited to events that specify casual attire, it is important to understand that the French definition of "casual" is not the same as the U.S. definition; the French definition is more formal.[24]

Holidays

France celebrates the following 11 public holidays:

- New Year's Day (January 1)
- Mardi Gras (Shrove Tuesday, dates vary)
- Easter Sunday and Monday (dates vary)
- Labor Day (May 1)
- WWII Victory Day (May 8)
- Ascension Day (dates vary)
- Bastille Day (July 14)
- Assumption of the Virgin Mary (August 15)
- All Saints' Day (November 1)
- World War I Armistice Day (dates vary)
- Christmas (December 25)[25]

Conversational Customs

Initial conversations with the French should be on such safe topics as art, music, books, the theater, and sports. Avoid topics that are personal; this includes questions about the person's family, profession, age, or income. Also avoid questions related to how much things cost and where they were purchased. Do not initiate discussions about French politics; however, be prepared for the French to ask you about your country's political situation. Learn something about the history and culture of France; the French will appreciate your interest in their country.

After you get to know them, the French may engage in some rather heated discussions by U.S. standards. However, this type of conversation is enjoyed by the French; they like a good debate. They seem to be able to detach themselves from the subject and do not let emotions or personal feelings become involved in the discussion. Although English is widely spoken, when conversing with the French it is wise to apologize if you do not speak French.[26]

Because the French are a high-context culture, they prefer being subtle, tactful, and talking around the point to being frank and open in their discussions. The French are known for being eloquent and logical in their communication.[27]

Humor

The French prefer humor that is intelligent and satirical; they also prefer jokes at another person's expense. They favor wit over a belly-laugh. Starting a meeting or a presentation with jokes to release tension is uncommon in France. The French rarely use humor in the business environment as they believe that conducting business is serious and that humor is inappropriate. On the rare occasions when humor is used during business presentations, it should be dignified and intelligent. Outside the office, the French do not sit around with their friends telling jokes or amusing personal stories.[28]

Attitude toward Women in Business

Few French women hold top positions in business; exceptions are found in the fields of art, cosmetics, fashion, and advertising as well as law, finance, and personnel. Although most French women do work outside the home, the majority hold low-level administrative support jobs. French women have not yet achieved equality with men in the business world. Although many people in France profess to believe in the equality of women, equality is not a reality. Women from other countries who conduct business in France, especially women from Canada and the United States, are usually accepted.[29]

On the Human Development Index (HDI), France ranks 16 out of 177 nations.[30] The HDI is a measure of empowerment; it is based on life expectancy, literacy, infant mortality, and real GDP. The assumption is that societies that provide an opportunity for education, access to healthcare, and adequate wages are inclined to be more democratic and exhibit a respect for human rights.[31]

Public Behavior

The French do not converse loudly in public; keep your voice low to avoid being conspicuous. Avoid walking on the street while drinking or smoking as this behavior is considered bad manners. The U.S. custom of smiling at strangers is inappropriate in France. In addition, do not chew gum or use personal items, such as combs, toothpicks, or nail clippers, in public. Greet sales personnel with *Bonjour* ("good day") upon entering a store and *Au revoir* ("goodbye") when leaving; this is customary.[32]

NONVERBAL COMMUNICATION

Gestures and Posture

The French do not gesture frequently in professional settings; however, they often use gestures in social situations. Gestures used in France include the "V" for Victory sign, which may be done with the palm facing toward you or away from you ("peace" or "victory"); playing an imaginary flute (questioning the truth of someone's story or signaling that the person is excessively verbose); and the U.S. O.K. sign ("worthless" or "zero"). The U.S. thumbs-up sign is the French gesture for O.K.; the "thumbs down" gesture means "bad." The gesture that suggests that a person is drunk is using the thumb and forefinger to form a circle, placing it over your nose, and making a twisting motion. The French kiss the fingertips to indicate that something is delicious. Gestures to avoid because of their vulgar meanings include taking an open palm and slapping it over a closed fist or snapping fingers on both hands. Other gestures to avoid include scratching or yawning in public and using the hand and fingers for pointing. Also avoid placing your finger beneath your eye, as this suggests that you think the other person is lying. Do not put your hands in your pockets during conversations.[33]

Good posture is considered important in France. Avoid slumping while seated in a chair; do not stretch your legs in front of you or place your feet on chairs or tables. Crossing the legs at the ankles is appropriate; women should sit with knees close together, with both feet on the floor or with legs crossed at the knee.[34]

Eye Contact and Facial Expressions

Eye contact is important to the French; it is intense and frequent. U.S. persons may interpret this gaze as rude but should understand that this is simply a French custom. When walking down the street, however, people do not make eye contact. Women should be especially careful to avoid smiling and making eye contact with male strangers on the street as the behavior is interpreted as an invitation. Giving eye contact, especially during business encounters, signifies equality. Refusing to give eye contact is inappropriate as it implies the person is beneath you and will be interpreted as a put down.[35]

Space and Touch

The French may stand closer to each other when conversing than U.S. persons are comfortable with. Do not touch the French during conversations; however, they may touch others they know.

Punctuality and Attitude toward Time

The French follow polychronic time, which means that they do a number of things simultaneously. They are quite comfortable with constant interruptions. Since they follow polychronic time, the French do not always keep strictly to schedule and may be lax when it comes to appointments; thus, visitors should be prepared to wait. They do, however, expect visitors to be on time for appointments. Do not expect your French colleagues to apologize for being late since they do not take time seriously. They also have a casual attitude toward deadlines and delivery dates. The French may also change plans at the last minute, which is very frustrating for people who follow monochronic time.

When conducting business with the French, international businesspeople should be aware that long-term planning is difficult for them. They know that something may happen to prevent their keeping a commitment a year in advance. The French believe in enjoying the moment. The present is more important to them than schedules and deadlines; thus, deadlines for them must allow for uncertainties.[36]

TRAVEL TIPS

- Passports are required; they should be valid for at least three months beyond the intended stay in France; no visa is required for a visit of up to three months.
- When making hotel reservations, confirm accommodations as many hotels do not have a bath in the room. In addition, hotels may not have such amenities as air conditioning or swimming pools.
- Avoid planning business trips in August; many businesses and shops close during that month. Also avoid business trips just before and after Easter and Christmas.
- Public transportation in France includes the Métro, a subway in Paris, Lyon, Lille, and Marseilles; keep your ticket to show agents who may check it. Reservations are required to ride the high-speed trains that travel 186 miles per

hour (300 kilometers per hour) and connect 36 cities in Europe. Car ferries are available between France and Corsica and Great Britain. Taxis are widely available; check for a sign on the roof indicating that it is an official taxi with a meter.

- An International Driver's License is not necessary for those who choose to drive; blowing your horn in cities is illegal, as is making a right turn on a red light.[37]
- Because of the numerous pickpockets in Paris, including children who are skilled at snatching purses, be especially cautious in train stations, at department stores, at the Paris Métro during rush hours, and at airports.[38]
- Some areas in Paris and in other French cities are unsafe for tourists; ask at your hotel for the location of the areas to avoid.[39]
- Public toilets may be unisex, indicated by OO on the door.
- The number to call for emergencies (police, ambulance) is 17 or 112. Call 15 or 112 for severe medical emergencies; for less severe, call 18 or 112. To call the fire department, dial 18 or 112.
- Do not be surprised to find dogs sitting beneath tables in French cafes. The dogs will be very well behaved. The French have no public health laws that prohibit animals in restaurants as is the case in the United States.
- When you give someone a compliment, do not expect the French to say thank you; they are modest about accepting compliments and will make some self-deprecating comment.[40]
- When you purchase fruits or vegetables in markets, let the vendor serve you; do not make your own selection.
- Additional information about France is available from the Embassy of France, 4101 Reservoir Road NW, Washington, D.C. 20007, (202-944-6000), or from the French Government Tourist Office, 444 Madison Avenue, 16th Floor, New York, NY 10022, (514-288-1904).

NOTES

1. U.S. Census Bureau, 2007 Export of Goods, http://www.census.gov/foreign-trade/statistics (accessed March 4, 2008).
2. U.S. Census Bureau, 2006 Export of Goods, http://www.census.gov/foreign-trade/statistics (accessed June 17, 2007).
3. Ann Marie Sabath, *International Business Etiquette: Europe* (Franklin Lakes, NJ: Career Press, 1999), 100.
4. *CultureGrams, Europe, France* (Ann Arbor, MI.: ProQuest CSA, 2008), 241.
5. List of countries by GDP (nominal) per capita, http://en.wikipedia.org/wiki/List_of_countries_by_GDP_(nominal)_per_capita (accessed March 5, 2008). Figures (in U.S. dollars) are estimates for 2007 from *The World Factbook* provided by the Central Intelligence Agency (updated February 12, 2008). These figures do not take into account cost-of-living differences; using additional economic data is advisable when making country comparisons.

6. Ibid., 244.
7. Ibid.; Economy of France, http://en.wikipedia.org/wiki/Economy_of_France (accessed May 28, 2007).
8. U.S. Census Bureau, "*IDB: Countries and Areas Ranked by Population,*" as of 2007, http://www.census.gov/cgi-bin/ipc/idbrank.pl (accessed January 16, 2008).
9. *CultureGrams, Europe, France*, 242.
10. Ibid.
11. Ibid.
12. Ibid.
13. Sabath, *International Business Etiquette: Europe*, 102.
14. Roger E. Axtell, *Gestures: The Do's and Taboos of Body Language Around the World* (New York: John Wiley & Sons, 1998), 138.
15. Carol Turkington, *The Complete Idiot's Guide to Cultural Etiquette* (Indianapolis, IN: Alpha Books, 1999), 90.
16. Sabath, *International Business Etiquette: Europe*, 104.
17. Nancy L. Braganti and Elizabeth Devine, *European Customs and Manners* (New York: Meadowbrook Press, 1992), 80–81; Sabath, *International Business Etiquette: Europe*, 104–106.
18. Braganti and Devine, *European Customs and Manners*, 74.
19. Axtell, *Gestures: The Do's and Taboos of Body Language Around the World*, 140; Mary M. Bosrock, *Put Your Best Foot Forward: Europe* (St. Paul, MN: International Education Systems, 1995), 209–210.
20. Bosrock, *Put Your Best Foot Forward: Europe*, 208.
21. Ibid.
22. Ibid., 108; Terri Morrison and Wayne A. Conaway, *Kiss, Bow, or Shake Hands*, 2nd ed. (Avon, MA: Adams Media, 2006), 176.
23. Richard D. Lewis, *When Cultures Collide: Leading Across Cultures*, 3rd ed. (Boston, MA: Nicholas Brealey International, 2006), 256–258.
24. Sabath, *International Business Etiquette: Europe*, 104.
25. Lillian H. Chaney and Jeanette S. Martin, *Intercultural Business Communication*, 4th ed. (Upper Saddle River, NJ: Prentice Hall, 2007), 194.
26. Braganti and Devine, *European Customs and Manners*, 71–72; Sabath, *International Business Etiquette: Europe*, 106.
27. Edward T. Hall and Mildred R. Hall, *Understanding Cultural Differences: Germans, French, and Americans* (Yarmouth, ME: Intercultural Press, 1990), 102.
28. John Mole, *Mind Your Manners* (London: Nicholas Brealey Publishing, 1998), 26.
29. Roger E. Axtell, Tami Briggs, Margaret Corcoran, and Mary Beth Lamb, *Do's and Taboos around the World for Women in Business* (New York: John Wiley & Sons, 1997), 57; Turkington, *The Complete Idiot's Guide to Cultural Etiquette*, 92; Mole, *Mind Your Manners*, 24.
30. *CultureGrams, Europe, France*, 244.
31. *CultureGrams, Concepts and Terminology* (Ann Arbor, MI: ProQuest CSA, 2008), A-14.
32. Braganti and Devine, *European Customs and Manners*, 73; Sabath, *International Business Etiquette: Europe*, 112.
33. Axtell, *Gestures: The Do's and Taboos of Body Language Around the World*, 139–140. Turkington, *The Complete Idiot's Guide to Cultural Etiquette*, 92.

34. Ibid., 139.
35. Turkington, *The Complete Idiot's Guide to Cultural Etiquette*, 91.
36. Hall and Hall, *Understanding Cultural Differences: Germans, French, and Americans*, 88–90; Morrison and Conaway, *Kiss, Bow, or Shake Hands*, 173.
37. Braganti and Devine, *European Customs and Manners*, 82–83.
38. Ibid., 83.
39. Ibid.
40. Ibid., 72.

CHAPTER 9
Germany

The Federal Republic of Germany, commonly referred to as Germany and once known as East Germany and West Germany, is the sixth largest export market of the United States.[1]

Major U.S. exports to Germany include agricultural and wood products, precious metals, chemicals, industrial supplies, electric apparatus, industrial engines, machine tools, electronics, medical equipment, aircraft parts, pharmaceuticals, toys, and military.[2]

COUNTRY SPECIFICS

A country's location, topography, economy, and population provide insight into understanding its culture. In addition, knowledge of ethnic groups, religions, time zones, and currency is helpful.

Location, Topography, and Land Mass

Germany is located in central Europe. On the country's western border are the Netherlands, Belgium, and Luxembourg; on the southwest is France; on the south and southeast are Switzerland and Austria; on the east are Poland and the Czech Republic; and on the north is Denmark. The capital is Berlin. The area of Germany is 137,803 square miles or 356,910 square kilometers.

Germany's primary geographic regions are the broad lowlands located in the north, the central uplands, the valley and gorge of the Rhine River in the southwest, and the plateaus and mountains of the south. Well-known rivers that flow through the country are the Elbe, Rhine, and Danube Rivers, which are useful transportation and trade routes. Almost one-third of the country is in forests; the Zugspitze (9,718 feet or 2,962 meters) is the tallest mountain.[3]

Economy

Germany is considered a top economic world power; its Gross Domestic Product (GDP) per capita is $36,699.[4]

Although Germany was divided into West and East at the end of World War II, the country was reunited on October 3, 1990. However, economic differences continue to exist in East and West Germany. The economy in the East is weaker than it is in the West; salaries and overall living conditions are still lower in the East. Overall, inflation in Germany is low.[5]

Germany is one of the largest exporters in the world; the country exports cars, steel, aluminum, televisions, and other manufactured goods. Construction, manufacturing, and service industries are also important to the economy.

Population, Languages Spoken, Ethnic Groups, and Religions

The population of Germany is 82.4 million;[6] it is not growing. Although German is the official language of the country, English is understood by most residents and is required in school. Russian is spoken by a number of Germans in the eastern part of the country.[7]

Approximately 91 percent of the population is ethnic German; Turks, Italians, Greeks, and Poles make up the remainder of the population.

About one-third of the population belongs to the Roman Catholic Church, and one-third is Protestant. The remainder of the population belongs to various religions; about 4 percent are Muslim.

Country Codes, Time Zones, and Currency

The country code for Germany is 49. City codes are 30 for Berlin, 228 for Bonn, 221 for Cologne, and 89 for Munich.

Germany is six hours ahead of U.S. Eastern Standard Time. Thus, when it is 5 PM in New York, it is 11 PM in Germany. In Universal Time, the times would be written as 1700 and 2300, respectively. In 1996 the European Union (EU) determined that Daylight Saving Time (DST) would be observed by its members from the last Sunday in March to the last Sunday in October. Since Germany is a member of the EU, the country observes DST.

The *euro* is the country's currency; it replaced the *Deutsche mark* in 2002. A currency converter is available at http://coinmill.com/AED_calculator.html that will convert any currency in the world to any other currency.

BUSINESS AND SOCIAL CUSTOMS

Greetings, Introductions, and Business Cards

When you greet people in Germany, remember to use their titles and last names and to give a firm handshake. The handshake is used both when greeting someone and upon departure.

Business cards should be printed in English on one side and in German on the other; include titles and advanced degrees since education is valued by Germans. Other information to include on your business card includes the date of the founding of your firm (if your company has been in business for a number of years) and the number of employees (if your company is a large one). Bring along a good supply of cards since your German business associates will probably expect to exchange business cards with you.[8]

Business Entertaining and Seating Customs

Germans usually do their business entertaining in restaurants, typically at lunch. Lunch is usually scheduled for noon or 1 PM and lasts about an hour and a half. Business breakfasts are uncommon. Business discussions precede the meal; however, no discussions take place during the meal. Actually, business entertaining is more social than business so you should wait for your German host to initiate a business discussion. Business dinners usually start about 6:30 PM—later (around 8 PM) if the meal is primarily a social event to which spouses are invited. Being entertained at a German home is uncommon; feel honored if you are invited to be a guest in the home.[9]

According to German seating etiquette, the most senior guest is given the center seat along the side of a table that is farthest from the door. The guest's counterpart is seated across from him or her. Rank is important in determining seating. The most senior German executive has the second most senior German seated to his or her immediate right, and the third in seniority sits to the immediate left. In business entertaining situations, the male guest of honor sits to the right of the hostess, and the female guest of honor sits to the host's right.

Seating etiquette in casual restaurants permits a stranger to approach your table and ask to join you. While you are not expected to converse with the stranger, you should say goodbye when he or she leaves.[10]

Dining, Toasting, and Tipping Customs

Germans use the Continental style of eating. Germans keep their hands on the table throughout the meal, not in the lap. Elbows, however, should be kept off the table. The edge of the fork is often used to cut food; use of a knife implies that the food is tough. Use only a fish knife to cut fish; however, two forks may be used when a fish knife is not available. Sandwiches and fruit are eaten with a knife and fork, rather than with the hands. In fact, few foods are considered finger foods. When in doubt about whether to use the fingers, follow your host's lead. Because you are expected to clean your plate, it is advisable to take small portions.[11]

Wine is usually served with meals, despite the fact that the Germans are well known for their beer. Serving wine, beer, and soft drinks at room temperature is not uncommon. After-dinner drinks, probably a choice of brandies, will be served with coffee. Those who wish to smoke after coffee has been served should ask permission.[12]

Germans consume the main meal of the day at noon; they eat a light meal in the evening. German food is rather heavy by U.S. standards; they eat a lot of meat, especially pork.[13]

The two toasts commonly used in Germany are *Prost* ("cheers!"), which is informal and used among friends when drinking beer, and *Zum Wohl*, meaning "To your health," which is typically used in more formal settings. Guests at dinner parties wait to drink until after the host has drunk. The higher-ranking person proposes the first toast to his lower-ranking colleague or guest; this person will return the toast later in the meal. The guest who returns the toast should be the highest-ranking person in the group.[14]

Tipping in most restaurants is 10 percent to 15 percent, which will be added to the bill. When the service has been exceptional, an additional tip is given directly to the server rather than leaving it on the table. Taxi drivers often charge extra for each piece of luggage; they are tipped 10 percent to 15 percent.[15]

Gift-Giving Customs

Although Germans do not usually exchange gifts at business meetings, it is acceptable to give small, inexpensive gifts of good quality at the end of successful negotiations. Appropriate gifts include imported liquor, U.S.-made gifts, and books, especially illustrated books featuring your city. Avoid giving gifts of wine, since Germans are proud of their own wine cellars. In addition, avoid knives, scissors, or other pointed objects since they are perceived to bring bad luck.[16]

When invited to a German home, you should bring a small gift, such as chocolates, for the hostess. Flowers make nice gifts, especially when invited to a large party. They may be sent the morning of the party or the day following the event. Yellow or tea roses in an uneven number, except 13, are appropriate. However, do not give carnations, calla lilies, or yellow and white chrysanthemums because of funereal connotations. Red roses are also inappropriate since they are associated with romance.[17]

Business Meetings

Make appointments with your German business colleagues at least a month in advance. The preferred appointment times are 9 AM to 12 PM and 1:30 PM to 4 PM—except for Friday afternoons as many companies close around 2 PM on Fridays.[18]

Germans expect you to be on time for meetings. Shake hands with those present; introduce yourself using your last name only. The person in charge will close the doors to the meeting room to signal the meeting is about to begin.[19]

Your German colleagues may or may not engage in light conversation prior to getting down to business. Thus, you would wait for your German associates to initiate the conversation. If there is chitchat, the questions you may be asked will probably relate to where you are from or where you are staying. They do not typically engage in humor. Any attempts to create a relaxed atmosphere by telling something humorous will not be appreciated.[20]

You will probably be offered something to drink before quickly getting down to business. Germans appreciate structure; you will want to have a well-organized presentation that includes visuals and perhaps product samples. Have proposals written in German; make sure offers are specific. Do not attempt to speed up the pace of meetings; Germans prefer to proceed slowly and are known for being thorough and cautious and for giving attention to every detail. It is important to remember that Germany is not a risk-oriented culture. Although a number of businesspeople will be involved at various stages, the final decision will be made by top management. Once Germans sign a contract, they will abide by it and expect others to do the same.[21]

Dress and Appearance

Germans usually follow European fashion trends. Business dress is conservative, including accessories. Both men and women should wear clothing of natural fibers and high-quality shoes. Men typically wear professional business attire—dark suits, white shirts, and coordinating ties—to business and formal social events. German men often keep their jackets on even in hot weather; follow your German colleague's example and wait to remove your jacket or tie until your German colleague does so. Women should wear dark suits in black, gray, or dark blue and white blouses; pantsuits are not customary except in casual restaurants. Women should wear jewelry that is elegant. However, avoid wearing flashy jewelry or clothing when visiting the former East Germany. Poverty still exists in that area; making a fashion statement would be perceived negatively. In warm weather women may wear short-sleeved dresses or suits but should not wear sleeveless attire. Casual clothing in Germany is similar to that worn by U.S. persons.[22]

Holidays

Germany celebrates the following public holidays:

- New Year's Day (January 1)
- Good Friday, Easter Sunday and Monday (late March/April)
- Labor Day (May 1)
- Ascension Day (five weeks after Easter)
- Whit Monday (eight weeks after Easter)
- German Unity Day (October 3)
- All Saints' Day (November 1)
- Christmas (December 25)
- New Year's Eve (December 31)

Conversational Customs

Germans rarely converse with strangers. In fact, they like their privacy and often keep to themselves. As they become acquainted with you, they will be more outgoing. During conversations avoid using your hands for emphasis; Germans prefer a calm demeanor without flamboyant gestures.

Being direct in their comments is characteristic of Germans; they rarely give compliments for doing a good job, but they are free with criticism for what was done incorrectly.[23]

When conversing with Germans, good topics include such sports as soccer, tennis, hiking, and skiing. Germans are also happy to answer questions about local beers as Germany is well known for making some of the world's finest beer. Do not ask personal questions. Inquiries into someone's family life, for example, are inappropriate. Other topics to avoid include anti-Semitism, World War II, or embarrassing political questions. Remember that Germans prefer conversations on topics of substance rather than engaging in small talk.[24]

Humor

In Germany, humor in business situations is inappropriate. They take business seriously and do not appreciate joking comments during business meetings. Germans see no need to lighten the atmosphere or to be entertained in a work environment. They lack the U.S. penchant for telling funny stories and are sometimes perceived as humorless and intense. However, Germans do have a good sense of humor and will tell jokes while relaxing at local bars or restaurants.[25]

Attitude toward Women in Business

On the Human Development Index (HDI), Germany ranks 21 out of 177 nations.[26] The HDI is a measure of empowerment; it is based on life expectancy, literacy, infant mortality, and real GDP. The assumption is that societies that provide an opportunity for education, access to healthcare, and adequate wages are inclined to be more democratic and exhibit a respect for human rights. [27]

Although German law guarantees gender equality, businessmen in Germany do not treat women equally. Women are not treated as equal to men in salary or status. Women have been perceived as lacking the ability to command male subordinates; however, this attitude seems to be changing. Evidence of this change was the election of Germany's first female chancellor, Angela Merkel, in 2005. To be successful in Germany, women will need to be self-confident and self-assured.[28]

Public Behavior

Do not be surprised if a German calls attention to your inappropriate public behavior. They do not mean to be rude; they simply feel that policing the behavior of other people is their social obligation.

When attending plays or concerts, Germans are quiet and respectful. Thus, you should remain very still during the performance and should not flip through the program, cough, sneeze, or make any other noises.

Other public behavior considered rude includes chewing gum and shouting or speaking loudly.[29]

NONVERBAL COMMUNICATION

Gestures and Posture

An important rule to remember while talking to Germans is to avoid standing with your hands in your pockets as it is considered insulting.

The "thumbs up" gesture is used both to signify agreement and to mean "one," such as when ordering one drink. Do not use the beckoning gesture or wave your hand; likewise, avoid using the U.S. O.K. gesture, which is considered quite rude by Germans. If you wish to get a person's attention, use a raised hand, index finger extended and palm facing outward. Avoid pointing your index finger to your temple accompanied by a twisting motion, since it means that the person is crazy. The German gesture for wishing someone good luck is to make a fist, with the thumb folded in, and pounding lightly on a surface. The gesture used when waving goodbye is extending the hand upward with the palm out, then waving the fingers up and down. (Waving the fingers from side to side means "no.")[30]

An upright posture is important. Posture while seated should consist of crossing one knee over the other; do not place one ankle on top of the opposite knee. In addition, placing your feet on the furniture is inappropriate.[31]

Eye Contact and Facial Expressions

Germans expect you to give direct eye contact during conversations. Eye contact is a sign of sincerity to Germans. If you avoid a German's gaze, this suggests you are untrustworthy.

Germans do not usually smile during business meetings; in fact, they typically smile only when talking with people they know well.

Space and Touch

Space is sacred to the Germans. Their territorial behavior can be attributed to the fact that they are geographically crowded. An example of the German sense of territoriality is their use of various barriers, such as fences, blinds, and hedges, to protect their homes from outsiders. In their offices, Germans maintain this territoriality by keeping their doors—usually thick and solid—closed. Knocking on the door and waiting for an invitation to enter is expected. The German need for space is also evidenced by their maintaining a greater distance when interacting than do people of the United States.[32]

Germans avoid touching each other; do not pat them on the back or engage in public displays of affection. This lack of touching extends to their cars; never touch someone's car or place any objects on it.

Punctuality and Attitude toward Time

Punctuality is very important to Germans. Being late will be pointed out by Germans, who equate tardiness with unreliability. Their definition of being late means arriving two or three minutes after the scheduled starting time. However, their concern with punctuality does not always include prompt delivery of products, which may arrive late with no apology or explanation.[33]

Germans are monochronic; they like to complete one thing before beginning another. Although U.S. Americans are also monochronic, differences exist between the two countries in their attitude toward time. Decision making, for example, is much slower in Germany; Germans do considerable background research and engage in lengthy discussions before reaching a decision.[34]

Being on time for business appointments and social engagements is a necessity. Being late by only five minutes may be viewed as an insult by German executives. Since making excuses for tardiness is unacceptable, make sure you allow plenty of time so that you will arrive early for all engagements.[35]

TRAVEL TIPS

- A passport is required for traveling to Germany; it should be valid for at least three months beyond your intended stay. No visa is needed for visits of up to three months.
- If you wish to use public transportation, purchase tickets for streetcars, buses, or subways at kiosks before boarding. Train tickets may also be purchased at a travel agency. Upon entering a train compartment, greet people and ask if the seat is reserved before sitting down. Bus stations in most German cities are conveniently located near railroad stations. Services offered by buses are excellent, including lavatories, nonsmoking sections, and adjustable seats.[36]
- Taxis are available at taxi stands; they may also be hailed on the street. Having the correct change is recommended as taxi drivers seldom carry change.
- If you drive in Germany, you will need an International Driver's License. Seat belts are mandatory. Do not drive while intoxicated as penalties are severe for drinking and driving.
- Always greet sales personnel with "good day" when entering a shop and say "goodbye" when departing. Bring your own bag when visiting a local market to purchase food. Otherwise, you may buy one for a small fee.[37]
- Since shops are required to close at 6:30 PM, go to the train station if you wish to purchase a paper, snack, or drink after 6:30 PM.[38]
- Jaywalking is illegal; you may be yelled at by local residents, especially in small towns, if you jaywalk. Before crossing a street, always wait for the signal for pedestrians to proceed.[39]
- The tap water is unsafe; always drink bottled water.

- Avoid being critical of telephones that do not work or making negative comments about the poor condition of hotels, bathrooms, and so forth.
- If you need to call the police, dial 110; to summon the help of the fire department or for medical emergencies, dial 112.
- A man customarily permits someone of higher status or an older woman to enter a room first. However, men precede women when entering a restaurant.
- A woman would not thank a man for giving her a compliment as this is not customary in Germany.
- Public restrooms, which are usually available in restaurants and bars, will be marked with an F (*Frauen*) for women and an H (*Herren*) for men.[40]
- Exercise caution in taking photographs. Do not photograph inside churches during services, near military installations, or inside galleries and museums that post signs forbidding the taking of photographs. Do not photograph strangers without first asking their permission.[41]
- Since prostitution is legal, you may see magazines that are sexually explicit prominently displayed in German newsstands.
- Additional information about Germany is available from the Embassy of Germany, 4645 Reservoir Road NW, Washington, D.C. 20007, (202-298-4000), or from the German National Tourist Office, 122 East 42nd Street, New York, NY 10168, (212-661-7200).

NOTES

1. U.S. Census Bureau Data, 2007, http://www.census.gov/foreign-trade/statistics (accessed March 4, 2008).
2. U.S. Census Bureau Data, 2006, http://census.gov/foreign-trade/statistics (accessed June 17, 2007).
3. *CultureGrams, Europe, Germany* (Ann Arbor, MI: ProQuest CSA, 2008), 261.
4. List of countries by GDP (nominal) per capita, http://en.wikipedia.org/wiki/List_of_countries_by_GDP_(nominal)_per_capita (accessed March 5, 2008). Figures (in U.S. dollars) are estimates for 2007 from *The World Factbook* provided by the Central Intelligence Agency (updated February 12, 2008). These figures do not take into account cost-of-living differences; using additional economic data is advisable when making country comparisons.
5. *CultureGrams, Europe, Germany*, 261.
6. U.S. Census Bureau, "*IDB: Countries and Areas Ranked by Population*," as of 2007, http://www.census.gov/cgi-bin/ipc/idbrank.pl (accessed January 16, 2008).
7. *CultureGrams, Europe, Germany*, 262.
8. Jeanette S. Martin and Lillian H. Chaney, *Global Business Etiquette* (Westport, CT: Praeger, 2006), 32–33.
9. Terri Morrison and Wayne A. Conaway, *Kiss, Bow, or Shake Hands*, 2nd ed. (Avon, MA: Adams Media, 2006), 185.
10. Ann Marie Sabath, *International Business Etiquette: Europe* (Franklin Lakes, NJ: Career Press, 1999), 124–125.

11. Ibid., 118–119; Mary Murray Bosrock, *Put Your Best Foot Forward: Europe* (St. Paul, MN: International Education Systems, 1994), 234–235.
12. Nancy L. Braganti and Elizabeth Devine, *European Customs and Manners* (New York: Meadowbrook Press, 1992), 89.
13. Martin and Chaney, *Global Business Etiquette*, 123; Sabath, *International Business Etiquette: Europe*, 118–119.
14. Bosrock, *Put Your Best Foot Forward: Europe*, 232–233; Michael Powell, *Behave Yourself! The Essential Guide to International Etiquette* (Guilford, CT: The Globe Pequot Press, 2005), 50.
15. Ibid.
16. Ibid., 236–237.
17. Ibid.; Terri Morrison and Wayne A. Conaway, *Kiss, Bow, or Shake Hands*, 2nd ed. (Avon, MA: Adams Media, 2006), 187–188.
18. Braganti and Devine, *European Customs and Manners*, 93.
19. Bosrock, *Put Your Best Foot Forward: Europe*, 225.
20. Braganti and Devine, *European Customs and Manners*, 93.
21. Ibid., 93–94; Sabath, *International Business Etiquette: Europe*, 122–123.
22. Martin and Chaney, *Global Business Etiquette*, 86; Sabath, *International Business Etiquette: Europe*, 117; Braganti and Devine, *European Customs and Manners*, 88.
23. Sabath, *International Business Etiquette: Europe*, 127.
24. Martin and Chaney, *Global Business Etiquette*, 141; Morrison and Conaway, *Kiss, Bow, or Shake Hands*, 185.
25. Richard D. Lewis, *When Cultures Collide: Leading Across Cultures*, 3rd ed. (Boston: Nicholas Brealey International, 2006), 227; Lillian H. Chaney and Jeanette S. Martin, *Intercultural Business Communication*, 4th ed. (Upper Saddle River, NJ, 2007), 188.
26. *CultureGrams, Europe, Germany*, 264.
27. *CultureGrams, Concepts and Terminology* (Ann Arbor, MI: ProQuest CSA, 2008), A-14.
28. Morrison and Conaway, *Kiss, Bow, or Shake Hands*, 182.
29. Bosrock, *Put Your Best Foot Forward: Europe*, 238–239.
30. Roger E. Axtell, *Gestures: The Do's and Taboos of Body Language Around the World* (New York: John Wiley & Sons, 1998), 143; Bosrock, *Put Your Best Foot Forward: Europe*, 228.
31. Ibid., 186.
32. Edward T. Hall and Mildred R. Hall, *Understanding Cultural Differences: Germans, French, and Americans* (Yarmouth, ME: 1990), 40–41; Lewis, *When Cultures Collide: Leading Across Cultures*, 224.
33. Lewis, *When Cultures Collide: Leading Across Cultures*, 225.
34. Ibid., 223; Morrison and Conaway, *Kiss, Bow, or Shake Hands*, 184.
35. Ibid., 35–36; Sabath, *International Business Etiquette: Europe*, 126.
36. Braganti and Devine, *European Customs and Manners*, 94–95.
37. Ibid., 87.
38. Ibid., 92.
39. Ibid., 96.
40. Ibid., 87–88.
41. Ibid., 89.

CHAPTER 10

Hong Kong

Hong Kong, more specifically referred to as the Hong Kong Special Administrative Region of the People's Republic of China, is the fourteenth largest export market of the United States.[1]

Major U.S. exports to Hong Kong are agricultural and wood products, plastics, chemicals, man-made cloth, leather and furs, industrial supplies, electric apparatus, instruments, industrial machinery, electronics, medical equipment, toys, jewelry, gem diamonds, generators, and art.[2]

Since Hong Kong was a British colony from 1842 to 1997, the British influence is apparent in many of the country's customs.

COUNTRY SPECIFICS

Location, Topography, and Land Mass

Hong Kong is located on the southeast coast of China; its area is about 421 square miles or 1,092 square kilometers. Hong Kong includes the two large islands of Lantau and Hong Kong, numerous smaller islands, the Kowloon Peninsula, and the New Territories, located adjacent to Guangdong Province on the mainland.[3] The capital is Victoria on Hong Kong Island; it is usually referred to as Central District. The new Chek Lap Kok Airport is located on Lantau Island.

Economy

Hong Kong exports equal $315.5 billion, primarily from watches and clocks, clothing, electronics, textiles, and office machinery. Its imports equal $333.3 billion, primarily in consumer goods, raw materials, food, and fuels.[4] Hong Kong has excellent shipping ports. In addition to shipping, tourism and financial services are becoming increasingly important to the economy. Other industries important to Hong Kong's economy are apparel, cement, electronics, iron, steel, and textiles. Most Hong Kong residents have a comfortable standard of living; the country's Gross Domestic Product (GDP) per capita is among the highest in the world at $29,296.[5]

U.S. ties with Hong Kong are substantial. About 1,100 U.S. firms conduct business with Hong Kong, and approximately 54,000 U.S. residents live there.[6]

Although SARS (severe acute respiratory syndrome) had a negative impact on Hong Kong's economy during the first half of 2003, it has rebounded. The country's unemployment rate in late 2006 and early 2007 was only 4.3 percent, which was the lowest since the middle of 1998.[7]

Population, Languages Spoken, Ethnic Groups, and Religions

Hong Kong has a population of almost 7 million;[8] it is growing at an annual rate of 0.6 percent. With the small land area, the country is one of the world's most densely populated areas. About half of Hong Kong residents live in the New Territories; almost one-third reside on Kowloon; and about one-fifth live on Hong Kong Island.[9]

The official language of Hong Kong is Mandarin Chinese; many dialects from various Chinese provinces are heard, including the *Yue* dialect (Cantonese), which is spoken by most Hong Kong residents. However, English is used in business and is also an official language; it is spoken by about one-third of the residents.[10] Now that Hong Kong has been incorporated into the People's Republic of China, more residents are learning Mandarin Chinese.[11]

The largest ethnic group in Hong Kong (95 percent) is Chinese; most are Cantonese who have roots in Guangdong Province. Other residents of Hong Kong are from Indonesia, Japan, Malaysia, the Philippines, Singapore, and Thailand. A number of residents are business professionals, many of whom have British citizenship.[12]

The religious life of the people of Hong Kong is diverse as they respect both moral philosophies and formal religions. The influence of Confucianism, which is a philosophy rather than a religion, is apparent. Taoism and Buddhism also have an influence on the religious life of the people of Hong Kong. In addition, most Christian religions and Islam are represented.[13]

Country Codes, Time Zones, and Currency

The country code for Hong Kong is 852. When calling from the United States to Hong Kong, for example, dial the International Access

Code (011), followed by the country code (852), and the local telephone number.

Hong Kong is 13 hours ahead of U.S. Eastern Standard time. When it is 5 PM in New York, it is 6 AM in Hong Kong the next day, as you lose a day when crossing the International Date Line. In Universal Time the times would be written as 1700 and 0600, respectively. Hong Kong does not observe Daylight Saving Time.

The currency is the *Hong Kong dollar*; one *Hong Kong dollar* is equal to 100 cents and is available in denominations of 10, 20, 50, 100, 500, and 1,000. Silver coins are available in denominations of HK$1, 2, and 5.[14] A currency converter is available at http://coinmill.com/AED_calculator.html that will convert any currency in the world to any other currency.

BUSINESS AND SOCIAL CUSTOMS

Greetings, Introductions, and Business Cards

When greeting others, people of Hong Kong will offer a light handshake and tend to stand closer to the other person than Europeans or U.S. Americans. Since women in Hong Kong typically do not shake hands, U.S. women should not expect Chinese men to extend their hands first.

During business introductions, introduce the person of higher rank before introducing someone of lower rank. Use the person's last name with title during introductions to avoid giving offense. Remember that in this culture the last name will be positioned before the first name; use a title and the name in the first position. After you have been introduced, you may be asked, "Have you eaten?" You would always reply "Yes." This is simply a ritual, similar to the U.S. ritual of "How are you?" They do not really have any interest in whether or not you have eaten, just as U.S. persons have no interest in another person's well-being.[15]

Business cards should be printed in Chinese on one side and in English on the other. In addition to your name and title and your company's name, include on the card your educational credentials and certifications, as rank and status are important in Hong Kong. Present your business card during introductions using both hands, Chinese side up, positioned so that it can be read by the person receiving the card. Examine the card carefully and make some comment about the information on it. Avoid writing on the card in the presence of your Hong Kong business associate.[16]

Business Entertaining and Seating Customs

Business entertaining is usually conducted in restaurants either at lunch or dinner; accept these invitations or suggest another time. Wives of your

Hong Kong associates usually do not attend these functions; Western wives may be invited but should probably decline since no business will be discussed when wives are present. Your Hong Kong host will usually invite you to a banquet to honor your visit; these banquets typically begin at 9 PM and end around 11 PM. You are expected to reciprocate and host a banquet before you leave.

Meals will be lengthy by Western standards; being served as many as 12 courses is not uncommon. To indicate that you are pleased with each course, leave some food on your plate. Do not refuse a course, except the last, which will be fried rice or noodles. (Eating this final course will signal that you are still hungry.) Rather than using a napkin for the entire meal, you will be given a hot towel before the meal and after it. Unusual foods you may be served include snake soup, shark's fin soup, Peking duck, roasted whole pigeon, or steamed whole ginger fish. (Eat the head to impress your host; he will view it as a compliment.) When you are served fruit and then given a finger towel, this signals the end of the meal.

Other aspects of Hong Kong dining etiquette with which you should be familiar are the acceptability of using toothpicks between courses and placing discarded items, such as bones or shells, on the tablecloth if no plate is provided. Unlike U.S. etiquette, in Hong Kong you would bring the rice bowl to your lips and use your chopsticks to move rice into your mouth. The concept of Dutch treat is unknown in Hong Kong; the person who issues the invitation pays the bill. The one who pays the bill checks it to confirm that a 10 percent charge had been added and adds the tip when no service charge was included. Requesting the bill from the server is done by making a writing motion on your left palm with your right hand.[17]

Seating etiquette is important in Hong Kong. If the host offers you the seat of honor, which is the center seat that faces the door, you would decline the honor before finally accepting it. By declining it initially, you are conveying that you do not feel worthy to occupy this seat of honor. Other people in attendance are seated according to rank.[18]

Dining, Toasting, and Tipping Customs

Dining practices are a mixture of Asian and Western customs; thus, you may be presented with chopsticks or with knives and forks. When using chopsticks, remember the following points: Do not place them upright in your rice; do not suck on them; and place them parallel across your dish when you have finished eating. When knives and forks are used, the Continental style of eating is the norm.[19] Making noises while eating, such as slurping soup and smacking your lips, is considered appropriate; such behavior indicates enjoyment of the food.[20]

Toasting is a common practice, both by the host and guest. An appropriate time for toasting is with the serving of shark's fin soup, which is considered a delicacy and the high point of the meal.[21] Try to learn the appropriate phrase in the local language, such as *Yum boui* for "Cheers." The guest with the highest rank proposes a toast near the end of the meal to thank the host for the evening. During the toast the guest expresses the desire for a successful business relationship and for continued friendship.[22]

Tipping is expected in Hong Kong. In restaurants a tip of 10 percent is included in the bill, but an additional amount of up to 5 percent is customary. Tips to taxi drivers vary from a small amount for short trips to 10 percent for longer rides that may include help with your luggage. Tips to porters should be HK$5 for each piece of luggage. Small tips to washroom attendants or other hotel personnel are appreciated [23]

Gift-Giving Customs

Giving gifts is important to building a business relationship in Hong Kong. Your gifts should be of equal value and quantity as those given by your Asian counterparts as reciprocity is important in this culture.

Appropriate gifts include imported brandy or cognac, U.S.-made cigarettes, candy, high-quality pens, or desk accessories. Framed paintings, DVDs, or books featuring pictures of your U.S. city also make good gifts. When you select gifts, remember that 3, 8, and 9 are considered lucky numbers, while four is a negative number. Avoid such gifts as clocks (considered bad luck) or knives and letter openers (interpreted as a desire to sever ties). Also avoid giving cheese as it is not a part of the native diet. Do not give gifts that are triangular in shape as the triangle has a negative connotation. Wrap gifts in red, green, and gold—after they have gone through customs, of course. In addition, do not use red ink to write a note or sign a card because of negative associations with the use of red ink. Avoid wrapping gifts in white (symbolizes death) or black (funereal connotations). Do not give white or red flowers; white symbolizes mourning and red symbolizes blood.[24]

Gifts may be given to individuals or to a group. When you give gifts to individuals, hand them to each member of the group in order of rank, starting with the person of highest rank. Group gifts from your company to theirs should be presented to the group's leader.

Gift-giving customs in Hong Kong are somewhat different from U.S. customs. For example, in Hong Kong gifts are presented and received with both hands. In addition, your gift may be refused one or two times before it is accepted. In Hong Kong gifts are not usually opened in front of the giver. Even if you are encouraged to open the gift they gave you in front of them, it is advisable to decline and open it in private.[25]

Business Meetings

Schedule meetings two to three months in advance; the best months for meetings are October, November, March, April, or May. Finding someone to introduce you either in person or in writing is recommended. When you select a team of negotiators, remember that people of Hong Kong respect people who are older and those with experience. Send the same people each time; otherwise, extra time is needed for your hosts to get to know a new member. Conducting business in Hong Kong will require numerous visits as establishing a personal relationship before conducting business is important.

Business meetings will start promptly; people of Hong Kong get right down to business. Top-level managers and specialists, except lawyers, should be present at the initial meeting. Greet others when you arrive, starting with the person with the highest rank. English is the language used for business discussions. You can expect small talk at the beginning of the meeting before getting down to business. Harmony should be maintained; do not ask a question that implies criticism. Do not say "no"; your hosts will always say "yes" even when they mean "no." Tea is usually served during business meetings. The host typically takes the first sip. When the host leaves the tea untouched for a period of time, this usually signals the conclusion of the meeting.[26]

Dress and Appearance

People of Hong Kong wear a mixture of styles of dress. Some dress in a traditional manner, while others may follow the clothing styles of Europeans. When you conduct business in Hong Kong, dress professionally, modestly, and well. Designer labels and quality jewelry are important. Light-weight suits in dark colors are typically worn by businessmen. Women should wear conservative suits in dark colors, dresses that give good coverage, or skirts and blouses. Because women may be required to sit on the floor, they should avoid wearing straight, tight skirts. Pantsuits or slacks are not typically worn for business. Shorts and tank tops are not worn except in resort areas. White or blue should not be worn to social events as these colors are funereal. Casual attire is more commonly worn at home rather than in public.[27]

Holidays

Hong Kong celebrates the following public holidays:

- New Years Day (January 1)
- Spring Festival and Chinese New Year (late January or February; dates of the three-day festival vary)
- Easter (spring)
- Ching Ming Festival (April 5)
- Dragon Boat Festival (May or June; the date varies)
- Liberation Day (*Tuen Ng*)
- Mid-Autumn Festival; (September or October; the date varies)
- Christmas Day (December 25)
- Boxing Day (December 26)

Conversational Customs

During conversations Hong Kong residents modulate their voices and respond negatively to loud voices. Appropriate topics of conversation include family, food, hobbies, and travel. Do not bring up unpleasant topics, such as death, failure, or poverty. Because Hong Kong Chinese are superstitious, bringing up such negative topics is offensive. In addition, do not speculate on Hong Kong's future under Chinese control or ask personal questions. People of Hong Kong may, however, ask you such personal questions as age, income, and marital status. You will want to be prepared with vague, indirect responses.[28]

Humor

Humor is not generally used in business presentations by Hong Kong Chinese. In fact, with the exception of Koreans, Asians do not understand the humor in jokes made by Americans or Europeans. Because of Confucian and Buddhist beliefs in politeness, sincerity, and truth, Asians would feel it inappropriate to make jokes about such topics as religion, minorities, or sex. Any attempts at humor should not rob people of their dignity. When humor is used, it should have international appeal (e.g., slapstick, restaurant and elephant jokes, and amusing stories about golfers).[29]

Attitude toward Women in Business

On the Human Development Index (HDI), Hong Kong ranks 22 out of 177 nations.[30] The HDI is a measure of empowerment; it is based on life expectancy, literacy, infant mortality, and real GDP. The assumption is that societies that provide an opportunity for education, access to healthcare, and adequate wages are inclined to be more democratic and exhibit a respect for human rights. [31]

Women in Hong Kong hold positions in government, business, and various professions; few, however, have top-level jobs in business. Businesswomen in other countries should have few problems conducting business in this country. They should understand, though, that women are not given equal access to some private clubs. In addition, while Chinese women do not usually consume alcohol in public, it is acceptable for Western women to do so.[32]

Foreign businesswomen will be taken seriously as long as their demeanor and attire are professional. Their actions should be above reproach, and their attire should consist of suits or tailored dresses of high quality.[33]

Public Behavior

When visiting Hong Kong, respect smoking customs and etiquette. Since smoking in public is acceptable, do not voice your annoyance when other people smoke without asking permission. Smokers are expected to offer a cigarette to others nearby before lighting their own cigarette.[34]

Do not chew gum or blow your nose in public. These behaviors are considered rude.[35]

Avoid showing affection or being physically demonstrative in public, such as hugging or kissing someone. Hong Kong residents are reserved and refrain from public displays of affection.[36]

NONVERBAL COMMUNICATION

Gestures and Posture

Because of the British influence for many years and the constant visitors from the United States, many gestures commonly used in England and the United States will be understood by people of Hong Kong.

Use the open hand to point to something rather than using a single finger. The beckoning gesture consists of extending the arm and hand, palm down, and making a scratching motion with the fingers. Beckoning someone using the index finger to make a curling motion toward you is to be avoided as it is used for animals only. Avoid numerous hand motions during conversations.[37]

Seated posture includes sitting quietly without wiggling the legs; hands should be kept in the lap. Slouching is disrespectful. Do not show the soles of your feet by crossing your legs or propping your feet on furniture. Men typically keep both feet on the floor and refrain from crossing their legs. Women, however, may cross their legs at the ankles or knees.[38]

Eye Contact and Facial Expressions

Eye contact is less important in Hong Kong than in Western countries. Hong Kong residents typically do not make eye contact while conversing. Constant eye blinking during conversations is interpreted as boredom and disrespect and should be avoided. Winking at someone is impolite.[39]

Space and Touch

People of Hong Kong prefer not to be touched during conversations; however, they tend to stand closer than U.S. persons are accustomed to. Touching a person of the opposite gender is inappropriate in public. However, when two Chinese of the same gender hold hands when walking, the behavior typically signifies only friendship.[40] Touching a person's head is inappropriate.

Punctuality and Attitude toward Time

Punctuality is expected for meetings and appointments. While you are expected to be on time, your Asian colleagues may be as much as 30 minutes late since Hong Kong traffic is heavy and often causes delays.

TRAVEL TIPS

- A passport is required; it should be valid for six months beyond your intended stay. A visa is also required.
- Transportation in Hong Kong includes buses, taxis, trains (connecting Kowloon and the New Territories), and a subway system (connecting Hong Kong Island and Kowloon). You may prefer to take the Star Ferry linking Hong Kong Island and Kowloon; it is inexpensive and takes less than 10 minutes. Rickshaws propelled by a bicycle are also available in central Hong Kong and Kowloon; bargain in advance for the best fare.[41]
- Avoid speaking in a loud voice in public or exhibiting any other conspicuous behaviors that would attract negative attention. Women in particular should be reserved, tactful, and avoid appearing aggressive.[42]
- Bargaining for items you plan to purchase, except in such stores as expensive boutiques and large department stores, is common.[43]
- You will not need to be concerned about personal safety when walking on the streets. However, women should take some precautions, such as keeping their purses close to their bodies and taking taxis after dark.[44]

- Should you need the help of an English-speaking police officer, look for one with a red patch on his sleeve—an indication that he speaks English.[45]
- Showing respect for the elderly is important, including opening doors for them and waiting to sit until invited to do so.[46]
- The number to call in emergency situations (police, fire department, or medical emergencies) is 999.
- Do not be offended if you hear Hong Kong residents refer to you as a *guei lou* (foreign devil) or if they refer to you as a European, even though you are from the United States. Residents of Hong Kong group all Western cultures together using that term.[47]
- Drink bottled water. Be careful of lettuce and other raw vegetables that have been washed in tap water. Do not purchase ice cream from street vendors.
- When you compliment someone, they will probably deny it. Although in the United States the correct response to a compliment is "thank you," in Hong Kong you would simply shrug it off to show humility.[48]
- Watch your language! Do not use obscenities; avoid using slang and jargon, as they will not be understood by Hong Kong residents.
- Before photographing someone, always ask their permission.
- When leaving Hong Kong, taxi drivers will charge HK$5 for each piece of luggage; and a departure tax of HK$100 will be charged at the airport. In addition, carry-on luggage may not exceed 22 inches by 14 inches by 9 inches.
- Additional information about Hong Kong is available from the Embassy of China, 2300 Connecticut Avenue NW, Washington, D.C. 20008, (202-328-2500), or from the Hong Kong Tourist Board, 115 East 54 Street, Second Floor, New York, NY 10022, (212-421-3382).

NOTES

1. U.S. Census Bureau, 2007 Export of Goods, http://www.census.gov/foreign-trade/statistics (accessed March 4, 2008).
2. U.S. Census Bureau, http://www.census.gov/foreign-trade/statistics (accessed June 17, 2007).
3. *CultureGrams, Asia, Hong Kong* (Ann Arbor, MI: ProQuest CSA, 2008), 305.
4. U.S. Department of State, Bureau of East Asian and Pacific Affairs, March 2007, http://www.state.gov/r/pa/ei/bgn/2747.htm (accessed May 22, 2007).
5. List of countries by GDP (nominal) per capita, http://en.wikipedia.org/wiki/List_of_countries_by_GDP_(nominal)_per_capita (accessed March 5, 2008). Figures (in U.S. dollars) are estimates for 2007 from *The World Factbook* provided by the Central Intelligence Agency (updated February 12, 2008). These figures do not take into account cost-of-living differences; using additional economic data is advisable when making country comparisons.
6. U.S. Department of State, Bureau of East Asian and Pacific Affairs, March 2007, http://www.state.gov/r/pa/ei/bgn/2747.htm (accessed May 22, 2007).

7. Ibid.
8. U.S. Census Bureau, "*IDB: Countries and Areas Ranked by Population*," as of 2007, http://www.census.gov/cgi-bin/ipc/idbrank.pl (accessed January 16, 2008).
9. *CultureGrams, Asia, Hong Kong*, 306; Terri Morrison and Wayne A. Conaway, *Kiss, Bow, or Shake Hands: Asia* (Avon, MA: Adams Media, 2007), 16.
10. *CultureGrams, Asia, Hong Kong*, 306.
11. Carol Turkington, *The Complete Idiot's Guide to Cultural Etiquette* (Indianapolis, IN: Alpha Books, 1999), 213.
12. Ibid.
13. Ibid.; Morrison and Wayne A. Conaway, *Kiss, Bow, or Shake Hands: Asia*, 19.
14. Ann Marie Sabath, *International Business Etiquette: Asia & the Pacific Rim* (New York: ASJA Press, 2002), 45.
15. Turkington, *The Complete Idiot's Guide to Cultural Etiquette*, 216.
16. Mary M. Bosrock, *Put Your Best Foot Forward: Asia* (St. Paul, MN: International Education Systems, 1997), 237–238; Turkington, *The Complete Idiot's Guide to Cultural Etiquette*, 216–217.
17. Elizabeth Devine and Nancy L. Braganti, *The Travelers' Guide to Asian Customs and Manners* (New York: St. Martin's Griffin, 1998), 46–48, 58; Sabath, *International Business Etiquette: Asia & the Pacific Rim*, 49–51, 60.
18. Sabath, *International Business Etiquette: Asia & the Pacific Rim*, 57.
19. Roger E. Axtell, *Gestures: The Do's and Taboos of Body Language around the World* (New York: John Wiley & Sons, 1998), 182.
20. Jeanette S. Martin and Lillian H. Chaney, *Global Business Etiquette: A Guide to International Communication and Customs* (Westport, CT: Praeger, 2006), 112.
21. Axtell, *Gestures: The Do's and Taboos of Body Language around the World*, 182.
22. Sabath, *International Business Etiquette: Asia & the Pacific Rim*, 59–60.
23. Bosrock, *Put Your Best Foot Forward: Asia*, 231.
24. Michael Powell, *Behave Yourself! The Essential Guide to International Etiquette* (Guilford, CT: The Globe Pequot Press, 2005), 58.
25. Ibid., 200–203, 236; Sabath, *International Business Etiquette: Asia & the Pacific Rim*,, 54–55.
26. Bosrock, *Put Your Best Foot Forward: Asia*, 239; Devine and Braganti, *The Travelers' Guide to Asian Customs and Manners*, 55.
27. *CultureGrams, Asia, Hong Kong*, 306; Martin and Chaney, *Global Business Etiquette: A Guide to International Communication and Customs*, 78; Turkington, *The Complete Idiot's Guide to Cultural Etiquette*, 218; Sabath, *International Business Etiquette: Asia & the Pacific Rim*, 48, 60.
28. Bosrock, *Put Your Best Foot Forward: Asia*, 236; Devine and Braganti, *The Travelers' Guide to Asian Customs and Manners*, 42; Sabath, *International Business Etiquette: Asia & the Pacific Rim*, 52.
29. Richard D. Lewis, *When Cultures Collide: Leading Across Cultures*, 3rd ed. (Boston: Nicholas Brealey International, 2006), 12–15.
30. *CultureGrams, Asia, Hong Kong*, 308.
31. *CultureGrams, Concepts and Terminology* (Ann Arbor, MI: ProQuest CSA, 2008), A-14.
32. Bosrock, *Put Your Best Foot Forward: Asia*, 242.
33. Sabath, *International Business Etiquette: Asia & the Pacific Rim*, 48
34. Ibid., 53.

35. Ibid., 60.

36. Devine and Braganti, *The Travelers' Guide to Asian Customs and Manners*, 43; Powell, *Behave Yourself! The Essential Guide to International Etiquette*, 58.

37. Bosrock, *Put Your Best Foot Forward: Asia*, 242.

38. Axtell, *Gestures: The Do's and Taboos of Body Language around the World*, 182.

39. Sabath, *International Business Etiquette: Asia & the Pacific Rim*, 53.

40. Ibid.

41. *CultureGrams, Asia, Hong Kong*, 308; Devine and Braganti, *The Travelers' Guide to Asian Customs and Manners*, 61.

42. Bosrock, *Put Your Best Foot Forward: Asia*, 236.

43. Ibid., 235.

44. Devine and Braganti, *The Travelers' Guide to Asian Customs and Manners*, 63.

45. Ibid.

46. Ibid., 43.

47. Ibid.

48. Bosrock, *Put Your Best Foot Forward: Asia*, 235.

CHAPTER 11

India

India, officially the Republic of India, is the sixteenth largest export market of the United States.[1]

The United States exports the following to India: oilseeds and food oils; fruit and frozen juices; nuts; nonagricultural foods; raw cotton; petroleum products; iron and steel; copper; nonferrous metals; finished metal shapes; pulpwood and wood pulp; newsprint; plastic materials; chemicals; cloth; industrial supplies; generators; electrical apparatus; drilling and oil field equipment; excavating equipment; industrial engines; metalworking machines; sewing machines; measuring, testing, and control instruments; material handling equipment; industrial machines; computers and accessories; semiconductors; telecommunication equipment; medicinal equipment; civilian aircraft, parts, and engines; pharmaceutical preparations; records, tapes, and disks; and jewelry and gem diamonds.[2]

COUNTRY SPECIFICS

A country's location, topography, economy, and population provide insight into understanding its culture. In addition, knowledge of ethnic groups, religions, time zones, and currency is helpful.

Location, Topography, and Land Mass

India is located on the continent of Asia and is bordered by the Arabian Sea, the Indian Ocean, the Bay of Bengal, Bangladesh, Bhutan, Nepal, China, and Pakistan. The capital is New Delhi. The size of India is 1,269,338 square miles or 3,287,590 square kilometers.[3]

Economy

India's Gross Domestic Product (GDP) per capita is $791.[4] The economy is still primarily agricultural; however, the service industries, particularly high technology, are enabling a middle class to develop. There are still large gaps between the wealthy and the poor. Health issues remain a major concern for the country.[5]

Population, Languages Spoken, Ethnic Groups, and Religions

The population of India is the second largest in the world at over 1.1 billion.[6] Many languages are spoken in India; however, Hindi and English are the main languages, with English being the language of business. English is taught all the way through school. India is one of the most ethnically diverse countries. The Indo-Aryan castes comprise 72 percent of the population; Dravidians make up 25 percent; and 3 percent is made up of other groups. In addition, 80 percent of the people are Hindu, 12 percent are Muslim, 3 percent are Christian, and 5 percent are of other religious faiths.[7]

Country Codes, Time Zones, and Currency

India's country code is 91. Some city codes are 44 for Chennai, 33 for Kolkatta, 22 for Mumbai, and 11 for New Delhi.[8] When calling from the United States to India, for example, dial the International Access Code (011), followed by the country code (91), the city code, and the local telephone number.

The time in India is 10.5 hours ahead of U.S. Eastern Standard Time. This means that when it is 8:30 AM in New York, it is 7:00 PM in India. In Universal Time the times would be written according to the 24-hour clock as 0830 and 1900. India does not observe Daylight Saving Time.[9]

The currency is the *rupee* (Rs). Rs1 is made up of 100 *paise* (p). The notes are in the denominations of Rs100, 50, 20, 10, 5, 2, and 1; and coins are 50, 25, 20, 10, and 5 *paise.*[10]A currency converter is available at http://coinmill.com/AED_calculator.html that will convert any currency in the world into any other currency in the world.

BUSINESS AND SOCIAL CUSTOMS

The customs of a country vary from greetings and introductions to dining and tipping customs. Becoming knowledgeable about a country's business and social customs is important to successful interactions with the people of the country.

Greetings, Introductions, and Business Cards

Namaste is the greeting that is said while you press your palms together with the fingers pointed up below the chin. While most women do not shake hands, men will greet Westerners with a handshake and "Hello." Professional titles are used in greetings.[11]

Business cards are exchanged at the first introduction. Have a good supply of cards when you travel to India. Since English is the language of business, they do not need to be translated into another language.[12] Titles and degrees are used on business cards.[13]

Business Entertaining and Seating Customs

Indians enjoy entertaining in their homes. While you do not touch food with your left hand, you may pass dishes with the left hand. Food in the common plates should not be touched with your hands or with your eating utensils. Do not offer food to someone from your plate or glass or take food from another's plate or glass. People of India customarily wash their hands before and after a meal; they also rinse the mouth after eating.[14]

Most Indians prefer business lunches to dinners. When you are hosting a business meal, remember that beef should not be served to Hindus, and pork should not be served to Muslims. While it is acceptable for a U.S. businesswoman to host Indian businessmen at a meal, she may wish to arrange for payment of the bill before the meal begins as the Indian businessman may otherwise try to pay. If you are being entertained, it is inappropriate to simply say "thank you." You are expected to reciprocate by treating the person to a meal at a later time as a demonstration of your appreciation.[15]

During business meetings you will be offered tea to drink. Although it is proper to refuse the offer of tea the first time, you should accept when you are asked the second time. Indians will offer both alcoholic and nonalcoholic drinks. Although Muslims and Sikhs do not typically drink alcoholic beverages, many do.

While there is no seating arrangement for informal meals, there are customs for formal occasions. If there is a guest of honor, he or she will be seated first next to the host. Also, women may be seated at one table and men at another table.[16]

Dining, Toasting, and Tipping Customs

Indian dining is more ritualistic than in the United States. Beef is not eaten by Muslims and Sihks, and pork is not eaten by the Hindu.[17] Meals will generally have chicken, lamb, or vegetables. While it is customary to wash hands before and after meals, the left hand is considered unclean because it is used for hygiene purposes; therefore, only the right hand is used at the dining table. The host serves everyone, and the guests should not touch the communal dishes or share food off of their plate with others. If you do touch the food, it is considered unclean.[18] You may use bread or your right hand to pick up items to eat because utensils will not always be provided. When you have finished eating, leave a little food on your plate; otherwise, your host will feel compelled to give you more food. Say *namaste* to indicate you have had enough to eat. Many times you will be served a betel nut or *paan*, which is made from the betel nut, to aid digestion.[19] Other seeds you may be offered at the end of a meal include anise or toasted fennel; chew these seeds to freshen your breath.[20]

For a dinner party you should arrive 15 minutes late; however, for official functions arrive at the time stated on the invitation.[21]

Toasts are used at formal events only, such as ceremonial banquets and weddings. Not all people in India participate in the toasting ritual because the Muslims and Hindus do not drink alcohol. Common toasts, when used, are "to your health" or "to your country."[22]

Tipping in India is a down payment for good service rather than a reward for good service. Tipping gets things done in a timely manner. For restaurants and taxis give 5 percent to 10 percent; for hired drivers give Rs10–25 per hour; for a tour guide give Rs5–10; and for a hotel maid leave Rs5 per day. Hotels will also include a 10-percent service charge. At temples and mosques, where you have to remove your shoes, it is customary to give the shoe guardian a few rupees for his service.[23] A *baksheesh* (bribe) will often open doors for you and will get things moving quickly.[24]

Gift-Giving Customs

Gift-giving is important to conducting business in India. Gifts are typically given once a relationship has been developed. Such gifts could be imported alcohol, ties, and nice pens. If you are invited to someone's home for dinner, bring chocolates, a basket of fruit, or flowers. However, do not bring frangipani blossoms as they are funereal.[25] Avoid gifts made of leather (the recipient may be a Hindu) or any gift featuring a picture of a dog (dogs are viewed as unclean by Indian Muslims). Small gifts for the family's children are appreciated.[26] Be sure to use a color other than white wrapping paper as white is the color of mourning in India.[27]

The wrapping of the gift is important. Appropriate colors for wrapping paper are red, green, and yellow. Avoid using black or white paper; these are considered unlucky colors. Do not unwrap a gift in the presence of the giver; this should be done in private.[28]

Business Meetings

As there are numerous holidays in India, check before you attempt to schedule a business meeting. While timeliness is appreciated, it is not always observed. Impromptu meetings are not uncommon. If offered refreshments during meetings, accept what you are offered; it is rude to refuse.[29] During negotiations keep in mind that the country is collectivistic; thus, business decisions are made by the group. The boss, however, will make the final decision. When negotiating, Indians do not usually change from their original offer.[30]

Indian meetings are very different from Western meetings. Because of the collectivistic nature of the country, there will be no open discussion with "give and take" as is customary in the West. Attendees of lesser rank will not offer their views at all, and differences will not be discussed. For Indians the purpose of a meeting is to avoid confrontation, to allow everyone to save face, and to avoid offending anyone. Meetings are for presenting the results of discussions and deliberations that occur in subgroups. Subgroups of equals are where the discussions happen. Most discussions are one-on-one conversations.[31]

Dress and Appearance

Business attire for men is similar to dress in the United States; men typically wear a suit and tie, and women wear a dress or pantsuit. Hindus will not wear leather and may wear their native dress, particularly in the warmer areas of the country.[32] Women wear dresses and long skirts or pants with long tops.[33] The native women will wear *saris* or pants with a tunic top. Shoes are not worn in the homes, temples, or mosques.

Holidays

Indian holidays to be aware of include:[34]

- New Year's Day (January 1)
- Republic Day (January 26)
- Ramadan (February/March)
- Hindu Fire Festival (March 7)
- Eid Al-Fitr (breaking of the fast of Ramadan; the date changes annually)
- Good Friday (March/April)

- Buddha Puvima (May 5)
- Hajj Season (approximately May 11–19)
- Eid Al-Adba (approximately May 20, culmination of the Hajj season)
- Sacrifice Feast (June 1–3)
- Islamic New Year (approximately June 21)
- Jonashtami (August 10)
- Independence Day (August 15)
- Mohandas K. Gandhi's Birthday (October 2)
- Dasheva (October 24)
- Festival of Lights (November 13)
- Guru Nanak's Birthday (November 29)
- Christmas (December 25)

Conversational Customs

Indians tend to have vague, open-ended conversations. "No" is seldom expressed. Indians feel that it is impolite to refuse someone's request; they prefer the more vague response of "I'll try" since they do not like to deliver bad news directly.[35]

Indians are very friendly, and conversations may include personal questions and discussions of family. It is permissible in India to discuss cricket, politics, and movies. Avoid discussing poverty, religion, or the caste system. Do not compare Indians and Pakistanis.[36]

Humor

Indians do not appreciate sarcasm or irony. It is best to avoid joking with them as they tend to take things seriously.[37]

Attitude Toward Women

On the Human Development Index (HDI), India ranks 126 out of 177 nations.[38] The HDI is a measure of empowerment; it is based on life expectancy, literacy, infant mortality, and real GDP. The assumption is that societies that provide an opportunity for education, access to healthcare, and adequate wages are inclined to be more democratic and exhibit a respect for human rights.[39]

The genders are more segregated in Indian society than in Western society. Hindu teaches subordination of women to men. Although India is democratic and has had a female prime minister, most women live lives of subordination in India. In government men and women are found working together; however, in other businesses you will see them segregated in the workforce. Today illiteracy is twice as high for girls, with girls dropping out of school 78 percent of the time. Indian men are less likely to open doors for women or to wait for women to enter or leave an elevator. Even today there are many arranged marriages in India.[40]

Indian women in business generally have to be more assertive than men to get the same level of attention and respect as their male colleagues. Because of the two-tiered system, it is difficult for women to be equal partners in a team situation unless they are outspoken and tougher than the men with whom they work. When a woman does become a manager over males, generally she will not have problems because of the work hierarchy in the country. Subordinates are viewed as subservient to the boss regardless of gender. Successful Indian women will generally be more competent than their male counterparts. Western women will probably have no problems with subordinates.[41]

Public Behavior

Public displays of affection, including hugging someone during greetings, should be avoided. Sikhs avoid all physical contact between the genders. Winking and whistling are considered impolite public behaviors and should likewise be avoided.[42] Do not sniff or touch the flowers that are displayed at bazaars; this is impolite. In addition, do not stare at the poor you may see while walking on the street.[43] Always cover your head when entering a Sikh shrine. (Women cover their heads in temples as well.) In addition, remove your shoes when entering a temple, Sikh shrine, or mosque.[44]

Public displays of affection between men and women in public are inappropriate. However, men may hold hands or walk arm in arm with men, and women may hold hands or walk arm in arm with women.[45]

NONVERBAL COMMUNICATION

Nonverbal communication can reinforce or negate what is said. In some cases, nonverbal communication is used instead of oral communication. Major sources of nonverbal communication are gestures and posture, facial expressions and eye contact, space and touch, punctuality and attitude toward time, and other nonverbal communicators, such as silence.

Gestures and Posture

Avoid excessive hand gestures. To beckon, hold your hand with the palm down and make a scooping motion with all fingers together. People of India often point with their chin.[46] Standing with your hands on your hips is an aggressive posture, and standing with arms crossed is an angry gesture; both should be avoided.[47]

The nonverbal motion for "yes" is the movement of the head in a side-to-side motion, almost like a figure 8 rather than the Western motion of the head from back to front. The Western side-to-side hand wave for hello means "no" or "go away" to an Indian. Holding the earlobe expresses remorse, repentance, or sincerity. When pointing, use the entire hand.[48]

Eye Contact and Facial Expressions

Eye contact is direct, with occasional breaks. Older Indians feel that it is impolite to look directly into the eyes of an older person or a person in a senior position. Younger Indians have more direct eye contact.[49]

Space and Touch

Indians appreciate a distance of approximately three feet of space when conversing; touching between men and women is inappropriate. However, Indian businessmen often engage in patting or slapping each other on the back as a sign of friendship. Even touching children on the head should be avoided since the head is considered sacred.[50] Indians stand closer than U.S. people do when they are conversing. Indians try not to point the sole of their feet towards another person, to step over another person, or to point their feet towards someone's head, as the feet are seen as unclean.[51]

Punctuality and Attitude toward Time

You are expected to be on time for meetings and appointments. However, your Indian hosts may be late or fail to arrive at all.[52] Indians are not as obsessed with time and are forgiving if someone is late. Deadlines are seen as loose commitments. When an Indian says "yes" to a question, it does not mean that what you are requesting can or will actually be done. Saying "yes" is the Indian's way of saving face for the boss at all costs. It is necessary to ask additional questions if the question is one of when something can be completed. Saying "no" in the Indian culture is problematic. Generally they will not answer at all rather than say "no."[53]

Punctuality is related to class; higher classes have more flexibility when it comes to being on time. Because of the belief in reincarnation, time is cyclical. If something does not happen in this life, it may happen in the next life. For this reason, opportunities are not always acted upon.[54]

TRAVEL TIPS

- A valid passport and Indian visa are required. Visas are effective for 180 days. Having the correct visa is important: missionary visa, work visa, or tourist visa.
- Dates are written with the day first, followed by the month and year. Thus, March 2, 2009, is written 2nd of March 2009.
- Health challenges exist in India. Diseases such as cholera, typhoid, polio, hepatitis, and malaria are common. You may wish to get a prescription for antimalarial tablets before you leave as malaria is still prevalent in some parts of India. Also bring insect repellent; mosquitoes can be a problem.
- Never drink the water or use ice cubes. Drink bottled water only; check the seal to make sure it is intact. All food that you eat should be cooked or peeled.
- Use auto-rickshaws or taxis for transportation. When you take a taxi, negotiate the rate before entering the vehicle. Do not share a taxi with a stranger or use a taxi that picks up other passengers. Subways are only available in Calcutta, and buses are very crowded. If riding a train, get a first- or second-class sleeper ticket. If you drive, you will need an International Driver's License. Remember that driving is on the left side of the road. Hiring a driver is recommended.[55]
- Bring along toilet paper and tissues as they are often unavailable in India.
- Between October and March is the best time period for meetings as this bypasses the extreme heat and monsoons in some parts of the country.
- For safety reasons women should not carry valuables in their purse and should avoid purses with a shoulder strap as they can be stolen easily. Men should avoid carrying their wallet in their front or back pockets. Both women and men should carry wallets that are concealed beneath their clothing.
- If you give money to one person asking for alms, others will expect the same treatment.
- Keep your hands in your pockets when you are near temples. Otherwise, street salespeople will hold out their hand as if wishing to shake hands, then quickly attach a religious bracelet to your arm and demand a donation.[56]
- When visiting temples, avoid wearing belts or other items made of leather as this may be offensive to Hindus.
- Always ask permission before you take a photograph of someone. Taking photographs in some places, such as airports, railway stations, and military installations, is prohibited.
- Emergency numbers in India are 100 for police (103 for the traffic police), 102 for medical emergencies, and 101 for the fire department.

- Additional information about travel to India is available from the Embassy of India, 2107 Massachusetts Avenue NW, Washington, D.C. 20008; (202-939-7000).

NOTES

1. U.S. Census Bureau, "Foreign Trade Statistics," http://www.census.gov/foreign-trade/statistics/highlights/top/top0612.html (accessed March 4, 2008).
2. U.S. Census Bureau, "Foreign Trade Statistics," http://www.census.gov/foreign-trade/statistics/product/enduse/exports/c5330.html (accessed February 9, 2008).
3. *CultureGrams, Asia, Republic of India* (Ann Arbor, MI: ProQuest CSA, 2008), 317.
4. List of countries by GDP (nominal) per capita, http://en.wikipedia.org/wiki/List_of_countries_by_GDP_(nominal)_per_capita (accessed March 5, 2008). Figures (in U.S. dollars) are estimates for 2007 from *The World Factbook* provided by the Central Intelligence Agency (updated February 12, 2008). These figures do not take into account cost-of-living differences; using additional economic data is advisable when making country comparisons.
5. *CultureGrams, Asia, Republic of India*, 320.
6. U.S. Census Bureau, "*IDB: Countries and Areas Ranked by Population*," as of 2007, http://www.census.gov/cgi-bin/ipc/idbrank.pl (accessed January 16, 2008).
7. *CultureGrams, Asia, Republic of India*, 318.
8. Country Calling Code, http://www.countrycallingcodes.com (accessed March 8, 2008).
9. U.S. Naval Observation, "What is Universal Time," as of October 30, 2003, http://aa.usno.navy.military.docs/T.html http://aa.usno.navy.mil/faq/docs/UT (accessed March 8, 2008).
10. Mary Murray Bosrock, *Put Your Best Foot Forward: Asia* (St. Paul, MN: International Education Systems, 1997), 246.
11. *CultureGrams, Asia, Republic of India*, 319.
12. Bosrock, *Put Your Best Foot Forward: Asia*, 268.
13. Craig Storti, *Speaking of India: Bridging the Communication Gap When Working with Indians* (Boston, MA: Intercultural Press, 2007), 175.
14. Ibid., 175–176.
15. Terri Morrison and Wayne A. Conaway, *Kiss, Bow, or Shake Hands*, 2nd ed. (Avon, MA: Adams Media, 20006), 228.
16. Bosrock, *Put Your Best Foot Forward*, 275–276.
17. Ibid., 257–258.
18. Morrison and. Conaway, *Kiss, Bow, or Shake Hands*, 228.
19. Bosrock, *Put Your Best Foot Forward*, 257–258.
20. Michael Powell, *Behave Yourself! The Essential Guide to International Etiquette* (Guilford, CT: The Globe Pequot Press, 2005), 65.
21. Ibid., 66.
22. Bosrock, *Put Your Best Foot Forward*, 261–262.
23. Ibid., 261–262.
24. Carol Turkington, *The Complete Idiot's Guide to Cultural Etiquette* (Indianapolis, IN: Alpha Books, 1999), 312.
25. Morrison and Conaway, *Kiss, Bow, or Shake Hands*, 231.

26. Turkington, *The Complete Idiot's Guide to Cultural Etiquette*, 310.
27. Storti, *Speaking of India: Bridging the Communication Gap When Working with Indians*, 176.
28. Morrison and Conaway, *Kiss, Bow, or Shake Hands*, 231.
29. Ibid., 227–228.
30. Storti, *Speaking of India: Bridging the Communication Gap When Working with Indians*, 96.
31. Ibid., 141–142.
32. *Bosrock, Put Your Best Foot Forward: Asia*, 261–263; Morrison and Conaway, *Kiss, Bow, or Shake Hands*, 232.
33. Storti, *Speaking of India: Bridging the Communication Gap When Working with Indians*, 175.
34. Bosrock, *Put Your Best Foot Forward*, 258.
35. Ibid., 254, 228.
36. Powell, *Behave Yourself! The Essential Guide to International Etiquette*, 64–65.
37. Richard D. Lewis, *When Cultures Collide: Leading Across Cultures*, 3rd ed. (Boston: Nicholas Brealey International, 2006), 439.
38. *CultureGrams, Asia, Republic of India*, 320.
39. *CultureGrams, Concepts and Terminology* (Ann Arbor, MI: ProQuest CSA, 2008), A-14.
40. Storti, *Speaking of India: Bridging the Communication Gap When Working with Indians*, 154–156.
41. Ibid., 157–161.
42. Powell, *Behave Yourself! The Essential Guide to International Etiquette*, 68.
43. Roger E. Axtell, *Gestures: The Do's and Taboos of Body Language around the World* (New York: John Wiley & Sons, 1998), 183.
44. *CultureGrams, Asia, Republic of India*, 319.
45. Storti, *Speaking of India: Bridging the Communication Gap When Working with Indians*, 177.
46. *CultureGrams, Asia, Republic of India*, 319.
47. Morrison and Conaway, *Kiss, Bow, or Shake Hands*, 231.
48. Bosrock, *Put Your Best Foot Forward*, 256.
49. Storti, *Speaking of India: Bridging the Communication Gap When Working with Indians*, 177.
50. Axtell, *Gestures: The Do's and Taboos of Body Language around the World*, 183.
51. Storti, *Speaking of India: Bridging the Communication Gap When Working with Indians*, 177.
52. Turkington, *The Complete Idiot's Guide to Cultural Etiquette*, 305.
53. Storti, *Speaking of India: Bridging the Communication Gap When Working with Indians*, 35–36, 178.
54. Lewis, *When Cultures Collide: Leading Across Cultures*, 436.
55. Elizabeth Devine and Nancy L. Braganti, *The Traveler's Guide to Asian Customs and Manners* (New York: St. Martin's Griffin, 1998), 87.
56. Axtell, *Gestures: The Do's and Taboos of Body Language around the World*, 183.

CHAPTER 12

Israel

The State of Israel, typically referred to as Israel, is the nineteenth largest export market of the United States.[1]

Major U.S. exports to Israel are agricultural, petroleum, and wood products; metals; plastics; electrical apparatus; industrial machines; electronics; medical equipment; aircraft; vehicles; pharmaceuticals; gems; and military.[2]

COUNTRY SPECIFICS

A country's location, topography, economy, and population provide insight into understanding its culture. In addition, knowledge of ethnic groups, religions, time zones, and currency is helpful.

Location, Topography, and Land Mass

Israel is located in the Middle East; it is bordered by Lebanon to the north, Syria and Jordan on the east, and Egypt on the southwest. The Mediterranean Sea is located along Israel's northwestern border. The capital is Jerusalem.

The terrain is quite varied, in spite of the country's small size. There are fertile valleys, hills, and deserts. The Dead Sea, which is the lowest point on earth, is on Israel's eastern border. The Negev Desert is located in southern Israel; it has numerous mountains, craters, and oases. The Jordan Rift Valley lies along the eastern part of Israel.[3]

Israel covers an area of 8,020 square miles or 20,770 square kilometers, excluding the occupied territories of the West Bank and Gaza.[4]

Economy

In spite of the dearth of natural resources, Israel has a modern, well-developed economy. Most Israelis enjoy a high standard of living. Israel's Gross Domestic Product (GDP) per capita is $20,617.[5]

Israel's natural resources include asphalt, bromide, clay, copper, manganese, phosphates, potash, sand, and sulfur. The country produces sufficient fruits, vegetables, beef, dairy, and poultry for both home consumption and export. Machinery, cut diamonds, high technology, and tourism are important aspects of the economy. Unemployment and inflation fluctuate; taxes are quite high.[6]

Population, Languages Spoken, Ethnic Groups, and Religions

The population of Israel is over 6.4 million,[7] which includes about 384,000 Israelis who have settled in the West Bank, the Golan Heights, and East Jerusalem. (Israelis use the biblical names of Judaea and Samaria when referring to the West Bank; in addition, they consider East Jerusalem part of Jerusalem rather than a separate occupied territory.) The largest metropolitan area is Tel Aviv, with a population of over 3 million. In addition to the capital of Jerusalem, other cities with large populations include Haifa and Beersheba. The annual rate of population growth is 1.2 percent.[8]

The official language of Israel is Hebrew. Arabic, which has official status, is spoken by the Arab minority. Most Israelis speak English, which is used in business. Both Arabic and English are taught in school beginning in the fifth grade. A majority of Israelis speak two or more languages.[9]

More than three-fourths of the population is Jewish, about half of which are Orthodox Jews; 17 percent are Palestinian Arabs and members of the Circassian and Druze ethnic groups.[10]

The dominant religion (85 percent) is Judaism; 13 percent of the population is Muslim, and 2 percent is Christian. Almost all of the Muslims, the largest religious minority group, are Sunni.[11]

Country Codes, Time Zones, and Currency

The country code for Israel is 972. City codes are 2 for Jerusalem; 3 for Tel Aviv, 4 for Haifa and Nazareth, and 8 for Beersheba. When calling from the United States to Nazareth, for example, dial the International Access Code (011), followed by the country code (972), the city code (4), and the local telephone number.

Israel is seven hours ahead of U.S. Eastern Standard Time (EST).[12] Thus, when it is 5 PM in New York, it is 12 AM in Israel. The times written in Universal Time would be 1700 and 2400, respectively. Daylight Saving Time begins the last Friday before April 2 and ends the Sunday between Rosh Hashana and Yom Kippur.

Israel's currency is the *new Israeli shekel* (NIS), which is linked closely to the *euro* and the U.S. dollar. In fact, most Automated Teller Machines (ATMs) in Israel provide options for receiving *euro* or dollar currencies. The U.S. dollar is accepted in most places, but you will usually need the local currency to buy items under $20. A currency converter is available at http://coinmill.com/AED_calculator.html that will convert any currency in the world into any other currency.

BUSINESS AND SOCIAL CUSTOMS

Greetings, Introductions, and Business Cards

The typical greeting in Israel is *Shalom* (peace), which is the English equivalent of "hello," along with a firm handshake.[13] *Shalom* is also used for goodbye. When people have known each other for some time, greetings may include an embrace and cheek kissing. Israelis do not typically speak to strangers as is common in the United States. In addition, they do not usually introduce themselves to a person they do not know unless it is at an initial business meeting.

In business situations, introduce and address Israelis by their title and surname. You will probably move to a first-name basis quickly. Visitors should be aware that when an Israeli man does not introduce his wife and/or daughters, it would be disrespectful to acknowledge them. Women are not typically included in introductions.

Business cards, preferably engraved, should be printed in English on one side and in Hebrew on the other side. While business cards are important to carry when you conduct business in Israel, you will find that many Israeli businessmen do not have them with them at all times.

Business Entertaining and Seating Customs

Business entertaining is usually conducted in restaurants over lunch rather than at dinner. Dinner events will usually be more social than business and will be held at finer restaurants.

When you are entertaining your Israeli guests, be sure to include all members of the negotiation team. Ask at your hotel for suggestions on the most popular restaurants, including good kosher restaurants, depending upon the preferences of your guests.[14]

Business entertaining can also include an invitation to join your Israeli hosts on a short sightseeing tour. Such tours provide an opportunity to enjoy Israel's history and beautiful scenery, to discuss business in an informal atmosphere, and to solidify relationships. Accepting such invitations will be viewed favorably by the Israelis, who will interpret your acceptance as having an interest in the history of their country.

Although there is no special restaurant seating etiquette in Israel, seating customs tend to be similar to those in many other countries, with the guest of honor seated to the left or right of the host.

Dining, Toasting, and Tipping Customs

The most commonly used style of eating is the Continental style, with the knife remaining in the right hand and the fork in the left, tines down. Leaving some food on your plate is acceptable; it indicates that you have had enough to eat. Alcoholic drinks are not usually served before dinner.

The main meal is eaten in the early afternoon (except Friday); the evening meal is light. Most Israelis, even those who are not religious, observe Jewish dietary laws. Many hotels and restaurants also observe the prohibition against serving meat and milk at the same meal. Some Jewish Israelis do not eat pork or seafood (except fish). Many Muslims do not eat pork or drink alcoholic beverages. When dining with Arabs, eat with your right hand even if you are left-handed; Arabs consider the left hand unclean.[15]

Toasts are usually given at the beginning of a meal. When toasting, say *L'Chaim*, which means "To Life!"

Tipping in restaurants is 10 percent to 15 percent, which may be added to the bill. Tour bus drivers and tour guides should also be tipped; the usual amount is $5 to $10 per person per day. Hotel maids are tipped the equivalent of $1 a day; porters receive $1 per bag. While tipping taxi drivers is not necessary, it is appreciated.[16]

Gift-Giving Customs

Business gift giving is not common in Israel; in fact, some companies do not permit their employees to accept gifts to avoid the appearance of bribery. However, small gifts that can be used in an office, such as desk accessories, are acceptable and appreciated. These gifts may contain your company's logo. Giving modest, tasteful gifts from your home country will demonstrate your thoughtfulness and kindness.

When invited to an Israeli's home, however, it is customary to bring candy or flowers and perhaps small gifts for the children. Giving and receiving gifts should be done with the right hand only or with both hands. Be sure that your gift is not in violation of the person's religious beliefs. For example, gifts of food to someone who is an Orthodox Jew should be kosher.[17]

Business Meetings

Meetings should be scheduled at least three weeks in advance. Keep in mind religious customs when making appointments. Most companies observe the Jewish week, which is Sunday through Thursday. (Businesses owned by Christians will be closed Sundays.) Although the Jewish and Islamic lunar calendars use 28-day months, Israelis use the Gregorian calendar for business.[18]

You are expected to be on time for meetings. The atmosphere of the meeting, as well as the attire, is somewhat casual. Israelis are direct and get to the point; they may at times be confrontational and emotional. They like to talk and argue. Expect Israelis to negotiate price and other aspects of the contract. They will eventually make concessions but will expect a *quid pro quo.* The decision-making process can take some time, so patience is needed.[19]

Israelis will serve coffee at the conclusion of business meetings; this is an indication that the meeting is coming to a close.[20]

Dress and Appearance

Business dress in Israel is rather casual; American- and European-style clothing is worn. Business attire for men is usually a jacket, a long-sleeved, open-collared shirt, and slacks. Many businessmen do not wear ties. For more formal events, men wear suits or jackets, ties, and slacks. Women executives wear pantsuits and designer dresses. Women should be aware of the standards of modesty that should be observed in public. Despite the hot weather, women are expected to keep most of their body covered. Modest clothing is especially important in churches, temples, mosques, and areas in which religious groups reside. Women should wear loose-fitting clothing with a high neckline and sleeves that are at least elbow-length. Dresses should preferably be to the ankle, but at least below the knee.[21] Taking along a scarf to use when the location or occasion requires covering the head is recommended.

Foreigners should not attempt to dress like the Israeli residents. For example, people who are not Arab should avoid wearing Arab headgear; and non-Jews should avoid wearing *kippah* caps or *yarmulkes.*[22]

Holidays

Dates of most holidays are based on a 28-day lunar month (since Judaism and Islam use lunar calendars rather than the Gregorian or Western calendar) and, therefore, vary from year to year. (Months following each holiday are estimates.)

- Jewish New Year—Rosh Hashanah (September/October)
- Day of Atonement—Yom Kippur (September/October)
- Feast of Tabernacles—Sukkot (September/October)
- Festival of Lights—Chanukah (November/December)
- Passover—Pesach (March/April)
- Independence Day—Yom Ha'Atzma'ut (April/May)
- Holocaust Remembrance Day (April/May)
- Pentecost—Shavuot (May/June)
- Celebration of the Law—Simhat Torah (October)
- Other holidays are celebrated in certain areas by specific religious groups. Check with your Israeli colleagues or a travel agent about holiday celebrations before planning travel to Israel.[23]

Conversational Customs

During conversation Israelis are very direct. This bluntness, called *doogri*, is often perceived as rudeness. Israelis are opinionated and are happy to enter into discussions on many topics, even controversial ones. However, it is best to avoid discussions about politics or religion. If conversations become heated, Israelis may suddenly end the discussion to avoid negative feelings.[24]

Israelis have a reputation for being poor listeners. Perhaps their desire to be heard, as well as their impatient nature, is responsible for their poor listening habits.[25]

Appropriate topics for conversation include sports, especially soccer, basketball, and swimming. You may be asked questions that are very personal, such as how much you earn or the amount you paid for a certain item. Your responses can be vague, such as "not very much" or "probably too much."

Humor

The humor of Israelis has been described as "strong, black, and very political in nature."[26] Israeli humor is based on happenings in their daily lives. When people must live in situations that pose a threat to their personal safety, they use humor to cope. Israelis are able to take a very tragic situation, such as the bombing of a restaurant, and make a joke about which restaurant to select for lunch based on the likelihood of its being blown up.[27]

While Israelis appreciate humor, they do not often understand U.S. humor. Thus, it is advisable to avoid sensitive issues involving religion, race, and politics and to refrain from telling jokes until you are well acquainted with a person and feel quite certain that your humor will be understood and appreciated.[28]

Attitude toward Women in Business

On the Human Development Index (HDI), Israel ranks 23 out of 177 nations.[29] The HDI is a measure of empowerment; it is based on life expectancy, literacy, infant mortality, and real GDP. The assumption is that societies that provide an opportunity for education, access to healthcare, and adequate wages are inclined to be more democratic and exhibit a respect for human rights.[30]

Of all the Middle Eastern countries, Israel is the most favorable toward women in business. In fact, Israel has a greater percentage of women in the workforce than many other countries. Evidence of the acceptability of women in the business and professional world is the fact that one-third of all dentists and doctors in Israel are women. In addition, one of its great leaders was a woman: Golda Meir.[31]

Businesswomen are, however, expected to observe strict codes of behavior. For example, businesswomen from other countries should not initiate a handshake with an Israeli and should not hand a business card directly to an Israeli businessman but should place it on a table within easy reach. Since some Israeli businessmen may have difficulty with women in business, foreign businesswomen may experience some teasing but should simply ignore it.[32]

Public Behavior

Smiling in public, which is customary in the United States, is not a good idea in Israel, especially by women. Since Israeli men might misconstrue this behavior, foreign women should avoid smiling in public places.[33] It is customary to give your seat on a bus or train to the elderly and to pregnant women.

NONVERBAL COMMUNICATION

Gestures and Posture

Some gestures that are common in the United States are used and understood in Israel. For example, the O.K. sign formed with the thumb and forefinger is positive and, unlike in a number of countries, is not considered vulgar. The "thumbs up" gesture also means O.K. The "V" signifies victory. Placing the thumb and other fingers together and making an up-and-down motion means to slow down. Exasperation is conveyed by shrugging the shoulders, often accompanied by open palms held up.

Some gestures are either rude or obscene and should be avoided. The extended middle finger should be avoided as it has a sexual connotation. Do not point with your index finger as this is rude.[34] When an Israeli uses the forefinger of one hand to point down to the upturned palm of the other hand, you should be aware that this is an insult. This gesture implies that "grass will grow on my hand" before what the speaker is saying comes true.[35]

Eye Contact and Facial Expressions

Eye contact is important in Israel, especially during business interactions. When people avoid eye contact, they are perceived as being less than truthful or as attempting to hide something. Smiling in public is uncommon.

Space and Touch

People of Israel stand close together; stepping back is rude. Touching between friends is common; holding hands signifies friendship. Arabs in Israel, however, do not engage in casual touching. Both men and women should not touch each other or shake hands with members of the opposite gender when interacting with Orthodox Jews.[36]

Punctuality and Attitude toward Time

Israelis are somewhat casual about punctuality, especially by U.S. standards. People generally show up for appointments on time but are not concerned when people are a little late. Allowances are made for delays due to heavy traffic or bad weather. Israelis do keep schedules but do not always observe deadlines.

Israelis are polychronic; they do several things simultaneously, such as answering the telephone while entertaining a visitor or interrupting the meeting to converse with another visitor who stops by during the meeting. This behavior should not be considered rude; it is characteristic of people of polychronic cultures.[37]

TRAVEL TIPS

- A passport is required for traveling to Israel; make sure it is valid for a minimum of six months after the scheduled return date. A visa is required for visits of longer than 90 days. You may be asked to show proof of sufficient funds.
- Do not bring plants, seeds, fruits, or vegetables into Israel.
- While tap water is reported to be potable, you may wish to drink bottled water because of the high mineral content of tap water.
- When making hotel reservations, keep in mind that Israel's five-star hotels may not be equal to five-star hotels in other countries. For example, rooms are smaller than hotel rooms in the United States. Ask about specific amenities, such as minibars, hair dryers, air conditioning, and room service. You may wish to investigate alternative accommodations; youth hostels, bed-and-breakfast pensions, and rental apartments are options.[38]
- Public transportation includes intra-city and intercity buses. Buy tickets ahead of time; keep the receipt until you reach your destination. Train service along the western coast that connects Nahariya, Haifa, Netanya, Tel Aviv, and Beersheba is very good; rates are reasonable. Taxis may be hailed along the streets or called from your hotel. Group taxis are sometimes a good choice; they operate between the airport and large cities as well as between major cities. They are faster than the bus and are sometimes less expensive.
- Driving in Israel is not recommended. The country has more automobile accidents than any other country. If you do decide to rent a car, be aware that people drive on the right and pass on the left, that seat belts are mandatory, and that punishment is stiff for violating the laws against drinking and driving. When you are fined for a traffic violation, you may be asked to pay the fine on the spot.[39]
- Public restrooms, often marked WC, may be found in good restaurants and hotels. Restrooms for both genders are labeled 00; pictures of a man or woman identify restrooms specifically geared for men or women. Bringing your own toilet tissue is recommended.[40]
- Remove your shoes before you enter an Arab building; follow your host's lead if you are unsure.
- The local emergency phone number to call if you need to summon the police is 100; for an ambulance or medical assistance, call 101; and for the fire department, call 102.
- Be aware of local customs before taking photographs. Do not photograph Orthodox Jews or Muslims as they may take offense. Do not photograph police officers or military personnel.[41]
- Always carry identification with you; authorities may ask for it. Soldiers are highly visible; their presence is for your protection.[42]

- Be sensitive to religious customs in Israel; the Sabbath (*Shabbat*) extends from sunset Friday to sunset Saturday. The Sabbath is strictly observed. Be prepared for restaurants and shops to be closed during this time and for public transportation and the national airline to suspend operations. Orthodox Jews do not even press elevator buttons or turn on light switches on Saturdays.[43]
- Exercise caution at pedestrian crossings since drivers cannot be counted on to stop. In addition, drivers may shout at you when you attempt to cross the street, even when you have the right of way. Road rage is not uncommon; Israelis dislike traffic jams just as much as U.S. persons do.[44]
- Getting in line and waiting to be served is not customary. Israelis are impatient and do not like to stand in line.
- Additional information about Israel is available from the Embassy of Israel, 3514 International Drive NW, Washington, D.C. 20008, (202-364-5500), or from the Israel Ministry of Tourism, 800 Second Avenue, New York, NY 10017, (212-499-5650).

NOTES

1. U.S. Census Bureau Data, 2007, http://www.census.gov/foreign-trade/statistics (accessed March 4, 2008).
2. U.S. Census Bureau Data, 2006, http://www.census.gov/foreign-trade/statistics (accessed June 17, 2007).
3. *CultureGrams, Middle East, Israel* (Ann Arbor, MI: ProQuest CSA, 2008), 337.
4. Ibid., 337.
5. List of countries by GDP (nominal) per capita, http://en.wikipedia.org/wiki/List_of_countries_by_GDP_(nominal)_per_capita (accessed March 5, 2008). Figures (in U.S. dollars) are estimates for 2007 from *The World Factbook* provided by the Central Intelligence Agency (updated February 12, 2008). These figures do not take into account cost-of-living differences; using additional economic data is advisable when making country comparisons.
6. Ibid., 340.
7. U.S. Census Bureau, "*IDB: Countries and Areas Ranked by Population*," as of 2007, http://www.census.gov/cgi-bin/ipc/idbrank.pl (accessed January 16, 2008).
8. *CultureGrams, Middle East, Israel*, 338.
9. Ibid.
10. Ibid.
11. Richard D. Lewis, *When Cultures Collide: Leading Across Cultures*, 3rd ed. (Boston, MA: Nicholas Brealey International, 2006), 428.
12. Terri Morrison, Wayne A. Conaway, and Joseph J. Douress, *Dun & Bradstreet's Guide to Doing Business Around the World* (Paramus, NJ: Prentice Hall, 1997), 210.
13. Michael Powell, *Behave Yourself! The Essential Guide to International Etiquette* (Guilford, CT: The Globe Pequot Press, 2005), 68.
14. Elizabeth Devine and Nancy L. Braganti, *The Travelers' Guide to Middle Eastern and North African Customs and Manners* (New York: St. Martin's Press, 1991), 121.
15. *CultureGrams, Middle East, Israel*, 339–340.

16. Devine and Braganti, *The Travelers' Guide to Middle Eastern and North African Customs and Manners*, 116.
17. Terri Morrison and Wayne A. Conaway, *Kiss, Bow, or Shake Hands*, 2nd ed. (Avon, MA: Adams Media, 2006), 265; Peggy Post and Peter Post, *Emily Post's The Etiquette Advantage in Business* (New York: HarperCollins Publishers, 1999), 507; Carol Turkington, *The Complete Idiot's Guide to Cultural Etiquette* (Indianapolis, IN: Alpha Books, 1999), 346.
18. Post and Post, *Emily Post's The Etiquette Advantage in Business*, 506.
19. Lewis, *When Cultures Collide: Leading Across Cultures*, 431–432.
20. Nan Leaptrott, *Rules of the Game: Global Business Protocol* (Cincinnati, OH: Thomson Executive Press, 1996), 207.
21. Morrison and Conaway, *Kiss, Bow, or Shake Hands*, 266.
22. Ibid.
23. *CultureGrams, Middle East, Israel*, 340; Morrison, Conaway, and Douress, *Dun & Bradstreet's Guide to Doing Business Around the World*, 210–211; Turkington, *The Complete Idiot's Guide to Cultural Etiquette*, 340–341.
24. Morrison and Conaway, *Kiss, Bow, or Shake Hands*, 266.
25. Lewis, *When Cultures Collide: Leading Across Cultures*, 431.
26. Dick Winter, *Israel (Culture Shock! A Survival Guide to Customs and Etiquette)* (New York: Graphic Arts Center Publishing Co., 1992), 47.
27. Ibid., 47–48.
28. Devine and Braganti, *The Travelers' Guide to Middle Eastern and North African Customs and Manners*, 107.
29. *CultureGrams, Middle East, Israel*, 340.
30. *CultureGrams, Concepts and Terminology* (Ann Arbor, MI: ProQuest CSA, 2008), A-14.
31. Roger E. Axtell, Tami Briggs, Margaret Corcoran, and Mary Beth Lamb, *Do's and Taboos Around the World for Women in Business* (New York: John Wiley & Sons, 1997), 124–125; Jan Yager, *Business Protocol: How to Survive and Succeed in Business*, 2nd ed. (Stamford, CT: Hannacroix Creek Books, 2001), 121–122.
32. Larry A. Samovar, Richard E. Porter, and Lisa A. Stefani, *Communication Between Cultures*, 3rd ed. (Belmont, CA: Wadsworth Publishing Company, 1998), 191.
33. Axtell, Briggs, Corcoran, and Lamb, *Do's and Taboos Around the World for Women in Business*, 126.
34. Roger E. Axtell, *Gestures: The Do's and Taboos of Body Language Around the World* (New York: John Wiley & Sons, 1998), 167; Leaptrott, *Rules of the Game: Global Business Protocol*, 208.
35. Axtell, *Gestures: The Do's and Taboos of Body Language Around the World*, 167.
36. Ibid., 166–167.
37. Lewis, *When Cultures Collide: Leading Across Cultures*, 430.
38. Devine and Braganti, *The Travelers' Guide to Middle Eastern and North African Customs and Manners*, 115.
39. Ibid., 125.
40. Ibid., 109.
41. Powell, *Behave Yourself! The Essential Guide to International Etiquette*, 69.
42. Ibid.
43. Ibid.
44. Ibid.

CHAPTER 13

Italy

The Italian Republic, commonly referred to as Italy, is the eighteenth largest export market of the United States.[1]

Major U.S. exports to Italy include agricultural, wood, steel, and iron products; precious metals; coal and fuel oil; chemicals; plastics; leather and furs; mineral supplies; generators; industrial engines; metalworking machinery tools; industrial machines; electronics; laboratory testing instruments; aircraft; vehicles and parts; boats and motors; toys; jewelry; art; and military goods.[2]

COUNTRY SPECIFICS

A country's location, topography, economy, and population provide insight into understanding its culture. In addition, knowledge of ethnic groups, religions, time zones, and currency is helpful.

Location, Topography, and Land Mass

Italy is located in southern Europe. In addition to the entire Italian Peninsula, Italy includes the islands of Sardinia and Sicily. The country surrounds the two independent nations of San Marino and Vatican City. On Italy's northern border are France, Switzerland, Austria, and Slovenia. The southern part of the country extends into the Mediterranean Sea. The capital is Rome.[3]

Italy's topography is varied. The Italian Alps are located to the north; coastal lowlands are in the south. The Apennines run along the length of Italy. The boot-shaped country is generally mountainous, as are the islands of Sardinia and Sicily. The land is flat in some of the coastal areas as well as in the boot's heel.[4]

The area of Italy, including the islands of Sicily and Sardinia, is 116,305 square miles or 301, 230 square kilometers.[5]

Economy

Italy's economy is agriculture-based in the south and industry-based in the north. The Gross Domestic Product (GDP) per capita is $32,022.[6] Two-thirds of the GDP comes from the service sector, while the remaining one-third of the GDP comes from industry.[7]

In addition to being a major producer of cheese and wine, Italy produces corn, fruits, olive oil, potatoes, and rice. The country also produces iron and steel. European Union (EU) nations are Italy's major trading partners.[8]

Italy's economic problems include a high rate of unemployment, corruption and organized crime, and the disparity between the economies of the northern and southern parts of the country. Those who live in the more prosperous north resent the high taxes they have to pay to subsidize projects in the south, while people in southern Italy resent the affluence of those in the north.[9]

Population, Languages Spoken, Ethnic Groups, and Religions

The population of Italy is over 58.1 million;[10] the growth rate is 0.04 percent annually. The official language of Italy is Italian, with numerous dialects being spoken in various parts of the country. The most common second language is English. French and German are also spoken, especially by those who do business with people of France or Germany.[11]

The ethnic makeup of the population of Italy is Italian. However, in the southern part of the country are small numbers of Greek Italians and Albanians, while in the north live small numbers of French, Germans, and Sloven-Italians.[12]

Religion is important in the life of the Italian people. Although there is no official religion, a majority of Italians are Roman Catholic. The fact that Vatican City, headquarters for the Roman Catholic Church, is located in Rome probably has an influence on the religious beliefs of the Italian people. Italians who are not Roman Catholic are either Jewish or Protestant.[13]

Country Codes, Time Zones, and Currency

The country code for Italy is 39. City codes include 81 for Capri, 31 for Como, 55 for Florence, 6 for Rome, 184 for San Remo, 942 for Taormina, 40 for Trieste, 11 for Turin, and 41 for Venice.[14]

Italy is six hours ahead of U.S. Eastern Standard Time. Thus, when it is 5 PM in New York, it is 11 PM in Italy. The Universal Time would be written as 1700 and 2300, respectively. In 1996 the European Union (EU) determined that members would observe Daylight Saving Time (DST) from the last Sunday in March to the last Sunday in October. Since Italy is a member of the EU, the country observes DST.

The *euro* is Italy's currency; it replaced the *lira* in 2002. A currency converter is available at http://coinmill.com/AED_calculator.html that will convert any currency in the world into any other currency.

BUSINESS AND SOCIAL CUSTOMS

Greetings, Introductions, and Business Cards

Italians greet each other by shaking hands, giving direct eye contact, and saying *Buon giorno* ("good day"). They also shake hands when they say goodbye. Women should remember to extend their hand first when greeting men. They should also be prepared to introduce themselves at business meetings. While you may observe people embracing and engaging in cheek-kissing when greeting others, this behavior is reserved for good friends.[15]

When you make introductions, remember to introduce those of higher rank first since showing respect for status is important in Italy. Italians tend to be formal in their introductions; you would wait to call people by their first names until they call you by your first name. Introduce people using their titles. Professors and doctors, for example, would be addressed as *Dottore* (man) or *Dottoressa* (woman) with their last name. Others would be addressed as *Signore* (Mr.), *Signora* (Mrs.), or *Signorina* (Miss) plus the last name.[16]

Business cards are an important part of Italian introductions. They are exchanged at the end of business meetings rather than at the beginning. Business cards are not exchanged on social occasions. Italian business cards are conservative; they are usually printed in black ink on a white card. Many Italians have a social card (listing only name, address, and phone number, which is used for social occasions). In addition, many Italians will have two business cards: one card will have complete information, including titles and degrees, and the other card will omit this information. The second card with less information is exchanged when business relationships have become more informal. Have your business card printed in English on one side and Italian on the reverse side.[17]

Business Entertaining and Seating Customs

Business entertaining is usually conducted in restaurants. Since hospitality is important to conducting business in Italy, you would always accept invitations to dine. Unlike some other European countries, however, business is not usually discussed while dining in restaurants. Italians prefer to concentrate on the food rather than on business. Business lunches can be quite lengthy, often lasting at least two hours.[18]

Italian seating etiquette differs from that of some other European countries. Instead of sitting at each end of a rectangular table, the hosts sit in the middle of the table across from each other. The ranking female guest takes the chair to the left of the host; the ranking male guest sits to the left of the host's spouse.[19]

Dining, Toasting, and Tipping Customs

Italians use the Continental style of eating. Throughout the meal, you should keep your hands on the table rather than in your lap. Although bread will be served with the meal, bread plates are not usually provided. In addition, rather than offering butter with the bread, olive oil in which to dip the bread will be served. Wine will typically be served with the meal; the wine will be poured by the host. (Women do not pour wine.) When cheese is served, it should be eaten with utensils; likewise, utensils are used for eating fruit, except for cherries or grapes.[20]

When toasting, simply say *Salute* (the equivalent of "to your health") as you raise your wine glass.

Tipping in most restaurants is 10 percent, which is added to the bill. Leaving an additional 5-percent tip when you received good service is appreciated. In cafés and bars, leave a tip of 15 percent when a tip is not included in the bill. Although taxi drivers include a tip in the fare, it is customary to give an extra 5-percent tip. Small tips are also given to hotel service personnel.[21]

Gift-Giving Customs

Business gifts may be exchanged when dealing with top-level managers. Rewarding business staff members with a small gift for being helpful is recommended. These small gifts may be pens, key chains, or electronic gadgets; secretaries appreciate chocolates or flowers. Additional recommended business gifts are American-made wines and crafts; illustrated coffee-table books featuring your country, region, or city; and quality desk accessories.

Avoid gifts containing your company's logo. Avoid flowers in even numbers (bad luck) or chrysanthemums (flowers for funerals). Handkerchiefs and knives should be avoided as they are associated with sadness.[22]

Business Meetings

Appointments with Italian business colleagues should be made several weeks in advance. Avoid making business trips during the six-week period starting the middle of July; this is vacation time for most Italians. The holiday period between Christmas and January 6 should also be avoided.

Be punctual for meetings; greet and shake hands with those present. Exchange business cards with people you have not met previously. Introduce yourself; remember that Italians are formal and do not use first names. The person in charge of the meeting will be seated at the head of the table. When you are in charge of the meeting, have an agenda. You may have little success with sticking to an agenda, however, as it is not uncommon for Italians to return to items you discussed previously or to skip to a topic listed later on the agenda. Meetings are often informal and sometimes appear to be social events; they usually start with small talk. The purpose of Italian meetings is more to get to know each other and to assess the mood of the participants; it is not usually used to make decisions. Participants, including junior-level attendees, are encouraged to offer their ideas; others listen. Interruptions are common; no offense should be taken when others interrupt you. If a proposal is to be presented, it should have been distributed in advance to all participants. Otherwise, the proposal will be met with objections. Those attending the meeting will convey major ideas presented at the meeting to top-level executives, who will make final decisions later.[23]

Dress and Appearance

Italy is renowned as a European fashion center. Famous Italian designers who have received international recognition include Ferragamo, Valentino, and Versace. Thus, dress is very important to Italians. People who wish to be successful in conducting business in Italy should be aware that they will be judged by their attire in addition to their knowledge and expertise. Wearing attire that is conservative, fashionable, and elegant is important. Fabric should be of high quality; accessories, including shoes and jewelry, should also be of top quality. Business attire for men should be dark suits; fashionable, conservative suits or dresses are recommended for women.[24]

Italians dress elegantly even for events that call for casual attire. Casual dress for men includes slacks and casual shirts; women wear pantsuits or skirts, but not shorts or worn jeans.[25]

Holidays

Although Italy has fewer holidays than a majority of other countries of Europe, various cities celebrate certain holidays honoring their patron saints. In celebration of the feast day of each city's patron saint—viewed as a legal holiday in that city—businesses close. Following are Italy's holidays:[26]

- New Year's Day (January 1)
- Easter Monday (Spring)
- Anniversary of the Liberation (April 25)
- Labor Day (May 1)
- St. John—in Genoa and Florence (June 24)
- Sts. Peter and Paul—in Rome (June 29)
- St. Rosalia—in Palermo (July 15)
- Ferragosto and Assumption (date varies)
- All Saints Day (November 1)
- St. Ambrogio—in Milan (December 7)
- St. Stephen's Day (December 26)
- New Year's Eve (December 31)

Conversational Customs

Italians are known for being excellent conversationalists, but they are not known for being good listeners. In fact, when conversing in a group, you may conclude that everyone seems to be talking at the same time. Italians are uncomfortable with more than about five seconds of silence. They are demonstrative and a bit dramatic by U.S. standards.

Appropriate topics during conversations include food, wine, films, art, family life, Italian culture, and sports, especially bicycling and soccer. Since Italians have strong opinions about sports teams, it is advisable to avoid making negative comments about regional or national teams.

Avoid discussions about religion, Italian politics, the Mafia, and World War II. Also avoid telling off-color jokes or criticizing anything about the country. Since Italians do not consider a person's occupation a suitable topic for small talk, avoid asking people you have just met about their profession.[27]

Humor

Italians enjoy their life and their work and do not believe that work should be taken too seriously. Although Italians value humor, they are not known for telling jokes (except for political ones). Italians enjoy irony. Their humor is often self-deprecating. Because they are concerned with public dignity, they do not inject humor in business presentations. In fact, they tend to be serious and formal in business settings.[28]

Attitude toward Women in Business

On the Human Development Index (HDI), Italy ranks 17 out of 177 nations.[29] The HDI is a measure of empowerment; it is based on life expectancy, literacy, infant mortality, and real GDP. The assumption is that societies that provide an opportunity for education, access to health-care, and adequate wages are inclined to be more democratic and exhibit a respect for human rights. [30]

Few women enjoy success in managerial positions in Italian businesses; likewise, there are few women in the professions. However, successful businesswomen can be found in family owned businesses; they are also found in the fashion industry. Slightly more than one-third of women who are under the age of 65 are in the labor market, which is less than several other European countries.[31]

Foreign women need to understand that Italian men tend to be flirtatious and charming. Thus, to be taken seriously foreign women who wish to do business in Italy will need to behave and dress in a professional manner.[32]

Public Behavior

Women should avoid wearing sleeveless attire or shorts when visiting churches; they will also need to wear a head covering when entering churches. Men should remember to remove their hats upon entering buildings.

Appropriate public behavior includes covering your mouth with your hand when sneezing or yawning. It is not unusual to see people of the same gender walk arm in arm in public.

The expression *bella figura* conveys the importance Italians place on projecting a positive image; it means conducting yourself with confidence, dignity, and pride when in public. Visitors would be wise to remember that their public behavior will be noticed and that they should comport themselves in a manner that conveys self-respect as well as respect for others.[33]

NONVERBAL COMMUNICATION

Gestures and Posture

Italians are among the world's most demonstrative people. They are well known for using gestures while conversing, especially those who live in southern Italy. Some gestures commonly used by Italians include the chin flick and flat hand flick (get lost), the "hook 'em horns" (unfaithfulness of one's spouse), the "cheek screw" (attractive woman), the "eyelid pull" (be careful, pay attention), the "hand purse" (careful — he may be a crook), the "forearm jerk" and the "finger" (insulting), the "flat hand flick" (get lost), the "nose tap" (be careful), the rubbing thumb and forefinger together (money), the "earlobe flick" (a person is effeminate), and the "fingertip kiss" (something or someone is beautiful). Because of the numerous gestures used by Italians, it is wise to use gestures with discretion and to review Italian gestures before traveling to this country.[34]

Eye Contact and Facial Expressions

Eye contact is expected during introductions and should be maintained during conversations. Eye contact is associated with honesty and sincerity. Failing to give eye contact implies that you have something to hide. Smiling to show acceptance of their demonstrations of affection during greetings and departures, including kissing on both cheeks, is recommended.[35]

Space and Touch

Italians tend to stand close during conversations; however, it is advisable to avoid stepping back as this may be interpreted as a wish to avoid them. Men usually shake hands when greeting other men; they will also hug each other and will lean close during conversations. When greeting women they know, they will kiss women on both cheeks. Women typically kiss each other on both cheeks when greeting other women they know.[36]

On a "touch/no touch" scale, Italians would be ranked high on the "touch" end of the scale. This touching, however, is usually done between Italian men; women in Italy rarely touch each other.

Punctuality and Attitude toward Time

Italians are not known for arriving for appointments on time; they tend to be more punctual in northern Italy than in the southern part of the country. People who are important may be late to business meetings. Visitors, however, are expected to be punctual. Italians are always punctual at such events as the theater or for church services.[37]

Italy is a polychronic culture; they are experts at multitasking. In other words, they are able to do several tasks simultaneously. These constant interruptions can be stressful to people from monochronic cultures, who do not allow interruptions and concentrate on doing only one thing at a time.[38]

TRAVEL TIPS

- A passport is required for traveling to Italy; it should be valid for at least three months beyond your intended stay. No visa is needed for visits of up to three months.
- When you leave your hotel, leave your room key at the front desk.
- Remain alert to potential robbers when walking on the streets in larger cities, such as Milan, Naples, and Rome. Pickpockets, including groups of children, are a problem in many areas. Purse-snatching is also a problem in some cities, so women should be especially vigilant in restaurants and while shopping. The best advice for women is probably to avoid carrying a purse.
- Public transportation in Italy includes buses, streetcars, subways, and trains. When using city buses, you usually pay a flat rate, regardless of your destination. Tickets for city buses and streetcars may be purchased at various places, including kiosks. Subways, like city buses, have flat rates. The types of trains available include express and semi-express that are used for both international and domestic service. You will want to inquire about certain amenities, such as whether the train is air conditioned, if food and drink are available, and whether both first- and second-class seating are provided. Tickets for all types of public transportation should be retained until debarking. [39]
- Taxis are available at taxi stands. Calling a taxi will involve being charged for the distance the driver travels to pick you up. Women are advised to take a taxi rather than to walk alone on the streets at night; they should, however, be prepared to pay extra for taxis at night.
- If you drive in Italy, you may use your U.S. driver's license; an International Driver's License is not required. Seat belts are mandatory. Be prepared for problems with parking, however, including the lack of on-the-street parking spaces as well as few parking garages. Do not drink and drive as laws prohibiting driving while intoxicated are strictly enforced.
- If you need to call a police officer, an ambulance, or the fire department, call 112, the number for emergencies in Italy.[40]
- Since it is customary to show respect to the elderly in Italy, stand when someone older enters the room.

- Bargaining with shopkeepers is common. Although you can bargain in English in larger cities, you will need to speak Italian when bargaining in smaller towns.
- Public restrooms, available in cafés and hotels, will be marked *W.C.* Those specifically for men will have a sign on the door that says *Uomini* or *Signori*; restrooms for women will be labeled *Donne* or *Signore*. *Gabinetti Publici* identifies a public restroom on the street. Take tissue with you as it may not be provided.[41]
- When you answer the telephone, say *pronto* ("ready") rather than *Buon giorno* ("good day') or *Buena sera* ("good evening").
- Do not take photographs of factories, military installations, or in any area that has a sign featuring an "X" across a picture of a camera. Should you wish to take a photo of people, ask permission before photographing them.[42]
- Do not approach the feral cats that are in many parts of Italy, especially in Rome. Since they are wild, they may carry disease.
- Avoid excessive drinking. Although Italians enjoy wine, they do not believe in drinking to excess. Italians seem to have a relaxed attitude toward alcohol consumption; alcoholic beverages are served 24 hours a day in bars and restaurants, and the country does not have a legal drinking age.[43]
- Additional information about Italy is available from the Embassy of Italy, 3000 Whitehaven Street NW, Washington, D.C. 20008, (202-612-4400), or from the Italian Tourist Board, 630 Fifth Avenue, Suite 1565, New York, NY 10111, (212-245-5618).

NOTES

1. U.S. Census Bureau Data, 2007, http://census.gov/foreign-trade/statistics (accessed March 4, 2008).
2. U.S. Census Bureau Data, 2006, http://census.gov/foreign-trade/statistics (accessed June 17, 2007).
3. *CultureGrams, Europe, Italy* (Ann Arbor, MI: ProQuest CSA, 2008), 341; Carol Turkington, *The Complete Idiot's Guide to Cultural Etiquette* (Indianapolis, IN: Alpha Books, 1999), 109.
4. *CultureGrams, Europe, Italy*, 341.
5. Ibid.
6. List of countries by GDP (nominal) per capita, http://en.wikipedia.org/wiki/List_of_countries_by_GDP_(nominal)_per_capita (accessed March 5, 2008). Figures (in U.S. dollars) are estimates for 2007 from *The World Factbook* provided by the Central Intelligence Agency (updated February 12, 2008). These figures do not take into account cost-of-living differences; using additional economic data is advisable when making country comparisons.
7. Ibid., 344.
8. Ibid.
9. Ibid.

10. U.S. Census Bureau, "*IDB: Countries and Areas Ranked by Population,*" as of 2007, http://www.census.gov/cgi-bin/ipc/idbrank.pl (accessed January 16, 2008).
11. Ann Marie Sabath, *International Business Etiquette: Europe* (Franklin Lakes, NJ: Career Press, 1999), 164.
12. Ibid., 163.
13. Ibid., 164–165.
14. Ibid., 163.
15. Roger E. Axtell, Tami Briggs, Margaret Corcoran, and Mary Beth Lamb, *Do's and Taboos Around the World for Women in Business* (New York: John Wiley & Sons, 1997), 79; Michael Powell, *Behave Yourself! The Essential Guide to International Etiquette* (Guilford, CT: The Globe Pequot Press, 2005), 70.
16. Powell, *Behave Yourself! The Essential Guide to International Etiquette*, 70; Sabath, *International Business Etiquette: Europe*, 170.
17. Turkington, *The Complete Idiot's Guide to Cultural Etiquette*, 114–115.
18. Sabath, *International Business Etiquette: Europe*, 166.
19. Ibid., 172.
20. Terri Morrison and Wayne A. Conaway, *Kiss, Bow, or Shake Hands*, 2nd ed. (Avon, MA: Adams Media, 2006), 273; Nancy L. Braganti and Devine, *European Customs and Manners* (New York: Meadowbrook Press, 1992), 146–147.
21. Braganti and Devine, *European Customs and Manners*, 149.
22. Morrison and Conaway, *Kiss, Bow, or Shake Hands*, 275.
23. Richard D. Lewis, *When Cultures Collide: Leading Across Cultures*, 3rd ed. (Boston: Nicholas Brealey International, 2006), 263–264; John Mole, *Mind Your Manners: Managing Business Cultures in Europe* (London: Nicholas Brealey Publishing, 1998), 54––55.
24. Morrison and Conaway, *Kiss, Bow, or Shake Hands*, 275; Sabath, *International Business Etiquette: Europe*, 165.
25. Braganti and Devine, *European Customs and Manners*, 145.
26. Turkington, *The Complete Idiot's Guide to Cultural Etiquette*, 111–112.
27. Braganti and Devine, *European Customs and Manners*, 143; Morrison and Conaway, *Kiss, Bow, or Shake Hands*, 272; Turkington, *The Complete Idiot's Guide to Cultural Etiquette*, 115.
28. Mole, *Mind Your Manners: Managing Business Cultures in Europe*, 60.
29. *CultureGrams, Europe, Italy*, 344.
30. *CultureGrams, Concepts and Terminology* (Ann Arbor, MI: ProQuest CSA, 2008), A-14.
31. Mole, *Mind Your Manners: Managing Business Cultures in Europe*, 58; Sabath, *International Business Etiquette: Europe*, 174.
32. Sabath, *International Business Etiquette: Europe*, 174.
33. Powell, *Behave Yourself! The Essential Guide to International Etiquette*, 72.
34. Roger E. Axtell, *Gestures: The Do's and Taboos of Body Language Around the World* (New York: John Wiley & Sons, 1998), 148; Jeanette S. Martin and Lillian H. Chaney, *Global Business Etiquette* (Westport, CT: Praeger, 2006), 69.
35. Ibid.
36. Axtell, Briggs, Corcoran, and Lamb, *Do's and Taboos Around the World for Women in Business*, 80; Martin and Chaney, *Global Business Etiquette*, 69; Philip R. Harris, Robert T. Moran, and Sarah V. Moran, *Managing Cultural Differences*, 6th ed. (Burlington, MA: Elsevier Butterworth-Heinemann, 2004), 483.

37. Lewis, *When Cultures Collide: Leading Across Cultures*, 220; Morrison and Conaway, *Kiss, Bow, or Shake Hands*, 271.
38. Harris, Moran, and Moran, *Managing Cultural Differences*, 482.
39. Ibid., 152
40. Braganti and Devine, *European Customs and Manners*, 144.
41. Ibid., 145; Sabath, *International Business Etiquette: Europe*, 173.
42. Braganti and Devine, *European Customs and Manners*, 145.
43. Ibid., 154.

CHAPTER 14

Japan

Japan, known as the Land of the Rising Sun, is the fourth largest export market of the United States.[1]

The largest categories of exports to Japan from the United States include agricultural products, coal, petroleum products, natural gas, nuclear fuel materials, steel materials, aluminum, metals, wood products, chemicals, man-made cloth, mineral supplies, industrial supplies, electrical apparatus, industrial engines, food/tobacco, machinery, metalworking machine tools, wood/glass/plastics, instruments, industrial machinery, photo machinery, electronics, laboratory instruments, aircraft, vehicles and parts, apparel, household goods, pharmaceuticals, toiletries, tobacco, art supplies, toys, records/tapes/disks, art, and military supplies and equipment.[2]

COUNTRY SPECIFICS

Japan's location contributed to its being isolated from the rest of the world for many years. This isolation, together with the fact that Japan comprises one ethnic group, is important to understanding the development of the Japanese culture.

Location, Topography, and Land Mass

Japan is located along the Pacific coast of Asia and is slightly smaller than the state of Montana. The capital of Japan is Tokyo. Japan has over 3,000 islands; the main ones are Hokkaido, Honshu, Shikoku, and Kyushu. The country is mountainous and has a great deal of seismic activity. Japan's size is approximately 145,882 square miles or 377,864 square kilometers.[3]

Economy

Japan is the second-largest economy in the world and is an industrialized, free-market economy. The country has a highly efficient economy and is very competitive in international trade. The per capita Gross Domestic Product (GDP) is $40,044.[4]

Japan has basically recovered from the economic slowdown of the early 1990s. Real growth in 2006 was 2.2 percent. Japan's labor force consists of 67 million workers; women make up 40 percent of the total. In addition to its well-educated and industrious workforce, Japan has a high savings rate and a global economy.[5]

Japan has very little in the way of natural resources. Fish is its most important natural resource. Agriculturally, the Japanese grow rice, vegetables, and fruit, but only 15 percent of the land is arable. In addition to milk, meat, and silk, the Japanese produce machinery, metal products, textiles, autos, chemicals, and electronic equipment.[6] Japanese tourist revenues are also important to the country's economy.[7]

Population, Languages Spoken, Ethnic Groups, and Religions

The population of Japan is estimated at 127.5 million. As the birth rate is currently falling, the population in Japan is actually declining.

The national language is Japanese; however, many Japanese businesspeople speak English.[8] Japanese is linked to the Altaic language group. The Japanese language has three sets of characters: Kanji, Hiragana, and Katakana. Due to word processing, text is written in the Western style (left to right in rows); however, you will also see the Japanese style of vertical columns starting at the right side of the page and moving to the left side of the page. Books are also read from what Westerners would consider the back of the book to the front.[9]

Japan has two ethnic groups: the Japanese and the Koreans. However, Koreans make up only 0.6 percent of the population.

Three main religions dominate Japan: Shintoism, Buddhism, and Confucianism. While there are 1.4 million Christians, Christianity is not a majority religion in Japan. It is not unusual for the Japanese to practice more than one religion; they often draw from the features of the different religions. In addition, a number of new religions are developing to meet the social needs of the population.[10]

Country Codes, Time Zones, and Currency

The country code for Japan is 81. City codes are 75 for Kyoto, 66 for Osaka, 11 for Sapporo, 3 for Tokyo, and 45 for Yokohama. When calling from the United States to Osaka, for example, dial the International Access Code (011), followed by the country code (81), the city code (66), and the local telephone number.

Japan is 14 hours ahead of U.S. Eastern Standard Time; the entire country is in one time zone. Thus, when the time is 5:00 PM in New York, in Japan it is 7 AM the following day. In Universal Time the times would be written according to the 24-hour clock as 1700 and 0700, respectively. Daylight Saving Time is not observed in Japan.[11]

The Japanese national currency is the *yen*, or JPY, whose symbol is ¥. A currency converter is available at http://coinmill.com/AED_calculator.html that will convert any currency in the world into any other currency.

BUSINESS AND SOCIAL CUSTOMS

Being knowledgeable about Japan's social and business customs is very important to doing business successfully in that country.

Greetings, Introductions, and Business Cards

Greetings are traditionally done with a bow. The length and depth of the bow are significant. People of equal standing bow for the same depth and same amount of time. If one is senior to the second, then the second person bows deeper and longer. During the bow, the hands are placed at the side of the thighs with the palms flat against the thighs. The eyes move toward the ground with the bow. Since the Japanese have been doing business with the West since World War II, they are also very accustomed to shaking hands. Sometimes a greeting involves both a bow and handshake. If the Japanese do shake hands, it will be a very gentle handshake.[12]

Introductions are similar to those made in the United States. The lower-ranking person is introduced to the higher ranking person first; however, the last name is used with the word *san*. Also, the person's company name, title, and how the person is related to the introducer would be included. An example of such an introduction would be, "I would like to introduce Tsuji-san of Hunter to you." First names are used by family and very close friends only.[13]

The business card exchange is very important in Japan. You should travel with a good supply of business cards, and they should be printed in English on one side and translated to Japanese on the other side. In a meeting, everyone present will receive a business card. If you are at a table, place the cards in front of you for quick reference. When receiving and giving a business card, present it with both hands while giving a slight bow. When presenting the card to a Japanese person, the Japanese-language side should be facing the recipient. After you receive the card, examine it carefully. Treat the card with respect; never place it in a pocket. Instead, place it in a business card holder or a briefcase.[14]

Business Entertaining and Seating Customs

Business entertaining is very important to the business deal and to getting to know each other well. Business entertaining is considered informal time and a time to discuss sports, politics, and families. Generally, very little business is discussed until the end of a meal and after drinks.[15]

Seating arrangements are very important to the Japanese, and they tend to be quite formal regarding such arrangements. When an interpreter is used, he or she would be placed at the corner of the table between the Japanese senior executive and the U.S. senior person. To the Japanese executive's right would be his executive staff members; to the staff member's right at the end of the table would be the lower-level Japanese executives. To the left of the U.S. senior executive would be that person's executive staff members. The Japanese senior executive should be seated as far from the door as possible. If chair sizes are not the same, the Japanese senior executive would be given the largest chair.[16]

Dining, Toasting, and Tipping Customs

If invited out to eat or to someone's home (which is rare), you will sit in a kneeling position on a *tatami* mat. Men should keep their knees a few inches apart, while women are expected to keep their knees together while kneeling. You should practice doing this so that you can assume the position and rise from the position with grace. The host will generally order for everyone at the table and pay the bill.[17] If you invite your Japanese hosts for dinner, they will say that you should not pay. However, you need to be insistent and pay the bill.[18]

The Japanese are not in a hurry when they are dining, and the evening meal may last until about 11:00 PM. Learn to use chopsticks. When you are not eating, the chopsticks should be positioned on the chopstick rest; chopsticks should not be used to point.[19] It is customary during meals to clean your plate. Sushi is eaten in one bite, and soups are sipped out of the bowl with the vegetables or noodles eaten with chopsticks.[20]

Toasting will occur after everyone has been served a drink. The host generally begins the toasting. When the Japanese toast, they say *Kampai*, which in the equivalent of "cheers."[21]

Tipping in Japan is not required and will not usually be accepted. Tipping in a nontipping culture can cause the person to lose face and is often embarrassing. If someone does something extra for you, however, you may tip; put the *yen* in an envelope rather than handing the money directly to the person. The Japanese consider helping you to be a gesture of hospitality.[22]

Gift-Giving Customs

Two major gift-giving times exist in Japan. The first is *Ochugen* (July 15), and the second is *Oseibo* (December). Gifts are given to customers as an expression of appreciation for past and future business. Gift giving has been an important part of Japanese business protocol in the past, but the custom is showing signs of changing.

Gift wrapping is as important as the gift itself. The paper should be colored, not all white; the folding of the corners should be perfect. Avoid red as this is a funereal color. Unwrap gifts carefully as a statement of politeness. You should thank the giver both in person and in writing. The host gives his or her gift first, and the visitor then reciprocates. Gifts should not be a surprise; check ahead of time to be sure that the gift you plan to give is not more expensive than the gift that will be given to you. Gifts are given in private rather than in front of others. Some good gift ideas include liquor, books, musical DVDs, neckties, silk scarves, handbags, and American art. Bringing a gift for your Japanese host's children is a nice gesture; appropriate gifts for children include cowboy and Indian outfits.[23]

Business Meetings

Punctuality is important when attending Japanese business meetings. These meetings will generally take place in the office, in restaurants, or in bars. In the office, the meetings are business related. Decisions will not happen quickly. The Japanese will want to discuss your proposal among themselves before giving you a response. The second meeting is meant to build a relationship and to discuss the issues in whatever business venture is being discussed. These second meetings may be planned or arranged on the spur of the moment. Typically you will go to a bar, a restaurant, or perhaps a "hostess" bar. In Japan the host always pays.[24] Drinking alcohol is part of these meetings, and it is considered rude if you do not participate.

When in a business meeting, everyone sits only after the highest-ranking person sits. It is also customary to avoid getting up while the highest ranking person is seated. Good manners dictate that you take notes during meetings; such behavior is appreciated by the Japanese.[25]

Connections are very important and can help one get appointments and negotiate business deals in Japan. Contracts are not seen as final and can be renegotiated at any time by either party. Because Japan is a group-oriented society, individuals are not complimented on a job well done; however, the whole group should be complimented. It would be rude to single out an individual for recognition or a reward. The Japanese respond to positive persuasion better than hard-sell techniques. When negotiating, look for common areas of agreement first; then build on those areas.[26]

Dress and Appearance

Clothing is conservative for both Japanese men and women. As Japan is a group-oriented culture, conformity in dress is important because it brings harmony to the group. Colors are subdued, and all white is worn only for mourning. Men wear dark suits and ties; women wear conservative dresses and suits. Women's dresses should be in subdued colors, not too short, and devoid of décolleté. Women should also avoid the overuse of jewelry, perfume, and makeup. Since shoes are removed often, wearing slip-on shoes is a good idea. Pantsuits for women are becoming more common. Women may wear high heels, but only if they will not be taller than their Japanese counterparts.[27] The traditional *kimono* is worn on special occasions.[28]

Holidays

Japan has three main holiday seasons: the New Year, Golden Week, and Bon Festival. Japanese holidays include the following:[29]

- New Year's Day (*shogatsu*) (January 1)—businesses are generally closed through January 3.
- Coming of Age Day (January 15)
- National Foundation Day (February 11)
- Vernal Equinox Day (March 21)—graves are visited during this week
- Greenery Day (April 29)
- Constitution Day (May 3)
- Children's Day (May 5)
- Bon Festival (August 15)
- Respect for the Aged Day (third Monday in September)
- Autumnal Equinox (September 23)

- Sports Day (October 10)
- Culture Day (November 3)
- Labor Thanksgiving Day (November 23)
- Emperor's Birthday (current emperor's date of birth is December 23)
- Visits to ancestral graves are made three weeks during the year (New Year's holidays, December 28–January 3; Golden Week, April 29–May 5; and Obon, mid-August)

Conversational Customs

The Japanese speak quietly at all times unless they are at a bar or during certain sporting events. A poker face is recommended when conversing with the Japanese as they tend to keep facial expressions to a minimum and do not show anger or irritation. The Japanese will apologize frequently out of politeness and have difficulty saying no. "No" will be indicated with such vague phrases as "I'll consider it," or "That is difficult." Silence is valued in the Japanese culture and does not indicate displeasure or disagreement with what has been said. The Japanese consider very carefully what they are going to say.[30]

Many times Westerners interpret the silence of the Japanese during discussions as disinterest or vagueness. However, the Japanese feel you should be able to sense feelings nonverbally and are often surprised by a Westerner's inability to be sensitive to the feelings of others.[31]

Humor

U.S. humor is difficult for the Japanese to understand as they interpret U.S. humor literally. The Japanese do not believe jokes that include sex, religion, or minorities are appropriate; however, they will laugh out of politeness. Due to their face-saving custom, they are very courteous towards others, use indirectness, and avoid self-deprecation. Humor is not used in business situations, but in a bar situation slapstick or golf jokes would be appropriate.[32]

Attitude toward Women in Business

Non-Japanese businesswomen are treated with respect because it is understood that foreign businesswomen hold higher positions in their companies than Japanese women hold in theirs. The Japanese expect a woman to be professional and to show her credibility and position of authority immediately. The male-dominated Japanese society makes it difficult for women to be in positions of power or to socialize with the men as equals.[33]

While the Human Development Index (HDI) ranking for Japan is 7 out of 177 countries, Japan still has a number of women who hold higher-ranking positions in their corporations.[34] The HDI is a measure of empowerment; it is based on life expectancy, literacy, infant mortality, and real GDP. The assumption is that societies that provide an opportunity for education, access to healthcare, and adequate wages are inclined to be more democratic and exhibit a respect for human rights. [35]

Public Behavior

Gum chewing in public is inappropriate in Japan. When using a toothpick, it is important to cover your mouth. Yawning in public is discourteous and should be avoided. Public displays of affection between young girls, such as walking hand in hand, are not uncommon. However, displays of touching in public between men and women are inappropriate. Silence should be interpreted with discretion as it can mean many things; it is used to show respect, to convey truthfulness, to show defiance, or to convey embarrassment.[36]

NONVERBAL COMMUNICATION

Gestures and Posture

Some gestures and postures have different meanings from those used in the United States. When beckoning someone in Japan, wave all of your fingers with the palm facing downward. Refer to yourself by using your index finger and pointing to your nose. Remember that a smile may mean pleasure, displeasure, or embarrassment. Another gesture of interest is the U.S. "O.K." sign, which means "money" to the Japanese. Other gestures include waving the hand with the palm up to point at something and waving the hand palm up with the palm facing left near the face, which indicates a negative response.[37]

Seated posture is important; sit straight with both feet flat on the floor. Only men may cross their legs at the knees or the ankles. Slouching may be interpreted as disinterest in what is being discussed.[38] Crossing your ankle over your knee is considered impolite.[39]

Eye Contact and Facial Expressions

Use indirect eye contact to show respect in Japan. Prolonged eye contact is frowned upon. Since Japan is a high-context culture, the signals that are sent between Japanese people are often missed by people from Western cultures. Very small changes in eye movement have meaning to the Japanese.

Facial expressions are kept as free of emotional expression as possible. Laughter has various meanings, ranging from amusement to embarrassment.

Space and Touch

Backslapping and touching in general are not recommended. Backslapping has a negative connotation; it is often used to convey that a person has done something incorrectly. Because they are a no-touch culture, the Japanese choose to bow during introductions and greetings. Only recently have the Japanese begun to be influenced by the West by shaking hands during introductions and by doing more touching in their business dealings with Westerners. Generally, the Japanese like more distance between themselves and others than Westerners prefer.

Punctuality and Attitude toward Time

Being punctual is important in the Japanese culture. Being tardy is impolite. Attitude toward time is influenced by rank. Japanese workers of lower rank do not go home before their boss goes home. Thus, those of the highest rank must go home before anyone else can leave. Doing otherwise is considered impolite.

TRAVEL TIPS

- Passports are required; visas are not required for short stays.
- Public transportation is very good but can be quite stressful because of impatient crowds. Taxis drivers have a reputation for driving erratically; therefore, pedestrians need to remain alert when crossing streets.[40]
- Since the Japanese people tend to be shorter than people of the United States and many other countries, visitors may find accommodations, including seating in public transportation, somewhat uncomfortable.[41]
- Visitors to Japan should be aware of the numerous natural disasters, including earthquakes, active volcanoes, typhoons, and tsunamis, that the country has experienced. They should also realize that Japanese citizens may view visitors with suspicion after these disasters.[42]
- Western-style hotel accommodations are available in the larger cities.
- Both genders often use the same public toilets.
- Electrical converters are not needed for small appliances.

- Numbers to call in case of emergencies include 110 for police and 119 for medical emergencies or for the fire department.
- Golf and baseball are good chitchat subjects to get to know people. These sports are also excellent venues to entertain your Japanese business associates when they visit the United States.
- Most Japanese receive 15 days of paid vacation per year; however, most only take an average of seven.[43]
- Conformity for the youth of Japan has a different meaning than for older Japanese. Young people are often seen in the latest fashions regardless of color. The younger generation is also revising some of society's views concerning family, politics, and male and female roles. Younger Japanese tend to be very materialistic, have lower moral standards, and show less devotion to their parents.[44]
- Additional information about travel in Japan is available from the Japan National Tourist Organization (212-757-5640), www.jnto.go.jp, or the Embassy of Japan (202-238-6700), www.us.emb-japan.go.jp.

NOTES

1. U.S. Census Bureau, "Foreign Trade Statistics," http://www.census.gov/foreign-trade/statistics/highlights/top/top0612.html (accessed March 4, 2008).
2. U.S. Census Bureau, "Foreign Trade Statistics," http://www.census.gov/foreign-trade/statistics/country/index.html (accessed June 17, 2007).
3. Ibid.
4. Ibid.
5. Ibid.
6. U.S. Department of State, "Background Note: Japan," as of October 2007, http://www.state.gov/r/pa/ei/bgn/4142.htm (accessed January 1, 2008).
7. Ibid.
8. Ibid.
9. Stefan Schauwecker, "Japan Travel and Living Guide," http://www.japan-guide.com (accessed March 17, 2007).
10. Ibid.
11. U.S. Naval Observatory, "What is Universal Time," as of October 30, 2003, http://aa.usno.navy.mil/faq/docs/UT (accessed May 9, 2007).
12. Terri Morrison and Wayne A. Conaway, *Kiss, Bow, or Shake Hands*, 2nd ed. (Avon, MA: Adams Media, 2006), 285.
13. Roger E. Axtell, *Do's and Taboos around the World*, 3rd ed.(New York: John Wiley & Sons, 1993), 89.
14. Ibid., 83; Letitia Baldrige, *Letitia Baldrige's New Complete Guide to Executive Manners* (New York: Rawson Associates, 1993), 262.
15. James Day Hodgson, Yoshihiro Sano, and John L. Graham, *Doing Business with the New Japan* (Lanham, MD: Rowman & Litterfield Publishers, 2008), 89–92.
16. Ibid., 92–94.
17. Axtell, *Do's and Taboos Around the World.*
18. Morrison and Conaway, *Kiss, Bow, or Shake Hands*, 285.

19. Ibid., 285.
20. Ibid.
21. Schauwecker, "Japan Travel and Living Guide."
22. Lillian H. Chaney and Jeanette S. Martin, *Intercultural Business Communication*, 4th ed. (Upper Saddle River, NJ: Prentice Hall, 2007), 169.
23. Baldrige, *Letitia Baldrige's New Complete Guide to Executive Manners*, 265–266.
24. Morrison and Conaway, *Kiss, Bow, or Shake Hands*, 284.
25. Ibid.
26. Ibid., 283.
27. Ibid., 287; Baldrige, *Letitia Baldrige's New Complete Guide to Executive Manners*, 263–264.
28. *CultureGrams, Asia, Japan* (Ann Arbor, MI: ProQuest CSA, 2008), 354.
29. Ibid.
30. Michael Powell, *Behave Yourself!: The Essential Guide to International Etiquette* (Guilford, CT: The Globe Pequot Press, 2005), 75.
31. *CultureGrams, Asia, Japan*, 354.
32. Jeanette S. Martin and Lillian H. Chaney, *Global Business Etiquette* (Westport, CT: Praeger, 2006), 139.
33. Mary Murray Bosrock, *Put Your Best Foot Forward: Asia* (St. Paul, MN: International Education Systems, 1994), 344.
34. *CultureGrams, Asia, Japan*, 356.
35. *CultureGrams, Concepts and Terminology* (Ann Arbor, MI: ProQuest CSA, 2008), A-14.
36. *CultureGrams, Asia, Japan*, 355.
37. Morrison and Conaway, *Kiss, Bow, or Shake Hands*, 286.
38. Bosrock, *Put Your Best Foot Forward: Asia*, 69.
39. *CultureGrams, Asia, Japan*, 355.
40. Morrison and Conaway, *Kiss, Bow, or Shake Hands: Asia*, 63.
41. Ibid.
42. Ibid.
43. Library of Congress, Federal Research Division, "Japan: Country Studies," as of November 8, 2005, http://lcweb2.loc.gov/frd/cs/jptoc.html (accessed March 17, 2007).
44. *CultureGrams, Asia, Japan*, 354.

CHAPTER 15
Malaysia

Malaysia is the twentieth largest export market of the United States.[1] The goods exported from the United States to Malaysia included agricultural products, steelmaking machinery, plastics, electrical apparatus, metal-working machine tools, instruments, industrial machines, electronics, medical equipment, and aircraft.[2]

COUNTRY SPECIFICS

Since Malaysia is geographically unique, understanding the land mass as well as the population and economy is helpful to doing business in Malaysia.

Location, Topography, and Land Mass

Malaysia is located in the South China Sea; it shares the Malay Peninsula with Thailand and a large island with Indonesia. Malaysia is made up of West or Peninsular Malaysia (about the size of Alabama) and East Malaysia on the Island of Borneo (approximately the size of Louisiana). The capital of Malaysia is Kuala Lumpur. The two states of East Malaysia are Sarawak and Sabah. Sarawak and Sabah have a coastal plain, but Sabah's coastal plain includes a mountainous jungle. Sabah is home to Mount Kinabalu, which is 13,455 feet, or 4,101 meters, high and is the tallest peak in Southeast Asia.[3]

The area of Malaysia is 127,316 square miles or 329,750 square kilometers.[4]

Economy

The Malaysian economy is growing. The per capita Gross Domestic Product (GDP) is $5,765.[5] The country does have some natural resources:

petroleum, liquefied natural gas, tin, minerals, palm oil, rubber, timber, cocoa, rice, tropical fruit, fish, and coconut. The main industries in Malaysia include electronics, electrical products, chemicals, food and beverages, metal and machine products, and apparel. Tourism is also important to the Malaysian economy. Major markets and suppliers for Malaysia include the United States, Singapore, and Japan.[6]

Almost two million migrant workers from Indonesia are employed in Malaysian agriculture, construction, and domestic work.[7] Since the 1970s, Malaysia has transformed itself into a multi-sector economy with a middle-income population. Growth has been in the industrial sector, mainly in the area of electronics for export. The government of Malaysia is very active in the nation's economic development. The government has tried to end the identification of economic function with ethnicity and thereby enhance the economic standing of its people. Prior business ownership had been in the hands of the Malay people only. With the new economic development plans, however, other ethnic groups can also be business owners. The National Vision Policy was released in 2001 and is a guide for development until 2010. The plan targets education for budget increases and focuses on higher technology products. Malaysia's goal is to be a fully developed economy by 2020.[8]

Population, Languages Spoken, Ethnic Groups, and Religions

The population of Malaysia in 2007 was 24.8 million people.[9] The population is growing at the rate of 1.8 percent per year.

The official language of the people is Bahasa Melayu (also called the Malay language); however, other languages are spoken such as Chinese (many dialects), English, Tamil, and indigenous languages. English is widely spoken. The Malay language must be used for official government business.

The population includes many ethnic groups: Malay, 50.2 percent; Chinese, 24.5 percent; Indigenous, 11.0 percent; Indian, 7.2 percent; non-Malaysian citizens, 5.9 percent; and others, 1.2 percent.

Religions tend to follow the ethnic groups. Malays are usually Muslim; the Chinese are typically Buddhists or Confucianists; Indians tend to be Hindus; and tribal/folk religions exist as well. Islam is the official religion of Malaysia.[10]

Country Codes, Time Zones, and Currency

The country code for Malaysia is 60. City codes include 5 for Ipoh, 7 for Johor Bahru, and 3 for Kajang and Kuala Lumpur. When calling from the United States to Kuala Lumpur, for example, dial the International Access Code (011), followed by the country code (60), the city code (3), and the local telephone number.[11]

Malaysia is 13 hours ahead of U.S. Eastern Standard Time. Thus, when the time is 5 PM in New York, in Malaysia the time is 6 AM the next day. In Universal Time the times would be written according to the 24-hour clock as 1700 and 0600, respectively. Daylight Saving Time is not observed in Malaysia.[12]

The Malaysian national currency is the *ringgit* or MYR (M$).[13] The *ringgit* was pegged to the U.S. dollar in July 2005 in order to stabilize the currency.[14] A currency converter is available at http://coinmill.com/AED_calculator.html that will convert any currency in the world into any other currency.

BUSINESS AND SOCIAL CUSTOMS

Greetings, Introductions, and Business Cards

Greetings and introductions depend upon the ethnic background, religion, age, and relationship to the addressee. Greeting someone with a handshake is common; however, do not attempt to shake hands with a woman unless she extends her hand first. If she does not extend her hand, a slight bow is appropriate.[15] A common greeting is to be asked, "Have you eaten?" The correct response is always "yes." Likewise, you may be asked "Where are you going?" The correct response is "Nowhere special."[16] Remember that people who are Muslim do not shake hands with the opposite gender.[17]

Women may or may not drop their father's name when they marry and use their husband's name. Generally, Malays do not have surnames but have a given name plus their father's name. To the given name add *bin* for men and *binti* for women plus the father's given name.[18]

Since age and seniority are respected in the Malay culture, introductions should begin by stating the name of the most important person first, accompanied by the person's position title (e.g., "Vice President Cheney, this is Senator Clinton."). If you do not know the person's title, you may use the Malay equivalents of Mr. (*Encik*), Mrs. or Madame (*Puan*), and Miss (*Cik*).

Business cards should be printed in English on one side of the card and in Chinese on the other. Business cards include as much information about you and your company as possible. The exchange of business cards is very formal in Malaysia. The visitor begins the exchange by offering his or her card either with both hands or with the right hand only; the print should be facing the recipient so he or she can read it. You would then study the card upon receiving it and place it in a card case. Never put a business card in a back pocket or write on it.[19]

Business Entertaining and Seating Customs

In social situations, Malays tend to arrive on time or slightly late, but never by more than a half hour. Foreigners should wait to be invited to a social event before hosting one. When invitations are received, it is proper to respond in writing. If spouses are present, business will not be discussed; otherwise, you can expect business discussions.[20] If the seating is on mats on the floor, men sit cross-legged and women fold their legs and feet to the left.[21] Guests are served first and are expected to begin eating first. The Malay culture is a clean-your-plate culture.[22]

Dining, Toasting, and Tipping Customs

Due to the different ethnic groups, dining customs vary. If an event is hosted by a Muslim, there will be no alcoholic beverages or pork served. The Hindus and Buddhists will not eat beef. However, both beef and pork are eaten by the Chinese, with pork being the main meat eaten. When they eat, Malays and Indians may use forks and spoons, spoons and their right hand, or only their right hand. Generally, the Chinese will use chopsticks and spoons to eat. The host will order the meal, and everyone will take what they want from serving dishes.[23]

Alcoholic beverages are not as common as in some other countries. When they are served, they are typically served after the meal. Therefore, there is no common toasting etiquette. What is more common is for fruit juice, tea, or coffee to be offered after dinner or with dessert. Use both hands to accept or offer beverages.[24]

Malays enjoy eating at restaurants. If invited to someone's home, you should be on time as the meal is served as the guests arrive. A cocktail hour before dinner is not the custom. The host may seat the guest of honor at the head of the table or to his right. Do not be surprised if the women are served after the men finish eating. A small bowl of water and a towel are provided to wash your hands before dinner.[25]

Malays do not generally tip. A service charge of 4 percent is automatically added to the restaurant bill; however, sometimes restaurant staff members expect additional gratuity from tourists. Tips for taxicab drivers are coin change. For gas station attendants, round up to the next *ringgit.* One *ringgit* per bag is normal for bellboys and porters. Toilet attendants receive 50 sen to 1 *ringgit.*[26]

Gift-Giving Customs

Because gifts may be perceived as bribes, they are not typically exchanged. If presented with a gift, accept it with both hands and wait until you return to your room to open it. Reciprocate with a gift of equal value so as not to lose face.[27] Gifts are typically given between friends, so you should not give someone a gift until a relationship has been established. The different ethnic groups have different gift-giving customs. Do not give gifts of pork or alcohol to Muslims. Gifts to ethnic Malays are wrapped in colored paper; avoid white paper as the color is considered funereal for some ethnic groups. Yellow is reserved for royalty. The Chinese appreciate a fruit basket as a thank-you gift after a dinner or party. When giving gifts to Indians, avoid a gift made of leather.[28] If invited to someone's home, bring some fruit, sweets, or crafts from your country. Gifts that are not considered appropriate include money, liquor, knives, scissors, or images of dogs.[29]

Business Meetings

Since relationships are important to Malays, it is important to build a relationship before trying to negotiate a deal. The pace of doing business will be slower than in the West. It is not unusual for a business deal to take several trips and many months to complete. Because many of the Malays are superstitious, they often consult astrologers before signing a contract.[30]

Letters of introduction help to start a business relationship, and without such a letter meeting requests may be ignored. When giving presentations, be sure they are very informative. When negotiating contracts, realize that Malays consider contracts to be open for further negotiation at any time. Due to this belief, escape clauses are common in Malay contracts. While it will be difficult to obtain concessions from Malays, the longer the negotiations take, the more concessions they will make.[31]

Dress and Appearance

Malaysia is north of the equator; therefore, it is hot and humid all the time. The monsoon season is from September through December, and there will be lots of rain during this time. However, showers are prevalent all year long, so people carry umbrellas every day. Even though the weather is hot, men should wear a suit and tie for initial visits. Just make sure the suit material is a light, summer-weight fabric. Women should also wear business suits for initial encounters. Normal business dress is somewhat more casual; dark pants and light-colored, long-sleeved shirts with a tie but without a coat is appropriate for men. Light-colored, long-sleeved blouses and skirts are appropriate for women. Jeans are not acceptable for work, and shorts are not worn. Because of the Muslim and Hindu populations, women should wear clothing that gives good coverage. The upper arms should be covered, and skirts should fall below the knee or longer. Since yellow is the color of royalty, avoid wearing this color.[32]

Holidays

Holidays vary from state to state within Malaysia and depend on whether the state is predominately Muslim or another religious faith. Avoid travel to Malaysia during January and February, which is the Chinese New Year; also avoid visits during Ramadan, which is the Muslim holy month and varies from year to year.[33]

Since many Malay holidays are determined by the lunar calendar, they will be different on the Western calendar every year. (The lunar calendar holidays are signified by an asterisk):

- New Year's Day (January 1)
- Chinese New Year* (January/February)
- Federal Territory Day (February 1)
- Ramadan* (March)
- Labor Day (May 1)
- Wesak Day* (May)
- Birthday of His Majesty the Yang Di Pertuan Agong (June 5)
- Hari Raya Haji* (June)
- Maal Hijrah* (July)
- National Day (August 31)
- Birthday of the Prophet Muhammad* (September)
- Deepavali* (November)
- Christmas (December 25).[34]

Conversational Customs

Malaysians will typically ask very personal questions during conversations; they seem unaware that Westerners find such questions a violation of their standards of polite conversation. Because saying "no" is not polite in Malaysia, the inflection that is used with the words "yes," "I agree," or "maybe" will tell you if the meaning is actually "yes" or "no." Another way to determine the exact meaning is by observing if Malays suck air in through their teeth. When they do, it is an indication of a problem. Conversational taboos include criticism of the Malaysian way of life, religion, government, sex, or the roles of the sexes. Topics that can be discussed include tourism, travel, the organization's successes, food, and future plans. Malaysians speak in quiet tones.[35] Malaysians are comfortable with silence as it gives them time for thought.

Humor

Humor will be somewhat different among the different ethnic groups. However, it is never proper to tell jokes that disparage others. Waiting to use humor until a relationship has been developed is recommended.[36] The Malay humor usually involves storytelling, parables, or proverbs.[37]

Attitude toward Women in Business

Because of the male-dominate religions in Malaysia, women of some ethnic groups have a more difficult time in business than do women of other ethnic groups. On the Human Development Index (HDI), Malaysia ranks 61 out of 177 nations.[38] The HDI is a measure of empowerment; it is based on life expectancy, literacy, infant mortality, and real GDP. The assumption is that societies that provide an opportunity for education, access to healthcare, and adequate wages are inclined to be more democratic and exhibit a respect for human rights. [39] While women are not barred from business, they are not currently being encouraged to take business positions.

While foreign women are generally accepted in the Malaysian business world, it would not be unusual for a Western woman to be hassled, especially one who is single. A woman traveling alone should eat in the hotel restaurant where she is staying. It is permissible for a woman to invite a Malay businessman to dinner with or without his wife.[40]

Public Behavior

Kissing in public is viewed as inappropriate by members of all ethnic groups. Even a brief kiss on the cheek when greeting someone is not customary. Losing your temper in public is unacceptable; individuals who do so are not trusted or respected.[41] Whistling, hissing, or shouting is also inappropriate public behavior. Malays are very modest and will decline compliments, but you should still give sincere compliments. Smoking in front of elderly people is rude. In public do not cross your legs or cross your ankle over your knee. You can expect everyone to rush for a seat on a bus or train rather than lining up in an orderly fashion. Criticizing a person or a company in public is impolite. When criticism is necessary, it should be done privately and tactfully. Harmony and face-saving are important; causing someone to lose face will be difficult to forgive.[42]

NONVERBAL COMMUNICATION

Gestures and Posture

Some gestures are viewed negatively and should be avoided. One such gesture is making a fist and hitting the other hand with it; this is considered obscene. Another gesture to avoid is placing your hands on your hips as this position conveys anger or aggression.[43] Putting your hands in your pockets also signifies anger.[44]

When pointing to someone or something, use the entire right hand with the palm up or out. To beckon someone, use the right hand with palm down and make a scooping motion with the fingers.[45]

Because of the variety of ethnic groups in Malaysia, you have to be aware of the various posture positions. To be on the safe side, do not cross your legs, point the bottom of your feet or shoes toward anyone, or put your feet up on a desk or chair.

Eye Contact and Facial Expressions

Eye contact will vary depending upon the ethnic group; however, overall you will have moderately direct eye contact. Eye contact will be broken if the person is asked for something that is not possible or if he or she is embarrassed.

A smile may mean embarrassment, shyness, or unhappiness, as well as the normal positive meaning of a smile in the West. If a Malay businessperson laughs during a serious business meeting, it could mean that he or she is anxious or happy.[46] If you have to yawn or use a toothpick, cover your mouth with your hand.

Space and Touch

Since the head is considered to be where the soul resides by many Malays, avoid touching anyone's head. While the space between people differs by ethnic group, generally three feet will be an acceptable distance.[47] Avoid touching the opposite gender. Malays will give a slight bow when entering or leaving a room or when passing by others, which means "excuse me."[48]

Punctuality and Attitude toward Time

Punctuality is very important in the Malay culture. Since the majority of the businesspeople are Chinese, promptness is expected of business associates. The Malay ethnic group holds the majority of the government offices; people in this group tend to be more flexible regarding time. As a foreigner in their country, however, you are expected to be on time whether or not the person you are meeting is on time. Some Muslim Malays work the traditional Muslim work week, where the weekend is Thursday and Friday.[49] Appointments should be made at least a month in advance.[50] Malays feel that today should be spent virtuously and that the past and future are in God's hands.[51]

TRAVEL TIPS

- Passports with a minimum of six months of validity remaining are required. Visas are only required for stays of more than three months.
- A medical exam is required for work permits. It is necessary for foreign workers to take tests for HIV, hepatitis, drugs, and pregnancy within one month of arrival and then repeat the tests on a yearly basis.[52]
- Since malaria, hepatitis A and B, and typhoid can be prevalent, check with your healthcare provider about vaccinations you will need before you travel and prescriptions that you may wish to take with you.
- Do not drink the tap water or use ice in your drinks; drink only bottled water.[53]
- If you swim while visiting Malaysia, swim only in the ocean or in well-chlorinated swimming pools due to schistosomiasis and leptospirosis.[54]
- As with all countries that are near the equator, visitors should take precautions to protect themselves from heat strokes and sunburn.[55]
- Visitors should be aware that credit card fraud is prevalent in Malaysia; they should also be aware that in major cities there are numerous pickpockets.[56]
- The number to call in case of emergencies (police, ambulance, or fire department) is 999.
- The most popular sports are *fútbol*, field hockey, cricket, rugby, badminton, and table tennis. Kite flying is also very popular. These are good topics for conversations.[57]
- Malays drive on the left side of the road as do the British.[58]
- The populous is well educated. Degrees from the United States, the United Kingdom, or Australia's universities are highly valued.[59]
- The Malaysian Embassy is at 3516 International Court, NW, Washington, D.C. 20008 (202-572-9700).

NOTES

1. U.S. Census Bureau, "Foreign Trade Statistics,"http://www.census.gov/foreign-trade/statistics/highlights/top/top0612.html (accessed March 4, 2008).

2. Ibid.

3. U.S. Department of State, "Background Note: Malaysia," as of December 2006, http://www.state.gov/r/pa/ei/bgn/4142.htm (accessed May 9, 2007);*CultureGrams, Asia, Malaysia* (Ann Arbor, MI: ProQuest CSA, 2008), 429.

4. *CultureGrams, Asia, Malaysia*, 429.

5. List of countries by GDP (nominal) per capita, http://en.wikipedia.org/wiki/List_of_countries_by_GDP_(nominal)_per_capita (accessed March 5, 2008). Figures (in U.S. dollars) are estimates for 2007 from *The World Factbook* provided by the Central Intelligence Agency (updated February 12, 2008).

6. Ibid.; CIA the World Factbook, "Malaysia," as of June 2007, https://www.cia.gov/library/publications/the-world-factbook/geos/my.html (accessed June 15, 2007); *CultureGrams, Asia, Malaysia*, 432.

7. *CultureGrams, Asia, Malaysia*, 432.

8. U.S. Department of State, "Background Note: Malaysia."

9. U.S. Census Bureau, *"IDB: Countries and Areas Ranked by Population,"* as of 2007, http://www.census.gov/cgi-bin/ipc/idbrank.pl (accessed January 16, 2008).

10. Ibid.; *CultureGrams, Asia, Malaysia*, 430.

11. Country Calling Codes, http://www.countrycallingcodes.com (accessed June 15, 2007).

12. U.S. Naval Observatory, "What is Universal Time," as of October 30, 2003, http://aa.usno.navy.mil/faq/docs/UT (accessed May 9, 2007).

13. Exchange Rates Table for Malaysian Ringgit, Malaysia, http://www.x-rates.com/d/MYR/table.html (accessed June 15, 2007).

14. U.S. Department of State, "Background Note: Malaysia."

15. Jodie R. Gorrill, Communicaid Global Communication, "Malaysian Business Culture," http://www.communicaid.com/malayasia-business-culture.asp (accessed June 15, 2007).

16. Carol Turkington, *The Complete Idiot's Guide to Cultural Etiquette* (Indianapolis, IN: Alpha Books, 1999), 242–243.

17. *CultureGrams, Asia, Malaysia*, 430.

18. Mary Murray Bosrock, *Put Your Best Foot Forward: Asia* (St. Paul, MN: International Education Systems, 1994), 355.

19. Terri Morrison and Wayne A. Conaway, *Kiss, Bow, or Shake Hands*, 2nd ed. (Avon, MA: Adams Media, 2006), 305.

20. Ibid., 307.

21. Bosrock, *Put Your Best Foot Forward: Asia*, 361–362.

22. *CultureGrams, Asia, Malaysia*, 431.

23. Bosrock, *Put Your Best Foot Forward: Asia*, 360.

24. Ibid.

25. Ibid., 362.

26. Ibid., 363.

27. Gorrill, Communicaid Global Communication, "Malaysian Business Culture."

28. Morrison and Conaway, *Kiss, Bow, or Shake Hands*, 311.

29. Bosrock, *Put Your Best Foot Forward: Asia*, 366.

30. Ibid., 306.
31. Bosrock, *Put Your Best Foot Forward: Asia*, 370–371.
32. Morrison and Conaway, *Kiss, Bow, or Shake Hands*, 311–312; Bosrock, *Put Your Best Foot Forward: Asia*, 364.
33. Bosrock, *Put Your Best Foot Forward: Asia*, 372.
34. Ibid., 375.
35. Gorrill, Communicaid Global Communication, "Malaysian Business Culture."
36. Elizabeth Devine and Nancy L. Braganti, *The Travelers' Guide to Asian Customs and Manners* (New York: St. Martin's Griffin, 1998), 142.
37. Roger E. Axtell, *Do's and Taboos of Humor Around the World* (New York: John Wiley & Sons, 1999), 77–78; Richard D. Lewis, *When Cultures Collide: Leading Across Cultures*, 3rd ed. (Boston: Nicholas Brealey Publishing, 2006), 13.
38. *CultureGrams, Asia, Malaysia*, 432.
39. *CultureGrams, Concepts and Terminology* (Ann Arbor, MI: ProQuest CSA, 2008), A-14.
40. Bosrock, *Put Your Best Foot Forward: Asia*, 373.
41. Gorrill, Communicaid Global Communication, "Malaysian Business Culture."
42. Bosrock, *Put Your Best Foot Forward: Asia*, 367–368.
43. Morrison and Conaway, *Kiss, Bow, or Shake Hands*, 300.
44. Bosrock, *Put Your Best Foot Forward: Asia*, 357.
45. *CultureGrams, Asia, Malaysia*, 431.
46. Bosrock, *Put Your Best Foot Forward: Asia*, 310.
47. Ibid.
48. Ibid., 357.
49. CIA the World Factbook, "Malaysia."
50. Bosrock, *Put Your Best Foot Forward: Asia*, 372.
51. Lewis, *When Cultures Collide: Leading Across Cultures*, 463.
52. Centers for Disease Control and Prevention, "Travelers' Health," as of May 14, 2007, http://www.cdc.gov/travel/seasia.htm (accessed June 15, 2007).
53. Ibid.
54. Ibid.
55. Morrison and Conaway, *Kiss, Bow, or Shake Hands: Asia*, 80.
56. Bosrock, *Put Your Best Foot Forward: Asia*, 374.
57. *CultureGrams, Asia, Malaysia*, 431.
58. Ibid., 432.
59. Ibid.

CHAPTER 16

Mexico

The United Mexican States are usually referred to as Mexico; the country is the second largest export market of the United States.[1] Items exported from the United States to Mexico include agricultural products, petroleum products, fuel oil, natural gas liquids, steelmaking materials, iron and steel products, aluminum, metals, finished metal shapes, wood products, chemicals, cotton fiber cloth, finished textiles, leather and furs, rubber products, industrial supplies, generators, electrical apparatus, machinery and engines, instruments, materials handling equipment, industrial machines, photo machinery, electronics, medical equipment, railway equipment, vehicles and parts, apparel, pharmaceuticals, books, toiletries, writing and art supplies, furniture, household appliances, toys, records/tapes/disks, art, and gem diamonds.[2]

COUNTRY SPECIFICS

Since Mexico is directly south of the United States, the northern part of the country is similar to the southwest part of the United States. Like the United States, Mexico has a varied topography.

Location, Topography, and Land Mass

Mexico, located in the southern part of the North American Continent, is bordered by the Caribbean Sea and the Gulf of Mexico to the east, the Pacific Ocean to the west, Guatemala and Belize to the south, and the United States to the north. The capital of Mexico is Mexico City. Mexico covers 761,602 square miles or about 1,972,550 square kilometers.

The topography includes high mountains, coastal plains, high plateaus, and deserts.[3] Mexico City, with over 20 million people, is one of the most populous cities in the world. The country has volcanoes and earthquakes from time to time, as well as hurricanes, floods, and mudslides. Because of the temperate climate and access to both the Gulf of Mexico and the Pacific Ocean, it is a wonderful place to vacation.[4]

Economy

Mexico's location in relationship to the United States and Canada has helped its economy to grow in recent years. Immigrants (legal and illegal) from Mexico to the United States have increased in recent years and are currently a much discussed topic between the two countries and within the U.S. Congress. Much of Mexico's industrialization has come from *maquiladoras*, privatizing state-owned companies, and encouraging foreign investment.

The Gross Domestic Product (GDP) per capita is $7,216.[5] The Mexican economy is a free-market economy and a mixture of modern and old industry and agricultural styles. Services have been expanded in the areas of seaports, railroads, telecommunications, electricity, natural gas, and airports to help the economy grow. The North American Free Trade Agreement (NAFTA) has caused increased trade among Mexico, Canada, and the United States. Mexico currently has 12 other free-trade agreements with over 40 countries in the world. Areas of the economy that need attention include more upgrades to infrastructure, a modern tax system, modern labor laws, private investment in the energy sector, creation of jobs, and reduction in poverty.[6]

Service industries employ the most people, with one-fifth of the labor force employed in agriculture. Several billion dollars are brought into the country by tourism. The other source of income in Mexico comes from Mexicans who live and work in the United States and send billions of dollars home annually to relatives.[7]

Population, Languages Spoken, Ethnic Groups, and Religions

The population is estimated at 108.7 million[8] and is currently growing at about 1.2 percent per year.[9]

While Spanish is the language of the country, other indigenous languages are also spoken, such as Mayan and Nahuatl. In the major metropolitan areas, many people also speak English.[10] English has replaced French as the second language of choice.

Ethnically, Mexico is made up of mestizos, who are an Amerindian-Spanish mix and make up 60 percent of the population; Amerindians comprise 30 percent of the population; whites make up 9 percent of the population; and other ethnic groups make up 1 percent.[11]

While most Mexicans profess to be religious, church attendance is similar to the United States in that few people attend services on a regular basis. The dominant religion in Mexico is Roman Catholic, practiced by 76.5 percent of the population. Protestants comprise 6.3 percent of the population.[12]

Country Codes, Time Zones, and Currency

The country code for Mexico is 52. City codes include 744 for Acapulco, 998 for Cancun, 33 for Guadalajara, 55 for Mexico City, 81 for Monterrey, 664 for Tijuana, and 229 for Vera Cruz. When calling from the United States to Cancun, for example, dial the International Access Code (011), followed by the country code (52), the city code (998), and the local telephone number. [13]

Mexico's single time zone is one hour behind U.S. Eastern Standard Time. This means that when the time is 5 PM in New York, in Mexico it is 4 PM. In Universal Time the times would be written according to the 24-hour clock as 1700 and 1600, respectively. Daylight Saving Time is observed in Mexico.[14]

The Peso ($) is the currency of Mexico.[15] A currency converter is available at http://coinmill.com/AED_calculator.html that will convert any currency in the world into any other currency.

BUSINESS AND SOCIAL CUSTOMS

Greetings, Introductions, and Business Cards

The handshake is used during greetings and introductions and is also exchanged when everyone leaves a meeting. The Mexican handshake is brisk and firm and is done upon arrival and departure. Men, if they know each other, may also include an *abrazo* (hug). As the *abrazo* shows acceptance, it is a compliment. Men should expect a hug on their second or third meeting if they are accepted. A woman will initiate a handshake if she wishes; otherwise, the man should bow slightly. Women will pat each other on the right forearm rather than shaking hands. If they are close, they will hug each other or exchange kisses on the cheek. As first names are not used on initial encounters, address people by the proper title (*Señor*, *Señora, or Señorita*) and his or her paternal last name. Names can be confusing in Mexico. Generally, single people will use their given names first, followed by their father's surname and mother's surname hyphenated together. When a woman marries, she drops her mother's surname and adds her husband's name.

During introductions, it is helpful to have a third party who knows both parties make initial introductions; this helps to build trust. As a people-oriented culture, Mexicans look for ways to build a relationship.[16] At a business meeting, the leader will introduce you to everyone else in the room. You would shake hands with each person in the room.

Business cards should be printed in English on one side and in Spanish on the other. Business cards are exchanged at the first meeting. Be sure to include your position title and university degrees on your business card. Respect is given to a person whose age, social status, or position is important.[17]

Business Entertaining and Seating Customs

Since Mexicans are very warm-hearted people, entertaining is part of doing business. The Mexican leader, or *patrón*, will be very courteous to guests. In Mexico it is not unusual for you to be invited to your host's home. Because family is so important, they will want you to meet their family. Being invited to someone's home is an honor, but you should not bring up business unless the host initiates the discussion. The Mexican leader will determine where everyone sits.[18]

Dining, Toasting, and Tipping Customs

Good manners are important while dining in Mexico. The Continental style of eating is generally used. Dining will be late whether in a home or restaurant; the evening meal could extend into the early morning hours. The largest meal of the day is generally eaten between 2 PM and 4 PM, which is the reason that the evening meal is eaten at a late hour.

In Mexico, whoever issues the invitation pays for the meal. If street food is purchased, it is proper to find a location to sit down and eat; it is inappropriate to walk and eat. At meals it is considered correct to leave a little food on your plate. Foods that you may be served could include tortillas, beans, various soups, eggs with salsa, various fish and shellfish, chicken in sauces, and beef and pork dishes. Foods may be highly spiced, and breads and rice are used to temper the hot seasonings.

A foreign woman would not invite a businessman to dinner unless other businesspeople or spouses were also invited. It is acceptable for a woman to invite a man to lunch by herself. If she wants to pay for the lunch, however, she will need to make arrangements before the meal to have the charges added to her hotel bill or charged to a credit card.[19]

Toasting is a very popular custom in the Mexican culture; the proper term to use is *Salud!* When tipping the server in a restaurant, leave 15 percent.

This gratuity should be placed directly in the server's hand rather than left on the table. A tax is included in the bill that is sometimes mistakenly assumed to be a tip since the amount of the tax is about 15 percent.[20]

Gift-Giving Customs

Gifts would not be expected at the first meeting. Foreign businesspeople are expected to give gifts to secretaries. A government secretary would be given a token gift; however, a private-sector secretary would be given a more substantial gift. A married man should indicate to the secretary that the gift is from his wife rather than from him.[21]

Gifts are very important in the Mexican culture, so choosing the correct gift, such as a gold pen, art book, or bottle of scotch, is important. If invited to your Mexican host's home, ask the hotel concierge or a florist for advice before selecting flowers. The number of flowers has particular significance in the Mexican culture as well as the variety and color of the flowers.[22] For example, yellow flowers are associated with death and, according to Mexican folklore, red flowers cast spells and white flowers lift spells.[23] The gift should be sent ahead of your arrival. Avoid giving gifts of knives as they signify your desire to sever the relationship. Also, do not give anything from your country that is made of silver because Mexico is known for its quality silver products. Bringing small gifts for the children would be appreciated.

Business Meetings

Meetings will always start with small talk about family, sports, current events, or travel experiences. The Mexican leader will be very visible and will direct the seating. Politeness is very important. Until a relationship has been established, surnames and titles will be used. This practice will change only if the leader initiates the change. When you make comments, direct them to the leader rather than to other members of the group or to the interpreter. Having credibility is very important in persuading Mexicans to your way of thinking. They are very skeptical of deceptive behaviors. Remember the *mañana* principle in relation to setting rigid deadlines. Mexicans look at business partnerships as long-term relationships in which both parties will look out for each other and make changes as conditions warrant.[24]

Dress and Appearance

Appearance and dress are very important in Mexico. Custom-tailored business suits are common for Mexican businessmen; it is important that the clothes fit the person well. Accessories should be of high quality also. The suits will be dark and worn with conservative ties and shirts. Women wear skirted suits or dresses; pantsuits are worn in some areas. Women should look feminine and should wear high heels. Fashion is very important.

While casual wear will be seen in resort areas, it is not acceptable when conducting business in Mexico City.[25] When wearing casual attire is appropriate, men would select trousers and a light shirt. Women would choose a skirt or nice pants. Only very tailored and pressed jeans would be considered proper casual wear. Do not wear excessive and/or expensive jewelry; Mexicans consider such displays of wealth as improper.

Holidays

The major national and religious holidays that need to be considered when planning business travel to Mexico include the following:[26]

- New Year's Day (January 1)
- St. Anthony's Day (January 17)
- Constitution Day (February 5)
- Carnival Week (varies)
- Birthday of Benito Juarez (March 21)
- Easter (March/April)
- Labor Day (May 1)
- Cinco de Mayo (May 5)
- Corpus Christi (varies)
- Assumption of the Virgin Mary (August 15)
- President's Annual Message (September 1)
- Independence Day (September 16)
- Columbus Day (October 12)
- All Saints' Day (November 1)
- All Souls Day (November 2)
- Revolution Day (November 20)
- Day of the Virgin Guadalupe (December 12)
- Christmas (December 25)

Conversational Customs

Getting to know each other is very important to the Mexican people. Topics for conversation include places you have visited, your family, personal topics, soccer (*fútbol*), or travel plans. Avoid comparisons between the United States and Mexico, particularly if the comparisons make one of the countries appear superior to the other. Before Mexicans can do business with you, they have to feel that a relationship exists.[27]

A term that is important to understand is *mañana*. While the term technically means "tomorrow," it should not be interpreted literally; it is used when Mexicans do not want to disappoint you. The word "maybe" has a similar meaning. In addition, Mexicans do not want to disappoint you by saying "I don't know" when asked a question. Thus, when you ask for directions, Mexicans would rather send you in the wrong direction than to seem unable to help you by saying "I don't know." If someone says "psst-psst" to you, they are trying to get your attention; they are not being rude.[28]

Speaking is considered an art in Mexico, but feelings are more important than facts. Therefore, you will see Mexicans use a lot of passion and eloquence when speaking, particularly if the issue is complex.[29] Embellishment of facts is not unusual, but Mexicans will also try to make things smaller and more intimate to minimize the importance of something.[30] Because of the need to be courteous, true feelings may be concealed; it is not unusual for a Mexican to say one thing and do something else.[31] Silence may be used to avoid an uncomfortable or embarrassing situation.

Being able to talk about Mexican history and historical sites will help you gain the respect of your host. Mexicans take a great deal of pride in their culture and appreciate it when others make an effort to become knowledgeable about it.

Humor

Humor is highly valued in the Mexican culture.[32] Mexicans find silly humor to be particularly to their liking. Disparaging comments about others or groups should not be made a part of humor.

Persuasiveness and verbal word play, along with the use of aphorisms, are used to make a concise statement of a principle, to settle arguments, or to inject humor into a conversation. Another way that Mexicans show their sense of humor is through proverbs, which have been passed down through the years.[33]

Provocative humor is also popular among men in the Mexican culture. Folk tales are told with a humorous storyline. Slapstick humor is also used. In social settings, men often tell each other jokes and use words or actions that lack seriousness. The buffoon laugh-makers are also a popular type of humor in the Mexican culture.[34]

Attitude toward Women in Business

On the Human Development Index (HDI), Mexico ranks 53 out of 177 nations.[35] The HDI is a measure of empowerment; it is based on life expectancy, literacy, infant mortality, and real GDP. The assumption is that societies that provide an opportunity for education, access to healthcare, and adequate wages are inclined to be more democratic and exhibit a respect for human rights.[36]

While Mexico does have some women in higher-level positions—and the numbers are increasing—there are still few by world standards. Women are treated well in business by their managers. Basically, the head of the company is a father figure for all of the employees, and the employees look to the head of the company as they would a father. For example, it is not unusual for a company to give short-term loans to employees who have money difficulties, just as a father might give a child a loan.

Public Behavior

Face saving is very important in the Mexican culture. People of position or wealth would not consider doing menial labor and would look down on someone who does. Status and appearance are very important to Mexicans. Apologizing is common if you have to walk between two people who are talking. Mexicans like a good conversation and can be seen talking on the street, in restaurants, and in business offices.

Mexicans are polite in public and are generally helpful to travelers to their country. While English is becoming more common, particularly in Mexico City and the tourist areas, speaking some Spanish can be very helpful. Displays of affection in public are not common; however, holding hands will be seen.

NONVERBAL COMMUNICATION

Gestures and Posture

Some gestures convey negative messages in Mexico and should be avoided. For example, the U.S. "O.K." sign is offensive to Mexicans and should not be used.[37] Avoid the thumbs-down gesture, as it is considered obscene; the thumbs-up gesture, however, is positive and means that everything is all right.[38] Using exaggerated gestures while talking is normal. Mexicans say everything with a lot of passion. When you are indicating how tall something or someone is, use your index finger; the whole hand is reserved for showing the height of an animal.

Use good posture when standing or sitting. Avoid standing with your hands on your hips or in your pockets as it is considered a confrontational posture.

Eye Contact and Facial Expressions

Mexicans value eye contact and are animated in their facial expressions. When you are talking, occasionally break eye contact since maintaining steady eye contact is considered confrontational. The facial expressions used will animate whatever Mexican people are talking about. Mexico is a high-context culture; as such, the people will be able to read nonverbal messages.

Space and Touch

Mexico's culture is very touch-oriented, so touching is common in this culture. During conversations someone may touch you on the arm or pat your back. Mexicans believe in standing close to someone when conversing. Remember not to back away from the person as this is considered rude.[39] Men and women who know each other exchange hugs when they meet, and women will exchange cheek air kisses. When standing in line, Mexicans will tend to push their way to the front of the line rather than await their turn.

Punctuality and Attitude toward Time

In Mexico time is fluid. Mexicans believe in finishing a meeting even if it means being late for the next meeting. While Mexicans would expect you to be on time and would try to be punctual themselves, it is not unusual for them to be late. Being late because of a prior commitment is completely acceptable in the Mexican culture. However, you are expected to give an explanation as to why you are late.

For private parties you should be at least 30 minutes late, and in Mexico City you would usually arrive one hour late. If you arrive earlier, you may find your hosts still preparing for the party.

TRAVEL TIPS

- Passports are required when traveling to Mexico; however, a visa is only necessary for stays of longer than three months.
- No vaccinations are required when traveling to Mexico; however, in certain parts of the country you may wish to get some vaccinations.

- Driving in Mexico is not recommended.
- Air pollution is extremely bad in Mexico City. If you have breathing problems, be sure to be prepared.
- Street crime, particularly in Mexico City, is high, including kidnapping those who look affluent.
- The numbers to call in case of emergencies (police, ambulance, or fire department) are 066, 060, or 080.
- High altitudes can cause altitude sickness or aggravate heart conditions; therefore, checking the altitude where you are going is advisable. You should know, for example, that because of the high altitude of Mexico City, the effects of alcoholic beverages are intensified.[40]
- Water may or may not be treated; drink bottled water to be on the safe side.
- Cooked foods are safe; however, raw fruits and vegetables may harbor bacteria and should be avoided.
- When paying for purchases, it is proper to place the money or credit card directly in the cashier's hand rather than place it on the counter for the cashier to pick up.[41]
- Wear swimwear on the beaches. Swimwear should not be worn to go shopping in the shopping district. Mexico has no nude or topless beaches.
- Maquiladoras are receiving criticism for not following the same guidelines as the United States for wages, safety, and environmental regulations.[42]
- People in Mexico are extremely friendly; they are very appreciative if you know something of the history and art of their country.
- The Mexican Embassy in the United States is located at 1911 Pennsylvania Avenue, NW, Washington D.C. 20006; (202-728-1600).

NOTES

1. U.S. Census Bureau, "Foreign Trade Statistics," http://www.census.gov/foreign-trade/statistics/highlights/top/top0612.html (accessed March 4, 2008).
2. Ibid.
3. CIA the World Factbook, "Mexico," as of June 14, 2007, https://www.cia.gov/library/publications/the-world-factbook/geos/my.html (accessed June 18, 2007).
4. *CultureGrams, North America, Mexico* (Ann Arbor, MI: ProQuest CSA, 2008), 457.
5. List of countries by GDP (nominal) per capita, http://en.wikipedia.org/wiki/List_of_countries_by_GDP_(nominal)_per_capita (accessed March 5, 2008). Figures (in U.S. dollars) are estimates for 2007 from *The World Factbook* provided by the Central Intelligence Agency (updated February 12, 2008).
6. CIA the World Factbook, "Mexico."
7. *CultureGrams, North America, Mexico*, 460.
8. U.S. Census Bureau, "*IDB: Countries and Areas Ranked by Population*," as of 2007, http://www.census.gov/cgi-bin/ipc/idbrank.pl (accessed January 16, 2008).
9. CIA the World Factbook, "Mexico."
10. Ibid.

11. Ibid.
12. Ibid.
13. Country Calling Codes, http://www.countrycallingcodes.com (accessed June 15, 2007).
14. U.S. Naval Observatory, "What is Universal Time," as of October 30, 2003, http://aa.usno.navy.mil/faq/docs/UT (accessed May 9, 2007).
15. Foreign Exchange, *The Commercial Appeal*, June 13, 2007, C4.
16. Ibid., 48.
17. Jeanette S. Martin and Lillian H. Chaney, *Global Business Etiquette: A Guide to International Communication and Customs* (Westport, CT: Praeger, 2006), 33.
18. Richard D. Lewis, *When Cultures Collide: Leading Across Cultures* (Boston: Nicholas Brealey International, 2006), 536; Terri Morrison and Wayne A. Conaway, *Kiss, Bow, or Shake Hands*, 2nd ed. (Avon, MA: Adams Media, 2006), 319–320.
19. Carol Turkington, *The Complete Idiot's Guide to Cultural Etiquette* (Indianapolis, IN: Alpha Books, 1999), 59.
20. Martin and Chaney, *Global Business Etiquette: A Guide to International Communication and Customs*, 124.
21. Turkington, *The Complete Idiot's Guide to Cultural Etiquette*, 61.
22. Ibid., 48.
23. Turkington, *The Complete Idiot's Guide to Cultural Etiquette*, 61.
24. Lewis, *When Cultures Collide: Leading Across Cultures*, 537.
25. Martin and Chaney, *Global Business Etiquette: A Guide to International Communication and Customs*, 86.
26. *CultureGrams, North America, Mexico*, 460.
27. Martin and Chaney, *Global Business Etiquette: A Guide to International Communication and Customs*, 142.
28. Michael Powell, *Behave Yourself! The Essential Guide to International Etiquette* (Guilford, CT: The Globe Pequot Press, 2005), 79.
29. Lewis, *When Cultures Collide: Leading Across Cultures*, 536.
30. Martin and Chaney, *Global Business Etiquette: A Guide to International Communication and Customs*, 160.
31. Morrison and Conaway, *Kiss, Bow, or Shake Hands*, 314.
32. Ann Marie Sabath, *International Business Etiquette: Latin America* (Franklin Lakes, NJ: Career Press, 2000), 143.
33. O. A. Ballesteros, *Mexican Proverbs: The Philosophy, Wisdom, and Humor of a People* (Austin, TX: Eakin Press, 1979).
34. M. R. Koller, *Humor and Society: Explorations in the Sociology of Humor* (Houston, TX: Cap and Gown Press, 1988).
35. *CultureGrams, North America, Mexico*, 460.
36. *CultureGrams, Concepts and Terminology* (Ann Arbor, MI: ProQuest CSA, 2008), A-14.
37. Sabath, *International Business Etiquette: Latin America*, 149.
38. Ibid., 70.
39. Martin and Chaney, *Global Business Etiquette: A Guide to International Communication and Customs*, 142.
40. Turkington, *The Complete Idiot's Guide to Cultural Etiquette*, 62.
41. Morrison and Conaway, *Kiss, Bow, or Shake Hands*, 320.
42. *CultureGrams, North America, Mexico*, 460.

CHAPTER 17

Netherlands

The official name for the Netherlands is The Kingdom of the Netherlands. The Netherlands is the eighth largest export market of the United States.[1] The United States exports the following goods to the Netherlands: agricultural products, coal, fuel oil, petroleum products, nuclear fuel materials, steelmaking materials, wood products, plastics, chemicals, industrial supplies, generators, electrical apparatus, industrial engines, instruments, material handling equipment, industrial machines, photo machinery, electronics, laboratory instruments, aircraft, vehicles and parts, pharmaceuticals, toiletries, toys, and art.[2]

COUNTRY SPECIFICS

A country's location, topography, economy, and population provide insight into understanding its culture. In addition, knowledge of ethnic groups, religions, time zones, and currency is helpful.

Location, Topography, and Land Mass

The Netherlands, located in Western Europe, includes the Netherlands Antilles and Aruba in the Caribbean. The Netherlands is bordered by the North Sea to the east and north, Belgium to the south, and Germany to the east. The country is less than twice the size of New Jersey. The capital of the Netherlands is Amsterdam. Most of the landmass is coastal lowland and land claimed from the sea, with a few hills in the southeast. Much of the country is below sea level; exceptions are in the eastern part of the country. The Netherlands is at the mouth of three major European Rivers: the Rhine, Maas, and Schelde Rivers.[3]

Dikes are used to keep much of the water from flooding the country. Since water pumping has caused some of the land to sink, the government is buying land and allowing it to return to marshes and wetlands.[4]

The area of the Netherlands is 16,036 square miles or 41,532 square kilometers.[5]

Economy

The Gross Domestic Product (GDP) per capita is $38,900.[6] Agriculture makes up 2.1 percent of GDP, industry 24.4 percent, and services 73.6 percent. As a member of the European Union (EU), the country exchanges 76.8 percent of its exports and 55.0 percent of its imports with the EU nations. Trade with the United States includes exports of 4.9 percent to the United States and imports of 8.0 percent from the United States.[7]

The country's labor costs caused the Netherlands to lose competitiveness during the early twenty-first century, and many companies lost market share to their major competitors. Low wage increases in 2004 and 2005 have enabled companies to regain part of that loss. More than 1,600 U.S. companies have subsidiaries of offices in the Netherlands. The Dutch are strong allies of the United States and proponents of free trade.[8]

Due to a dependency on trade for centuries, the Dutch are very internationally oriented.[9] Many multinational conglomerates have headquarters in the Netherlands; the country has made it very lucrative for businesses to be centered there.[10]

Population, Languages Spoken, Ethnic Groups, and Religions

The population of the Netherlands is about 16.6 million; it is growing annually at .53 percent.

The official language of the Netherlands is Dutch. Frisian, a combination of English and Dutch, is spoken by the people who live on the island of Frisia. English is a common second or third language that is spoken by people in the Netherlands.

Many ethnic groups reside in the country. The Dutch ethnic group comprises 83 percent of the population, with 9 percent consisting of Turks, Moroccans, Antilleans, Surinamese, and Indonesians; 8 percent of the population is made up of other nationalities.[11]

The Dutch have a decreasing percentage of their population attending church on a regular basis; this reflects figures for regular church attendance for the other countries of Europe. A total of 41 percent of the population report that they do not belong to any religion; 31 percent consider themselves Roman Catholic; 20 percent are Protestant (primarily Dutch

Reformed); 5.5 percent are Muslim; and 2.5 percent report that they are members of other religions.[12]

Country Codes, Time Zones, and Currency

The country code to make telephone calls to the Netherlands is 31. City codes include 20 for Amsterdam, 70 for Hague, and 10 for Rotterdam. When calling from the United States to Amsterdam, for example, dial the International Access Code (011), followed by the country code (31), the city code (20), and the local telephone number.

The Netherlands is six hours ahead of U.S. Eastern Standard Time. This means that when the time is 3 PM in New York, in the Netherlands it is 9 PM. In Universal Time (UT) these times would be written according to the 24-hour clock as 1500 and 2100, respectively. Daylight Saving Time is observed in The Netherlands.[13]

The Netherlands is a member of the European Union (EU) and uses the *euro* (€) as its currency; the *euro* replaced the *guilder* (NLG) as the unit of currency in 2002. A currency converter is available at http://coinmill.com/AED calculator.html that will convert any currency in the world into any other currency.

BUSINESS AND SOCIAL CUSTOMS

Greetings, Introductions, and Business Cards

The Dutch greeting is typically a handshake that is swift and firm, generally accompanied by a smile. The Dutch are very sensitive to equality so it is important to shake hands with everyone in the room. Friends will also give each other several small kisses on the cheek. As etiquette is very important, the Dutch will use a title and surname until invited to use first names.[14] Waving to a person in the distance is acceptable; however, shouting is impolite.[15]

Introductions are very important. Academic titles are not used in introductions; however, a professional title would be used. No differences exist between introducing the two genders, but it is important to introduce the younger person to the older person. If at a meeting or dinner party, the host will introduce the guests to one another. In other situations it would be permissible for you to introduce yourself.[16]

Business cards are generally exchanged at the end of the business meeting. If you have a degree beyond the bachelor's degree, this should be included on your business card. Because most businesspeople in the Netherlands speak English, it is not necessary to translate the card into Dutch.[17]

Business Entertaining and Seating Customs

Being on time for an engagement is important in the Netherlands. Close friends may invite you to their home for mid-morning coffee on weekends. Coffee with milk and sugar, along with a biscuit, would be served. After you are offered a second coffee and biscuit, you are expected to leave. The Dutch like strong coffee and tend to drink a lot of it.

All business social events are carefully planned and scheduled; the Dutch do not do things on the spur of the moment. Dinners are used to entertain more than lunches because the lunch hour is very short in the Netherlands. Dinners tend to be held at restaurants; however, the Dutch like to host informal gatherings before or after dinner in their homes.[18]

Seating is similar to that in many other European countries. The host and hostess will be seated at the opposite ends of the table. The guests of honor will be seated at the right hand of the host and hostess. The male guest of honor is seated to the host's right, and the female guest of honor is seated to the right of the hostess. Everyone remains standing until the host invites everyone to sit down. Women are seated first; then the men will sit down.[19]

Dining, Toasting, and Tipping Customs

Business meals are not central to the culture of the Netherlands; this is particularly true of lunch. When business lunches are held, they can take up to three hours, with decisions being made during lunch.[20]

During the meal the Continental style of eating is customary. While at the table, you should keep your hands above the table. You may rest your wrists on the edge of the table, but you should not rest your hands in your lap. Foods typically eaten with the fingers in the United States—such as cheese, fruits, pizza, and sandwiches—are eaten with a knife and fork in the Netherlands. The only foods that are eaten from the hand are rolls, French fries, and small snack foods. Some Dutch people even eat these foods with a knife and fork as well. If you need to leave the table, place your crossed fork and knife in the middle of the plate with the fork over the knife. To indicate that you have finished, place the fork and knife on the right side of the plate in a parallel position. Since the Netherlands is a clean-your-plate culture, do not take more than you can eat.[21]

Toasting is popular in the Netherlands. The host will be the first to propose a toast. If it is beer or soft drinks, the host will probably say *Proost*, which means "Cheers!" If everyone is drinking wine with dinner, the host will probably say *Santé* or nothing at all. What is important is the raising of your glass and friendly glances to each person who is present. Other toasts may follow after everyone takes the first sip.[22]

Tipping is expected in the Netherlands. Generally, in restaurants a tip of 5 to 10 percent is sufficient. However, there will be a gratuity added to your bill, so you are leaving an additional tip for particularly good service. When using a taxi, round your tip to the nearest *euro*; do not give a taxicab driver small change. Maids should be given one to two *euros* per day. If the washroom has an attendant, the attendant should receive 50 *euro* cents. Bellmen should receive one *euro* per bag.[23]

Gift-Giving Customs

Gifts given to the Dutch should always be modest. While the Dutch appreciate quality items, they frown on gifts that are obviously expensive.[24] Appropriate gifts when invited to a person's home include flowers, a small assortment of chocolates, decorative candles, or a book about your country. If you bring flowers, be sure you have an odd number (but not 13, as 13 flowers would be viewed as unlucky). In addition, do not choose white lilies or chrysanthemums as they are associated with funerals. Other items to avoid include scissors or knives. While U.S. people often give a bottle of wine, this is not an appropriate gift in the Netherlands as the Dutch are wine collectors. Your bringing a bottle of wine to your host may be perceived as a criticism of the host's wine cellar.[25] Gifts are usually wrapped, except for flowers. If there are children in the home, a gift of candy or a small toy will be appreciated.

Business gifts are given only after a relationship has been developed. Business gift ideas include desk accessories, books, and imported liquor.[26]

Business Meetings

The typical workday is from 8:30 AM to 5:30 PM. Appointments should be made at least one to two weeks in advance and should not be cancelled at the last minute. E-mails and letters should be written in a formal manner whether you are just beginning a relationship or have become friends. Always use the person's surname in correspondence.[27]

Being a cautious people, the Dutch are skeptical listeners. Meetings should be used to present factual information with no show of emotion. The Dutch want to find mutual goals and work toward them without confrontation.[28] The Dutch are profit oriented, will want preliminary discussions, and will be very pragmatic in their discussions and decisions.[29]

The Dutch believe in teamwork and make decisions and solve problems as a team rather than individually. While they will be very direct and pragmatic, it is not a contentious work situation. Negotiations will move slower because of the consensus building.[30]

You are expected to back up what you say with facts. Be willing to debate points and brainstorm a great deal before coming up with solutions to problems. Driving a hard bargain is expected, but keeping promises is also expected. Show that you are honest, dependable, rational, and egalitarian. While you should appear convincing, you should not appear aggressive. Ideas are seen as independent of the person expressing them. The Dutch do their homework and will probably know more about you than you will know about them.[31]

Dress and Appearance

The Dutch are very conservative in their business dress, with European fashions being popular. If you are undecided about what to wear, dress up for the event. Businessmen wear dark suits and muted ties. Businesswomen wear dark suits with white blouses. Many people remove their jackets while working. In the Netherlands, someone who is of higher rank in the company is more likely to be dressed casually than someone of a lower rank in the company. In social situations men tend to dress less formally, often wearing nice slacks and a sport coat rather than a suit and tie.[32]

The Dutch enjoy wearing tuxedos and evening gowns for formal social events. Casual wear is similar to the United States; however, shorts are only worn for jogging or hiking.[33]

Holidays

July and August are used for summer vacations; it is difficult to make appointments during this time period. In addition to avoiding the months of July and August for business travel, it is best to avoid the following holidays:

- New Year's Day (January 1)
- Easter (March/April)
- Queen's Day (April 30)
- Memorial Day (May 4)
- Liberation Day (May 5)
- St. Nicholas Eve (December 5)
- Christmas (December 25–26)

Conversational Customs

When conversing with the Dutch, do not stand too close. They prefer to stand about an arm's length away during conversations. Appropriate topics of conversation include sports, travel, or world affairs. They enjoy discussing Dutch politics. However, asking about their voting record would be impolite. The Dutch prefer not to discuss money or prices. Eye contact is important during conversations.[34]

The Dutch always speak very logically and factually. They do not understand emotional speeches, so it is important to be calm and composed in your conversations. The Dutch appreciate people who are direct and honest. Complimenting someone during conversations is not customary in the Netherlands because it makes someone stand out; the Dutch feel that everyone in the group should be treated equally.[35]

Humor

Humor is not appreciated in business correspondence. Irony and sarcasm are not enjoyed; however, a jesting or playful humor is appreciated.[36] The Dutch are serious and do not smile a lot when conducting business.[37] During dinner, weekends, or free time, however, they are much more jovial.

Attitude toward Women in Business

On the Human Development Index (HDI), the Netherlands ranks 10 out of 177 nations. The HDI is a measure of empowerment; it is based on life expectancy, literacy, infant mortality, and real GDP. The assumption is that societies that provide an opportunity for education, access to healthcare, and adequate wages are inclined to be more democratic and exhibit a respect for human rights.[38]

The Gender-Empowerment Measure (GEM) of the HDI lists the Netherlands as 7 out of 75 countries for the share of seats held in government by women, the number of professional women, the earned income disparity between the genders, and economic independence.[39] The Dutch are very equalitarian when it comes to the genders. They rank very high on the HDI and GEM because women have equal pay, equal jobs, and are not discriminated against in the workforce. Their egalitarianism has lead to one of the most comprehensive welfare states in Europe, with an immigration policy that has allowed 15 percent of the population to be of other than Dutch descent.[40]

Public Behavior

Since what is acceptable public behavior in one country is inappropriate in another, it is wise to do some research before traveling to determine appropriate and inappropriate behavior.

As the Dutch are a shy people, they would not say "Hi" to a stranger or to someone older than themselves. Public behaviors to avoid include not using toothpicks or chewing gum. If you sneeze or cough, simply say you are sorry or smile apologetically. If you have to yawn, be sure to cover your mouth. You are expected to wait your turn in line when shopping. The Dutch expect others to be as open-minded and frank as they are; they freely express their opinions. The Dutch do not boast, show off, or wear status symbols because they feel respect is achieved through effort and a modest attitude.[41]

NONVERBAL COMMUNICATION

Gestures and Posture

The Dutch do not use a lot of gestures to make their points. Very few hand movements or body language will be used. However, they do use certain gestures. If they place a hand under the chin and stroke an imaginary beard, it means the story being told is old. Making a circular motion with the index finger near your ear signals that a person has a telephone call. Tapping the middle of the forehead indicates someone is crazy.[42]

The posture of the Dutch is very erect. When standing, do not put your hands in your pockets. Carrying on a conversation with your hands in your pockets is considered rude.

Eye Contact and Facial Expressions

Eye contact is maintained during a conversation. If you look away for too long a period, the Dutch will think that you are not interested or that you are being dishonest. The Dutch are very business oriented and do not display a lot of facial expressions when conversing with someone with whom they are doing business. They have a stoic demeanor that is often misinterpreted. The Dutch are simply very businesslike during business encounters and, like their German neighbors, are very serious minded while conducting business. The Dutch prefer to say what is on their minds; they do not use silence. They feel that everyone should be given the courtesy of expressing an opinion.

Space and Touch

The Dutch do not stand close during conversations. They prefer a distance of about an arm's length when interacting. It is also impolite to touch or hug in public.

Punctuality and Attitude toward Time

Being on time and being prepared are very important in the Dutch culture. Punctuality is expected; if you are not on time, your tardiness can break a business deal. If you are going to be late, call ahead with an explanation. The Dutch are very organized and place a great deal of importance on scheduling, planning, and keeping appointments. Chaos is to be avoided. Efficiency is a mantra of the Dutch culture, and they take great pride in using time efficiently.[43]

The Dutch are a monochromatic people; they believe you should finish one thing before beginning another. They also believe in doing only one thing at a time.

TRAVEL TIPS

- A passport is required to visit the Netherlands; however, a visa is not needed for visits of less than six months.
- Inoculations to consider include tetanus and hepatitis A and B.
- Ask whether the water supply is safe to drink; otherwise, drink bottled water.
- English is widely spoken in hotels and shops.
- Public transportation is among the best in Europe. Trains connect the cities, and buses and streetcars provide excellent local transportation. Subways are available in Amsterdam and Rotterdam.
- Private transportation includes cars and bicycles, which create numerous traffic problems. Bicycles are a favorite form of transportation for the Dutch; in fact, there are bicycle parking lots in Amsterdam.
- Pedestrians in Amsterdam must respect the bicycle paths throughout the city; walking on one of the paths may cause angry shouts from the cyclists.
- Smoking marijuana in coffeehouses is legal.
- While illicit drugs are legal in the Netherlands, they tend to be restricted to certain areas of the city. Even though drugs are legal, there does not seem to be an abundance of use among the locals.
- People of the Netherlands tend to be liberal on legalized prostitution, euthanasia, and homosexual marriages.[44]
- Smoking in public places has been illegal since January 2004.
- The number to call in case of emergencies (police, ambulance, or fire department) is 112.
- The Netherlands has taken a strong stand against terrorist activities.
- While many people refer to the country as "Holland," this is incorrect as North and South Holland are two of the provinces in the Netherlands.
- The Dutch admire honesty, humor outside of business, modesty, and a good education; they measure social status by occupation.[45]

- Additional information about the Netherlands is available from the Embassy of the Netherlands, 4200 Linnean Avenue NW, Washington, D.C. 20008 (202-244-5300) or the Netherlands Board of Tourism, 355 Lexington Avenue, 19th Floor, New York, NY 10017 (212-370-7360).

NOTES

1. U.S. Census Bureau, "Foreign Trade Statistics," http://www.census.gov/foreign-trade/statistics/highlights/top/top0612.html (accessed March 4, 2008).
2. Ibid.
3. CIA the World Factbook, "Netherlands," as of June 19, 2007, https://www.cia.gov/library/publications/the-world-factbook/geos/my.html (accessed June 25, 2007).
4. *CultureGrams, Europe, Netherlands* (Ann Arbor, MI: ProQuest CSA, 2008), 509.
5. Ibid.
6. List of countries by GDP (nominal) per capita, http://en.wikipedia.org/wiki/List_of_countries_by_GDP_(nominal)_per_capita (accessed March 5, 2008). Figures (in U.S. dollars) are estimates for 2007 from *The World Factbook* provided by the Central Intelligence Agency (updated February 12, 2008).
7. U.S. Department of State, "Background Note: The Netherlands," as of January 2007, http://www.state.gov/r/pa/ei/bgn/3204.htm (accessed May 9, 2007).
8. Ibid.
9. Lillian H. Chaney and Jeanette S. Martin, *Intercultural Business Communication*, 4th ed. (Upper Saddle River, NJ: Prentice Hall, 2007), 227.
10. Richard D. Lewis, *When Cultures Collide: Leading Across Cultures* (Boston: Nicholas Brealey International, 2006), 244.
11. Ibid.
12. Ibid.
13. U.S. Naval Observatory, "What is Universal Time," as of October 30, 2003, http://aa.usno.navy.mil/faq/docs/UT (accessed May 9, 2007).
14. Netherlands, http://kwintessential.co.uk/resources/global-etiquette/netherlands.html (accessed June 26, 2007).
15. Chaney and Martin, *Intercultural Business Communication*, 177.
16. Jacob Vossestein, "Netherlands," http://executiveplanet.com/index.php?title=Netherlands (accessed June 26, 2007).
17. Ibid.
18. Ibid.
19. Ibid.
20. Lewis, *When Cultures Collide: Leading Across Cultures*, 244.
21. Vossestein, "Netherlands."
22. Ibid.
23. Ibid.
24. Ibid.
25. Netherlands, http://kwintessential.co.uk/resources/global-etiquette/netherlands.html (accessed June 26, 2007); Terri Morrison and Wayne A. Conaway, *Kiss, Bow, or Shake Hands*, 2nd ed. (Avon, MA: Adams Media, 2006), 330–331.
26. Chaney and Martin, *Intercultural Business Communication*, 177; Morrison and Conaway, *Kiss, Bow, or Shake Hands*, 330.

27. Vossestein, "Netherlands."
28. Lewis, *When Cultures Collide: Leading Across Cultures*, 243–250.
29. Ibid., 248.
30. Chaney and Martin, *Intercultural Business Communication*, 254.
31. Lewis, *When Cultures Collide: Leading Across Cultures*, 249–251.
32. Ibid.
33. Morrison and Conaway, *Kiss, Bow, or Shake Hands*, 331.
34. Jeanette S. Martin, and Lillian H. Chaney, *Global Business Etiquette* (Westport, CT: Praeger, 2006), 142.
35. Michael Powell, *Behave Yourself!: The Essential Guide to International Etiquette* (Guilford, CT: The Globe Pequot Press, 2005), 85.
36. Lewis, *When Cultures Collide: Leading Across Cultures*, 250.
37. Vossestein, "Netherlands."
38. *CultureGrams, Concepts and Terminology* (Ann Arbor, MI: ProQuest CSA, 2008), A-14.
39. Human Development Report 2006, http://hdr.undp.org/hdr2006/statistics/countries/ (accessed June 16, 2007).
40. Lewis, *When Cultures Collide: Leading Across Cultures*, 244.
41. Ibid.
42. Ibid.
43. Vossestein, "Netherlands."
44. *CultureGrams, Europe, Netherlands*, 510.
45 Ibid.

CHAPTER 18

Singapore

The Republic of Singapore, commonly referred to as Singapore, is the eleventh largest export market of the United States.[1]

U.S. exports to Singapore include agricultural products, fuel oil, petroleum products, finished metal shapes, plastics, chemicals, tapes (audio and video), industrial supplies, generators, electrical apparatus, oil field equipment, excavating machinery, industrial engines, metalworking machine tools, instruments, industrial machines, materials handling equipment, photo machinery, electronics, aircraft engines and parts, pharmaceuticals, toys, and military.[2]

COUNTRY SPECIFICS

A country's location, topography, economy, and population provide insight into understanding its culture. In addition, knowledge of ethnic groups, religions, time zones, and currency is helpful.

Location, Topography, and Land Mass

Singapore is an island located off the southern coast of Malaysia across the Singapore Strait from Indonesia. Singapore is a city-state; thus, there are no rural areas. The capital of Singapore is Singapore since it is an island state. The terrain is mainly lowlands, with rolling hills in the middle of the island.[3] Singapore occupies 685 square kilometers or 264 square miles.

Economy

The economy of Singapore is very robust. The Gross Domestic Product (GDP) per capita is $29,475.[4] The island has no natural resources. Singapore's exports include petroleum products, food/beverages, chemicals, textile/garments, electronic components, telecommunication apparatus, and transport equipment. The major export markets for Singapore in order are Malaysia, the United States, the European Union (EU), Hong Kong, China, and Japan. The majority of Singapore's imports come from Malaysia, the United States, Japan, China, and the EU.[5]

Little corruption exists in the government; Singapore has a skilled workforce and good infrastructure, with more than 7,000 multinational corporations having offices there. A total of 1,500 of the companies are U.S.-based corporations. The multinational corporations account for two-thirds of the manufacturing and exports. While manufacturing accounts for 26.9 percent of the economy, services account for 63.2 percent of the economy. The government has negotiated 16 free trade agreements; the U.S. agreement became effective January 1, 2004. Singapore's location on the Southeast Asian sea routes is very important to the country's economy.[6]

Population, Languages Spoken, Ethnic Groups, and Religions

The population of Singapore is approximately 4.55 million people.[7] The growth rate of residents is approximately 1.8 percent per year. When sojourners are included, the rate is 3.3 percent annually. The island is densely populated, with about 18,400 persons per square mile (or 7,100 people per square kilometer).[8] The people of Singapore are known as Singaporeans.

The national language is Malay; however, Chinese, English, and Tamil are also official languages. English is the language of the professions, businesses, and schools. English has been mandated as the language to be used at all levels in the school system. Most Singaporeans speak at least two languages.

The ethnic distribution of the people is 75.2 percent Chinese, 13.6 percent Malay, 8.8 percent Indian, and 2.4 percent consist of other ethnic groups.

Singaporeans have religious freedom. The religious breakdown of the population follows ethnic origin, with Malays tending to be Muslim; Indians are Hindu or Sikh; and Chinese are Taoists, Buddhists, and Confucianists. There are also some Christians.[9] Religions are permitted to make laws governing such family matters as marriage for their members.[10]

Country Codes, Time Zones, and Currency

The country code for Singapore is 65. When calling from the United States to Singapore, dial the International Access Code (011), followed by the country code (65), and the local telephone number.

Singapore is 13 hours ahead of U.S. Eastern Standard Time. Thus, when it is 8 AM in New York, it is 9 PM in Singapore. In Universal Time the times would be written according to the 24-hour clock as 0800 and 2100, respectively. Daylight Saving Time is not observed in Singapore.[11]

The Singapore dollar (S$) is the currency of Singapore. A currency converter is available at http://coinmill.com/AED_calculator.html that will convert any currency in the world into any other currency.

BUSINESS AND SOCIAL CUSTOMS

Business and social customs are very important in order to avoid getting off on the wrong foot. Since there are three ethnic groups in Singapore, there is much to learn when doing business in this country.

Greetings, Introductions, and Business Cards

Greetings vary according to ethnicity and age. The Chinese greet each other by shaking hands; they sometimes add a bow when greeting older people. They will say *Whei*, which means "Hello," or *Ni hao ma*, which means "How are you?" The Malays greet each other with the *salaam;* the two people involved place their right palms together as they would if they were shaking hands. After sliding their hands apart, they each touch the palm of their hand to their heart. Malays will say *Selamat pagi*, meaning "Good morning," when greeting each other. Indians put their palms together at chest level; they then put them in front of their face, bow, and say *Vanakkam*, which means "Hello" in Tamil.[12] Rather than introducing yourself, it is customary to be introduced by a third party. The handshake is held for about 10 seconds and is softer than those in the West; it is also maintained longer than is customary in the West. It would not be unusual for people to use both hands when they shake your hand.[13]

Since English is spoken fluently in the business world of Singapore, you may use English when addressing people. Use the appropriate courtesy title of Mr., Mrs., Miss, or Ms. with their surname or given name. Many of the ethnic Malays do not have surnames. They have a given name plus *bin*, meaning "son of," or *binti*, meaning "daughter of," and their father's given name. Use the courtesy title with the first name for Malays. Women do not typically take their husband's name. The Chinese Singaporeans will have three parts to their name: the family name and the two-part given name. Use the courtesy title and the family name, which will be the first name you hear. Many of the Indians in Singapore also do not have surnames; use their given name with the courtesy title.[14]

Business cards will be exchanged during introductions. Since the language of business is English, business cards may be printed in English only. If you plan to do business with the Chinese, however, you may wish to include the Chinese translation on one side. Use gold ink to make a good impression; it is a prestigious color for Chinese characters. As is customary in most Asian countries, give a card to everyone present and present it with the text facing the recipient using both hands. The other person will receive the card with both hands as well. The card is reviewed carefully before placing it in a card holder; placing it in your back pocket is rude. Business cards should be treated with respect; do not write on them. Enclose a business card in your correspondence with your Singaporean colleague.[15]

Business Entertaining and Seating Customs

Most business entertaining is done in restaurants. If you need to get a waiter's attention, simply raise your hand. Raising one finger, whistling, hissing, or shouting to get the attention of the server is impolite. Business lunches are popular, but breakfasts are not. Most business entertainment will be around dinner. Meals will be a time to build relationships and socialize rather than discuss business. Generally, spouses are not invited to business meals.[16]

Seating customs of the Chinese include having the host and hostess seated opposite each other. Guests will be seated to the host's left facing the entrance. If a Malay or Indian is entertaining, he or she will seat the guest of honor to the host's right or put the honored person at the head of the table.[17]

Dining, Toasting, and Tipping Customs

Some dining customs in Singapore are quite different from those in the United States. When dining in a crowded restaurant, for example, strangers may feel free to share a table with you. When this occurs, you are not expected to carry on a conversation with them. Another custom when dining in a restaurant is that the host orders all dishes and everyone shares, rather than each guest's ordering what he or she prefers. Complimenting the host on the selection of dishes is appropriate. Because of the different eating habits of the various ethnic groups, make sure that when you are the host you avoid ordering beef for Buddhists or Hindus or pork for Muslims. Muslims will not use utensils that have ever touched pork.

When dining in Singapore, you may be given many different types of utensils with which to eat, depending upon where you go and the ethnic group with whom you are dining. You may be expected to eat with your fingers. Remember to avoid the use of the left hand for eating as it is considered unclean. Malays and Indians wash their hands before and after each meal using a small bowl of water and a towel that will be provided. Do not refuse initial offers of food or drink as this is rude. Always try some of everything that is offered. After the meal it is customary to sit and converse for about an hour before leaving the restaurant.[18]

If your host is Chinese and you are in a Chinese restaurant, chopsticks will be used. Use the broad end to put food on your plate and the small end to eat if serving spoons are not provided. Alcohol or beer is a common drink provided during the meal, with tea served before or after the meal. Singaporeans do not drink water with their meals.[19]

Toasts are not very common in Singapore; Muslims do not toast or drink alcohol at all. When given a drink, accept it with both hands or with your right hand only. At Chinese banquets they will have a toast, *Yam Seng*, which means "to your continuing success." If you propose a toast, stand up. If you are the recipient of a toast, rise and say "thank you."[20]

Tipping at a restaurant is not necessary since a service charge is included in the bill. You are not expected to leave an additional amount. Tipping in other situations is not usually expected. However, it is customary to tip taxi drivers a small amount by rounding to the nearest dollar on your fare. Bellmen receive S$1 or S$2 for their services.[21]

Gift-Giving Customs

Because of the three different ethnic groups in Singapore, three different gift-giving protocols are used. Gift-giving protocol that is the same for all three groups includes using both hands to give someone a gift and not opening a gift in the presence of the giver. Business gifts are not routinely exchanged. Only if you are invited to someone's home are you expected to bring a gift. Government officials are never to be given gifts. Gifts should be wrapped nicely and should be high-quality gifts but not expensive.[22]

Some gift-giving customs are different for the three ethnic groups. When you give gifts to the Chinese, give either single items or pairs. Do not give odd numbers. Thus, when you give flowers, be sure to have an even number. The gift wrap should not be blue or black; however, red is a good color for gift wrapping. Some good gift ideas include candy, cakes, fruit, scotch whiskey, brandy, or something from your country. When you present gifts to Indians, use your right hand only. Gifts to Indians should be wrapped in a color other than white, navy, or black. Candy or fruit make good gifts. Gifts should be in an uneven quantity, unlike Chinese customs. Gifts for Malays should be wrapped in green, red, or yellow paper. Gift ideas for Malays include shirts or other clothing items, candy, or perfume for women.[23]

You are expected to refuse a gift at least twice before accepting it as this shows your humility. Singaporeans will also refuse gifts that you offer them at least twice before finally accepting.[24]

Business Meetings

Business meetings should be scheduled well in advance of your arrival in Singapore.[25]

People enter the meeting room in rank order, with the most senior person entering first. There is little chitchat, as Singaporeans like to get right down to business. The meetings will be well organized, and Singaporeans like to make decisions quickly. Avoid correcting people in front of their colleagues; this would be embarrassing and cause a loss of face.[26] Speak calmly and quietly. After making a statement or proposal, allow sufficient time for your Singaporean colleague to respond. Pausing for a few seconds before responding is polite. Impatient Westerners often speak too soon as they are generally uncomfortable with silence.[27]

As with other Asian cultures, it will take multiple trips to build a relationship and to conclude a business negotiation.

Dress and Appearance

In the Singaporean work environment, men will tend to wear white shirts, ties, and dark trousers with no jacket. However, men will wear a jacket to a nice restaurant. Women wear skirts (which should be no shorter than knee length) and blouses with sleeves or pantsuits. When meeting with government officials, dress is a little more formal. Evening attire at nightspots is a suit for men and an evening dress for the women. If invited to someone's home, remember to remove your shoes before entering their home.[28] Since this is a tropical climate, clothing of natural fibers will be cooler than synthetic fabrics. Lightweight, Western-style clothing is worn by most of the people.[29]

If a woman goes into a temple, she should cover her shoulders as a sign of respect. Clothing that is revealing, including shorts, should not be worn.[30] If you go jogging, which is a popular Singaporean activity, you are permitted to wear jogging shorts.

Holidays

The best months to schedule business meetings are March through July. The period from November through February is when many of the people of Singapore take their vacations.[31] The primary holidays include:

- New Year's Day (January 1)
- Chinese New Year (lunar calendar) (January/February)
- Easter (Good Friday through Easter Sunday) (March/April)
- Hari Raya Puasa (April 16)
- Labor Day (May 10)
- Buddha's Birthday (May 28)
- Hari Raya Haji (June 24)
- National Day (August 9)
- Deepavali (November 5)
- Christmas (December 25)
- During the Chinese New Year, many companies will close for a week.[32] The Chinese New Year is probably one of the main holidays during the calendar year to be concerned with because it changes date from year to year. The company closings are for more than just a day, and the holiday will include many celebrations.

Conversational Customs

Singapore is a face-saving culture so it is very difficult for them to say no. "No" will be said in a very indirect manner. Assertiveness and directness are considered rude. Everything should be understated and diplomatic at all times. Expressing disagreement could be viewed very negatively.[33] It is improper to cause someone to lose face in public. Conformity is stressed in the Singaporean culture.[34]

Appropriate topics of conversation are travel, local sights, and the arts. Compliments about the local cuisine are appreciated. Avoid discussing religion, politics, or any topic that could be viewed as a criticism of Singaporean customs. People of Singapore may ask you personal questions about your age, weight, and salary. If you do not want to answer, you should evade the question politely. People should only be complimented on their performance and not on their personal appearance. When asked a question, do not answer immediately; it is proper to wait a few seconds to think about what has been said before you respond.[35] Westerners need to remember that Easterners are more comfortable with silence than Westerners.

Humor

Unless you know the people you are working with very well, do not attempt humor or jokes of any kind. Risqué jokes are out of place in Singapore.[36] One of the problems with humor in Singapore is the presence of people from so many different ethnic backgrounds. You would need to understand all of the nuances that separate the ethnic groups before you could interject humor into your business talk.

Attitude toward Women in Business

On the Human Development Index (HDI), Singapore ranks 25 out of 177 nations.[37] The HDI is a measure of empowerment; it is based on life expectancy, literacy, infant mortality, and real GDP. The assumption is that societies that provide an opportunity for education, access to health-care, and adequate wages are inclined to be more democratic and exhibit a respect for human rights.[38]

Women in Singapore enjoy equality and can travel alone safely. Sexual harassment is rare, and Singapore has official policies against gender discrimination. While women are accepted in business, a Western woman may encounter some bias initially.[39] Women will need to initiate handshakes; otherwise, men will acknowledge them with a nod and smile.

Public Behavior

Since behavior in public is highly visible, learning the rules for polite behavior in a country is important. In Singapore, if you have to use a toothpick, cover your mouth while using it.[40] Smoking is not permitted in public areas, including on public transportation. Public displays of affection are considered inappropriate. Showing anger or raising your voice in public is not acceptable.[41] Fines are common for spitting in public, dropping trash on sidewalks, chewing or selling gum, and failing to flush toilets. Singapore is a very clean country because its strict laws are enforced. You may pay a harsh fine for simply dropping a candy wrapper or a cigarette butt on the street.[42]

NONVERBAL COMMUNICATION

Knowledge of nonverbal communication is helpful in interpreting nonverbal messages. The areas that will be especially useful are gestures and posture, eye contact and facial expressions, space and touch, punctuality, and attitude toward time.

Gestures and Posture

Many gestures are negative and should be avoided. To Muslims, the foot is considered unclean. Thus, it is rude to point the bottom of your foot toward someone. In addition, tapping your foot or swinging a leg while sitting is considered rude. Pounding your fist into an open palm is obscene in Singapore. Using the forefinger to point is considered rude.[43] When you need to point, you may use your knuckle rather than extending a finger. If you want to beckon someone, use your whole hand, palm facing down. Give a slight bow when passing someone; this is a sign of courtesy. Posture is also important. Standing with your hands on your hips is an aggressive posture and should be avoided.[44]

Eye Contact and Facial Expressions

Eye contact is not as constant in Singapore as it is in the West; you are expected to break eye contact more often. A smile or laugh has various meanings in Singapore; people may laugh because they are embarrassed rather than because they think something is humorous. Silence may be used to convey different meanings: to indicate a negative reaction to something, to indicate thought about what has been said, or to convey disagreement with what has been said. Facial expressions should not show disagreement, disgust, or other emotions.[45] Singaporeans expect you to maintain control of your emotions at all times and to show this through your facial expressions and voice tone.

Space and Touch

The preferred distance between people when interacting varies with the ethnic group. The general rule is to stand two to three feet apart. However, Indians prefer more space and will stand about three to three-and-a-half feet apart.[46]

Touching the opposite gender, with the exception of the handshake, or displays of affection, are considered inappropriate in public. However, touch between people of the same gender, including holding hands, is common and is simply a sign of friendship.[47] Since the head is considered sacred, never touch another person's head. Even patting a small child on the head is inappropriate.[48]

Punctuality and Attitude toward Time

You are expected to be on time for both business and social occasions. Being late is seen as disrespectful. For social events the guest of honor should arrive last. Because of congestion, you may get stuck in traffic. If this happens, call to say you have been delayed.[49]

TRAVEL TIPS

- Passports are necessary for travel to Singapore.
- Prescriptions should be carried in their original containers.
- Remember that littering, jaywalking, and chewing gum in public are illegal; laws are strictly enforced. Even bringing gum into the country is illegal. Possession of illegal drugs is extremely serious; it carries a death sentence.
- Queuing in line is very important in Singapore; cutting in line, including when you line up for taxis, is considered rude.
- Medical services are very good in Singapore. Prescriptions are easily filled but must be written by local doctors.
- Singapore is a very safe country.
- The numbers to call for emergencies include 999 for police and 995 for medical emergencies or for the fire department.
- In food courts the food will be rated by the Ministry of Health and Environment with ratings of either A, B, C, or D; do not eat anything that is rated D.
- Renting a car requires an International Driver's License; driving is on the left of the road.
- Tap water is reported to be safe to drink in Singapore.
- Bring an umbrella for the frequent showers.
- Show respect for the elderly by opening doors for them, by standing when they enter a room, and by relinquishing your seat on public transportation to them.
- For additional travel information, contact the Embassy of the Republic of Singapore, 3501 International Place NW, Washington, D.C. 20008; the telephone number (202-537-3100).

NOTES

1. U.S. Census Bureau, "Foreign Trade Statistics," http://www.census.gov/foreign-trade/statistics/highlights/top/top0612.html (accessed March 4, 2008).
2. Ibid.
3. CIA the World Factbook, "Singapore," as of June 19, 2007, https://www.cia.gov/library/publications/the-world-factbook/geos/my.html (accessed June 25, 2007).
4. List of countries by GDP (nominal) per capita, http://en.wikipedia.org/wiki/List_of_countries_by_GDP_(nominal)_per_capita (accessed March 5, 2008). Figures (in U.S. dollars) are estimates for 2007 from *The World Factbook* provided by the Central Intelligence Agency (updated February 12, 2008).
5. U.S. Department of State, "Background Note: Singapore," as of January 2007, http://www.state.gov/r/pa/ei/bgn/3204.htm (accessed May 9, 2007).
6. Ibid.
7. U.S. Census Bureau, "*IDB: Countries and Areas Ranked by Population*," as of 2007, http://www.census.gov/cgi-bin/ipc/idbrank.pl (accessed January 16, 2008).

8. U.S. Department of State, "Background Note: Singapore."
9. Ibid.
10. *CultureGrams, Asia, Singapore* (Ann Arbor, MI: ProQuest CSA, 2008), 642.
11. U.S. Naval Observatory, "What is Universal Time," as of October 30, 2003, http://aa.usno.navy.mil/faq/docs/UT (accessed May 9, 2007).
12. *CultureGrams, Asia, Singapore*, 642.
13. Michael Powell, *Behave Yourself!: The Essential Guide to International Etiquette* (Guilford, CT: The Globe Pequot Press, 2005), 108.
14. Mary Murray Bosrock, *Put Your Best Foot Forward: Asia* (St. Paul, MN: International Education Systems, 1994), 407–408.
15. Ibid., 421.
16. Ibid., 423.
17. Bosrock, *Put Your Best Foot Forward: Asia*, 412–413.
18. Ibid., 411–414.
19. Ann Marie Sabath, *International Business Etiquette: Asia & the Pacific Rim* (New York: ASJA Press, 2002), 141–142.
20. Bosrock, *Put Your Best Foot Forward: Asia*, 414–415.
21. Ibid., 415.
22. Ibid., 417.
23. Ibid., 417–418; Sabath, *International Business Etiquette: Asia & the Pacific Rim*, 145.
24. Sabath, *International Business Etiquette: Asia & The Pacific Rim*, 145.
25. Ibid., 425; Powell, *Behave Yourself!: The Essential Guide to International Etiquette*, 108.
26. Bosrock, *Put Your Best Foot Forward: Asia*, 422–423.
27. Terri Morrison and Wayne A. Conaway, *Kiss, Bow, or Shake Hands: Asia* (Avon, MA: Adams Media, 2007), 118.
28. Bosrock, *Put Your Best Foot Forward: Asia*, 416–417.
29. *CultureGrams, Asia, Singapore*, 642.
30. Ibid.
31. Ibid.
32. Ibid., 426.
33. Powell, *Behave Yourself!: The Essential Guide to International Etiquette*, 109.
34. *CultureGrams, Asia, Singapore*, 642.
35. Sabath, *International Business Etiquette: Asia & The Pacific Rim*, 143–144.
36. Elizabeth Devine and Nancy L. Braganti, *The Travelers' Guide to Asian Customs and Manners* (New York: St. Martin's Griffin, 1998), 142.
37. *CultureGrams, Asia, Singapore*, 644.
38. *CultureGrams, Concepts and Terminology* (Ann Arbor, MI: ProQuest CSA, 2008), A-14.
39. Bosrock, *Put Your Best Foot Forward: Asia*, 424
40. Ibid., 411.
41. Ibid., 421.
42. Roger E. Axtell, *Do's and Taboos around the World*, 3rd ed. (New York: John Wiley & Sons, 1993), 92.
43. Bosrock, *Put Your Best Foot Forward: Asia*, 409–410.
44. Powell, *Behave Yourself!: The Essential Guide to International Etiquette*, 110.

45. Sabath, *International Business Etiquette: Asia & the Pacific Rim*, 144.
46. Morrison and Conaway, *Kiss, Bow, or Shake Hands: Asia*, 122.
47. Ibid.
48. Bosrock, *Put Your Best Foot Forward: Asia*, 409.
49. Ibid., 421.

CHAPTER 19

South Korea

The Republic of Korea is South Korea's official title; the country is known as the Land of the Morning Calm. South Korea is the seventh largest export market of the United States.[1]

Product categories exported to South Korea from the United States include agricultural products, fuel oil, petroleum products, nuclear fuel materials, steelmaking machinery, metals, finished metal shapes, wood products, plastics, chemicals, mineral supplies, industrial supplies, generators, electrical apparatus, industrial engines, metalworking machine tools, instruments, electronics aircrafts, vehicles and parts, pharmaceuticals, toiletries, toys, and records/tapes/disks.[2]

COUNTRY SPECIFICS

The connection between South Korea and the United States makes it an important country to study.

Location, Topography, and Land Mass

South Korea is located in Eastern Asia on the southern half of the Korean Peninsula between China and Japan; it borders North Korea to the north and the Sea of Japan and the Yellow Sea on its other borders. The capital of South Korea is Seoul. South Korea is located only 123 miles, or 196 kilometers, from Japan. The land is forested mountains, narrow valleys, and cultivated plains near the coast. The terrain is hilly on the east; plains dominate the west and south.[3] The land mass of South Korea is approximately 38,022 square miles or 98,480 square kilometers.

Economy

The Gross Domestic Product (GDP) per capita is $16,979.[4] The South Korean economy has grown moderately at about 4 percent to 5 percent. Although consumer spending has slowed down, moderate inflation, low unemployment, surplus exports, and equal income distribution have produced a strong economy in South Korea. The government has encouraged the importing of raw materials and technology over consumer goods; the government has also encouraged the people to save and invest rather than to consume. South Korea has very close government and business relationships.[5]

During the 1960s South Korea's economy grew so rapidly that it earned the position as one of the Four Dragons of East Asia. In the late 1990s, many economic problems beset South Korea. Approximately 6 percent of the labor force is in agriculture; 40 percent is in mining and manufacturing; and over 50 percent is involved in the service industry.[6]

Population, Languages Spoken, Ethnic Groups, and Religions

The 2007 estimate of the population is a little over 49 million.[7] The population is growing at a modest rate of almost 0.4 percent per year.[8]

Korean is the language of South Korea. English is taught in the junior and senior high schools, as is Japanese and Chinese. The Korean language uses only approximately 1,300 Chinese characters for clarification; the rest of the Korean language's phonetic writing system uses Hangul. Most of the people are Korean; however, Korea is also home to about 20,000 Chinese.[9]

The half of the population that practices religious beliefs consist of Christians, at 49 percent, and Buddhists, at 47 percent. Another 3 percent practice the Confucian philosophy, while 1 percent are Shamanists and Chondogyoists. Confucianist ideals are strong within the South Korean culture.[10] Confucianism orders social behavior and stresses virtue, morality, and filial piety. Confucianism is very ancestor-oriented, so parents are respected in both this life and the afterlife. Even those who are Christian will practice the Confucian cultural rites.[11]

Country Codes, Time Zones, and Currency

The country code for South Korea is 82. City codes include 32 for Inchon, 51 for Pusan, 2 for Seoul, and 53 for Taegu. When calling from the United States to Seoul, for example, dial the International Access

Code (011), followed by the country code (82), the city code (2), and the local telephone number.[12]

South Korea is 14 hours ahead of U.S. Eastern Standard Time. Thus, when it is 8 AM in New York, the time in South Korea is 10 PM. These times in Universal Time would be written according to the 24-hour clock as 0800 and 2200, respectively. Daylight Saving Time is not observed in South Korea.[13]

The currency of South Korea is the *won* (KW). When you exchange traveler's checks, you will need your passport as identification.[14] A currency converter is available at http://coinmill.com/AED_calculator.html that will convert any currency in the world into any other currency.

BUSINESS AND SOCIAL CUSTOMS

Greetings, Introductions, and Business Cards

Greeting behavior depends upon age and social standing. The typical greeting is a bow; however, men usually add a handshake. When shaking hands, the left hand is often placed beneath the right forearm to show respect. Women are usually greeted only with a slight bow. Bows are done upon arrival and departure.[15] Lower-ranking individuals, those who are younger, or those whose social class is less will execute a deeper bow.[16] The greeting terminology used with the bow and/or handshake is *man-na-suh pan-gop-sumnida*, which means "pleased to meet you."[17]

Introductions by a third party are recommended when you are meeting the people in the company with whom you anticipate doing business.[18] Visitors should be aware that Koreans have three names. First is the surname, then the clan name, and then the given name. The term *songsaeng-nim* is added at the end of the name, which means "respected person." If the person has a title, such as doctor, professor, or engineer, you would use his or her title rather than *songsaengnim*.[19] It is not unusual for women in South Korea to maintain their own surname rather than using their husband's name.[20]

After greetings, business cards will be exchanged. The cards are to be given and received with both hands, with the card printed in Korean on one side and in English on the other side.[21] Writing on a business card in front of the person who has given you the card is rude. The card information should include information that will allow your South Korean counterpart to discern the hierarchical relationship between the two of you. If it does not, the conversation will quickly turn to questions concerning age, schools, and family.[22] Be sure to take plenty of cards (a box of 500 may not be too many) as you will exchange business cards with everyone you meet.[23]

Business Entertaining and Seating Customs

Business entertaining is generally done in a restaurant and does not include spouses. Business dinners begin between 7 PM to 9 PM and will continue into the night. Drinking generally begins the meal. If urged to continue drinking, you should do so in order not to lose face, even if it means getting intoxicated.

Wait for your host to initiate business discussions, which will usually be at the end of the meal. Singing typically follows dinner; it is one of the ways South Koreans unwind and have fun. Play along and submit to the singing requests of superiors. By joining in, you are showing a willingness to participate in elevating their *Kibun* ("feeling" or "mood"), which will help you be successful.[24] When your host asks you to go drinking after the meal, always accept. If invited to a home, you should not discuss business in the presence of the family, unless the host initiates the discussion. Arriving up to 30 minutes late for home entertaining is considered polite. Remove your shoes upon entering the house.

As seating protocol is very strict, wait to be told where to sit. The best seat is considered the center seat facing the door and is usually given to the most senior person present. The eldest person will be served first, then everyone else will eat.[25]

Dining, Toasting, and Tipping Customs

Review the rules for Korean table manners before you visit the country to be prepared for some different dining experiences. Guidelines for use of eating utensils are similar to those in other Asian countries. For example, it is considered rude to point your chopsticks at someone or to pierce your food with them. In addition, place the chopsticks on the rest rather than across the rice bowl when you have finished eating. While most of the meal is eaten with chopsticks, the rice is eaten with a metal spoon. Also, do not eat with your fingers as this is considered rude.

South Koreans are proud of their cuisine and will want you to sample spicy foods such as *putlog* (strips of beef that are marinated and barbecued) as well as their alcoholic drink, *soju*.[26] Making slurping sounds while eating your soup is acceptable. In the South Korean culture, you are not expected to clean your plate.[27] After dinner the host will accompany everyone to their car or to the gate because it is insulting to wish guests farewell indoors.[28]

The common toast in South Korea is *Gun-hei*. Raise your glass with your right hand. To confer more respect to the person being toasted, support your right forearm with your left hand. If you drain your glass, your host will immediately refill it. Therefore, if you do not want it refilled, leave some liquid in your glass.[29] Drinking alcohol is inappropriate for women; however, males who do not wish to drink alcoholic beverages will need to decline for reasons of health or religion.[30] A man may fill another man's glass with whatever is being drunk (alcoholic or nonalcoholic); a man may fill a woman's glass; a woman may fill a man's glass; but a woman does not fill another woman's glass, nor do you fill your own glass.[31]

High-end hotels and restaurants will add a 10 percent tip or service charge to the bill. Individual tipping is not usually done unless someone has gone out of his or her way to help you.[32]

Gift-Giving Customs

Bringing a gift is acceptable when invited to a dinner party. Suggestions for gifts include fruit, chocolate, or flowers. Gifts should not be in multiples of four since four is considered an unlucky number. When wrapping gifts, use red or yellow paper; do not use green, white, or black paper. Gifts are given and received with both hands. The recipient does not open the gift in front of the giver but opens it later.[33]

Using gift giving as a way to obtain favors is common in business. Reciprocity is expected with business gifts.[34] Business gifts are not necessary but will be appreciated. Appropriate business gift ideas include something with your organization's logo or something from your city. The gift should be of good quality but not so expensive that it would embarrass the receiver. If you are giving gifts to several people within the organization, be sure to give the senior person the gift of greater value. Gifts to subordinates may be similar as long as they are not of the same value as the superior's gift.[35]

Business Meetings

Make business appointments well in advance, approximately three to four weeks before your intended travel. Before making travel plans, remember that Koreans typically take vacations from mid-July through mid-August, so this is not a good time to plan business meetings. You may also wish to avoid October because of the holidays in that month as well as the two weeks before and after Christmas.[36] The best times to make appointments are between 10 AM and 11 AM or 2 PM and 3 PM. Meetings may extend beyond the normal business hours.

To make a good first impression, be on time, use good manners, and be somewhat formal until a working relationship has been formed.[37] Jackets are worn during meetings unless the most senior South Korean removes his or her jacket. The purpose of the first meeting will be primarily to get to know you rather than for conducting business.[38]

As relationships are very important, work on building a positive relationship and boosting your business colleagues' *Kibun*. Show respect by standing when a visitor arrives; however, a higher-level official may not stand up.[39]

Business negotiations can be very emotional and aggressive with the South Koreans. Use of theatrics to achieve their goals is not unusual. Contracts are viewed as a guideline, and the interpersonal relationship between the parties is viewed as more important than the contract. You should not sign anything in red ink in South Korea.[40]

If silence is encountered during negotiations, it could indicate a lack of understanding. At that point it would be necessary to add additional information, rephrase the information, or ask if there are questions.[41] South Koreans will tend to be louder and more forward than many other Asian groups. South Koreans are also not as group-oriented as the Japanese, so you will be doing business with a person rather than a group. South Koreans will also be very direct with their comments, and interrupting someone while they are speaking is viewed positively.[42]

Dress and Appearance

Western-style clothing is worn; the exception is the elderly in rural areas, who may wear native clothing. U.S. conservative business dress is appropriate in South Korea. Conservative colors are suggested for initial meetings; if you like brighter colors, reserve them until you have gained credibility and a relationship has been developed. Attire for men should be conservative and includes a dark suit, white shirt, and conservative tie. Attire for women should likewise be conservative. A skirt and blouse combination is appropriate; however, the skirts should not be short or tight. Since people sit on the floor in homes and in restaurants, women would be wise to wear long, full skirts. Blouses should also be sleeved; sleeveless tops are not considered professional.[43]

Holidays

South Korean holidays are different depending on the solar or lunar calendars. The following holidays are observed according to the solar calendar:

- New Year's Day (January 1 and 2)
- Independence Movement Day (March 1)
- Arbor Day (April 1)
- Children's Day (May 5)
- Memorial Day (June 6)
- Constitution Day (July 17)
- Liberation Day (August 15)
- National Foundation Day (October 3)
- Christmas Day (December 25)

According to the lunar calendar, the following holidays are observed:

- Lunar New Year (the first day of the first month plus the day before and after the first day)
- Buddha's Birthday (the eighth day of the fourth lunar month, usually May)
- Harvest Moon Festival (the 15th day of the eighth lunar month; 14 and 16 are also holidays)

Conversational Customs

When conversing with South Koreans, maintain appropriate eye contact. Remember that eye contact is maintained about 50 percent of the time while conversing with people of equal status. However, people of lower rank will tend to avert their gaze often during conversations.

If someone pays you a compliment, simply say that you are not worthy of such praise. Be careful not to single out a person for praise, but instead praise the group so the individual will not be embarrassed. Direct and concise conversation is appreciated as South Koreans tend to avoid asking questions if they do not understand.

Appropriate topics for conversation include South Korea's cultural heritage, its economic success, sports, and personal hobbies. Topics that are to be avoided include Korean politics, the Korean War, socialism, communism, your host's wife, and personal matters.[44]

Humor

Using humor during business meetings in South Korea is inappropriate. Although people in this country—unlike many other Asians—seem to appreciate humor of all cultures, they believe that humor has no place during negotiations. Business is serious; even making joking comments during meetings may be viewed negatively.[45]

Attitude toward Women in Business

On the Human Development Index (HDI), South Korea ranks 26 out of 177 nations.[46] The HDI is a measure of empowerment; it is based on life expectancy, literacy, infant mortality, and real GDP. The assumption is that societies that provide an opportunity for education, access to healthcare, and adequate wages are inclined to be more democratic and exhibit a respect for human rights.[47]

Korea tends to be a male-dominated society, so women are somewhat restricted. In 1945, women were given the rights by law that men traditionally had. However, attitudes do not change overnight. Although 47.7 percent of the women work outside the home, women earn 63.4 percent of what men earn doing the same job.[48] Only businesswomen who have expertise, seniority, or rank can be expected to be successful in South Korea.[49]

Public Behavior

When interacting with superiors in public, South Koreans will be very courteous; when interacting with friends or acquaintances of equal social status, they will be very outgoing and friendly.[50] South Koreans have strong feelings for family, schoolmates, teachers, work colleagues, and those they grew up with; these feelings will be shown publicly. Because South Koreans tend to be modest, they will deny compliments and speak very modestly about themselves. It is not acceptable to have heated discussions in public places.[51]

An inappropriate behavior is eating while walking on the street.[52] In addition, it is customary to walk on the left side of the street or stairs when in public places.

Public restrooms that are intended to be used by both men and women are not uncommon. A woman would walk past the urinals to use the stalls. If someone knocks on the stall door, the correct response is to knock back to indicate it is occupied.[53]

NONVERBAL COMMUNICATION

Gestures and Posture

Certain gestures are impolite in South Korea and should be avoided. Blowing your nose in public, for example, is rude. If spicy food makes your nose run, you should leave the table before wiping or blowing your nose. People will often wear surgical masks when they have a cold to avoid spreading germs.[54]

Another gesture, the beckoning gesture, has negative connotations when done in a certain manner. Using the index finger to beckon someone would be rude. Beckoning a younger or junior-level person is done by extending the arm with the palm down and moving the fingers up and down.[55]

When South Koreans suck air through their teeth, they are saying "no." Since it is difficult for South Koreans to say "no," you will need to be able to read their nonverbal messages. Also, if South Koreans say "maybe" and squint their eyes or tilt their head back, they are really saying "no."[56] Avoiding hand motions during conversations is recommended; they are considered too animated to be acceptable in South Korea.[57]

Posture is important; do not slouch when you are seated. In addition, it is inappropriate to put your feet on a table or chair.[58] When seated, both feet should be flat on the floor. The feet are viewed as dirty; they should not be permitted to touch others.

Eye Contact and Facial Expressions

South Koreans prefer intermittent eye contact. Not looking directly into the eyes of the person to whom they are speaking is a sign of respect and is done when the hierarchy or age between the two people is not equal. In addition to hierarchy and age, gender is a consideration in eye contact. Males will avoid eye contact with women as a sign of respect. An international businessperson needs to make eye contact as a show of sincerity and attentiveness to the speaker.[59]

Facial expressions are very important and can communicate an entire message. South Koreans may laugh when they are embarrassed or frustrated as well as when something is funny. Any type of discomfort is usually expressed by laughter. When Korean women laugh, they cover their mouth. Smiling is a way of maintaining harmony, so South Koreans will smile a lot.[60]

Space and Touch

South Koreans stand closer together than Westerners do since their country is so crowded. Because of the crowding, you may be bumped by others on the streets, in the stores, in train stations, or at the airport. South Koreans feel no need to apologize since the behavior was unintentional; visitors often perceive their failure to apologize as rude.[61]

Pushing and shoving are also common when waiting in line, since queuing does not exist in South Korea.[62]

Desk space is very private; no materials should be placed on anyone's desk. Instead, you would hand the materials to the person.[63]

Touching someone on the back or arm is not proper unless the individuals are friends or peers. Touching between people who are not good friends or family members is inappropriate. Touching someone who is older is inappropriate, as is touching someone of the opposite gender; however, people of the same gender often hold hands.[64]

Punctuality and Attitude toward Time

While punctuality is important in South Korea, it is permissible for a top-level executive to be late for meetings or appointments occasionally.[65] However, Westerners are expected to be on time.[66] Time is cyclical in South Korea; it is considered on the continuum of past, present, and future rather than the Western continuum of future, present, and past.

TRAVEL TIPS

- Passports are required; they should be valid for at least six months past the anticipated return date. Visas are also required for stays of 30 days or more.
- Hotel accommodations may be Western or Korean style. Since accommodations can be quite different, specify your preference when making reservations.
- Transportation includes rail, subways, buses, taxis, and private cars. Hiring a driver is recommended over driving a car yourself. A bullet train operates between Pusan and Seoul.
- Although South Korea has a low crime rate, visitors should be alert for burglars and pickpockets.[67]
- Do not take photographs of airports, military facilities, or harbors; observe signs prohibiting the taking of photographs.
- Emergency telephone numbers are 112 for police and 119 for the fire department or ambulance.
- Weather problems include typhoons; air pollution is a problem in the larger cities.
- Visitors should remember to remove their shoes before entering a temple and to avoid sitting with their back to the temple when putting their shoes back on.[68]
- Save your money-exchange receipts so that you can reconvert *won* into dollars before you leave the country.
- The legal drinking age in South Korea is 20.
- Drink only bottled water.
- For additional information on South Korea, contact the Embassy of the Republic of Korea (202-939-5600), www.koreaembassyusa.org, or Korea National Tourism Organization (201-585-0909), www.knot.or.kr.

NOTES

1. U.S. Census Bureau, "Foreign Trade Statistics," http://www.census.gov/foreign-trade/statistics/highlights/top/top0612.html (accessed March 4, 2008).
2. Ibid.
3. U.S. Department of State, "Background Note: South Korea," as of January 2007, http://www.state.gov/r/pa/ei/bgn/3204.htm (accessed May 9, 2007).
4. List of countries by GDP (nominal) per capita, http://en.wikipedia.org/wiki/List_of_countries_by_GDP_(nominal)_per_capita (accessed March 5, 2008). Figures (in U.S. dollars) are estimates for 2007 from *The World Factbook* provided by the Central Intelligence Agency (updated February 12, 2008). These figures do not take into account cost-of-living differences; using additional economic data is advisable when making country comparisons.
5. CIA the World Factbook, "South Korea," as of June 19, 2007, https://www.cia.gov/library/publications/the-world-factbook/geos/my.html (accessed June 25, 2007).
6. *CultureGrams, Asia, South Korea* (Ann Arbor, MI: ProQuest CSA, 2008), 668.
7. U.S. Census Bureau, "*IDB: Countries and Areas Ranked by Population*," as of 2007, http://www.census.gov/cgi-bin/ipc/idbrank.pl (accessed January 16, 2008).
8. CIA the World Factbook, "South Korea."
9. U.S. Department of State, "Background Note: South Korea."
10. Ibid.
11. *CultureGrams, Asia, South Korea*, 666.
12. Country Calling Codes, http://www.countrycallingcodes.com (accessed June 15, 2007).
13. U.S. Naval Observatory, "What is Universal Time," as of October 30, 2003, http://aa.usno.navy.mil/faq/docs/UT (accessed May 9, 2007).
14. Ann Marie Sabath, *International Business Etiquette: Asia and the Pacific Rim* (New York: ASJA Press, 2002), 154.
15. Roger E. Axtell, *Do's and Taboos Around the World* (New York: John Wiley and Sons, 1993), 87.
16. Boyd DeMente, *NTC's Dictionary of Korea's Business and Cultural Code Words* (Lincolnwood, IL: NTC Publishing Group, 1998), 82.
17. Kwintessential Language and Culture Specialists, "South Korea-Language, Culture, Customs, and Etiquette," http://www.kwintessential.co.uk/resources/global-etiquette/south-korea-country-profile.html (accessed March 25, 2007).
18. Ibid.
19. Elizabeth Devine and Nancy L. Braganti, *The Traveler's Guide to Asian Customs and Manners* (New York: St. Martin's Griffin, 1998), 222.
20. Sabath, *International Business Etiquette: Asia and the Pacific Rim*, 164.
21. Lillian H. Chaney and Jeanette S. Martin, *Intercultural Business Communication*, 4th ed. (Upper Saddle River, NJ: Prentice Hall, 2007), 177.
22. DeMente, *NTC's Dictionary of Korea's Business and Cultural Code Words*, 85.
23. Sabath, *International Business Etiquette: Asia and the Pacific Rim*, 157.
24. DeMente, *NTC's Dictionary of Korea's Business and Cultural Code Words*, 20.
25. Eun Y. Kim, "Executive Planet" South Korea, http://www.executiveplanet.com/index.php?title+South_Korea.
26. Chaney and Martin, *Intercultural Business Communication*, 177.

27. Devine and Braganti, *The Traveler's Guide to Asian Customs and Manners*, 228.
28. Kwintessential Language and Culture Specialists, "South Korea-Language, Culture, Customs, and Etiquette."
29. Ibid.
30. Sabath, *International Business Etiquette: Asia and the Pacific*, 159.
31. Mary Murray Bosrock, *Put Your Best Foot Forward: Asia* (St. Paul, MN: International Education Systems, 1994), 441.
32. Trip Advisor, "Inside South Korea: Tipping and Etiquette," as of 2007, http://www.tripadvisor.com/Travel-g294196-s606/South-Korea:Tipping.And.Etiquette.html (accessed March 25, 2007.
33. DeMente, *NTC's Dictionary of Korea's Business and Cultural Code Words*, 119.
34. *CultureGrams, Asia, South Korea*, 666.
35. Sabath, *International Business Etiquette: Asia and the Pacific Rim*, 161.
36. Devine and Braganti, *The Traveler's Guide to Asian Customs and Manners*, 233.
37. Ibid., 234.
38. Kwintessential Language and Culture Specialists, "South Korea-Language, Culture, Customs, and Etiquette."
39. DeMente, *NTC's Dictionary of Korea's Business and Cultural Code Words*, 85.
40. Ibid., 87.
41. Chaney and Martin, *Intercultural Business Communication*, 228.
42. Devine and Braganti, *The Traveler's Guide to Asian Customs and Manners*, 235.
43. Kim, "Executive Plant."
44. Kwintessential Language and Culture Specialists, "South Korea-Language, Culture, Customs, and Etiquette."
45. Carol Turkington, *The Complete Idiot's Guide to Cultural Etiquette* (Indianapolis, IN: Alpha Books, 1999), 279.
46. Ibid., 668.
47. *CultureGrams, Concepts and Terminology* (Ann Arbor, MI: ProQuest CSA, 2008), A-14.
48. DeMente, *NTC's Dictionary of Korea's Business and Cultural Code Words*, 317.
49. Devine and Braganti, *The Traveler's Guide to Asian Customs and Manners*, 235.
50. Chunghee Sarah Soh, "Countries and Their Cultures, Culture of South Korea," http://www.everyculture.com/Ja-Ma/South-Korea.html (accessed March 22, 2007).
51. *CultureGrams, Asia, South Korea*, 666.
52. Devine and Braganti, *The Traveler's Guide to Asian Customs and Manners*, 225.
53. Ibid.
54. Kim, "Executive Planet."
55. Ibid.
56. Chaney and Martin, *Intercultural Business Communication*, 135.
57. Sabath, *International Business Etiquette: Asia and the Pacific Rim*, 159.
58. Roger E. Axtell, *Gestures: The Do's and Taboos of Body Language around the World* (New York: John Wiley & Sons, 1998), 193.
59. Kim, "Executive Planet."
60. Chaney and Martin, *Intercultural Business Communication*, 135; Sabath, *International Business Etiquette: Asia and the Pacific Rim*, 159.
61. Soh, "Countries and Their Cultures, Culture of South Korea."
62. Sabath, *International Business Etiquette: Asia and the Pacific Rim*, 160.

63. Terri Morrison and Wayne A. Conaway, *Kiss, Bow, or Shake Hands*, 2nd ed. (Avon, MA: Adams Media, 2006), 458.
64. Kim, "Executive Planet."
65. Chaney and Martin, *Intercultural Business Communication*, 134.
66. Sabath, *International Business Etiquette: Asia and the Pacific Rim*, 151.
67. Morrison and Conaway, *Kiss, Bow, or Shake Hands: Asia*, 130.
68. Turkington, *The Complete Idiot's Guide to Cultural Etiquette*, 286.

CHAPTER 20
Switzerland

Switzerland, officially the Swiss Confederation, is the seventeenth largest export market of the United States.[1] The following categories of items are exported from the United States to Switzerland: agricultural products, metals, precious metals, chemicals, industrial engines, instruments, industrial machines, electronics, aircraft, pharmaceuticals, jewelry, art, and gem diamonds.[2]

COUNTRY SPECIFICS

A country's location, topography, economy, and population provide insight into understanding its culture. In addition, knowledge of ethnic groups, religions, time zones, and currency is helpful.

Location, Topography, and Land Mass

Switzerland is landlocked in the middle of the continent of Europe. The country is bordered on the north by France and Germany, on the south by Italy, on the west by France, and on the east by Austria and Liechtenstein.[3] The capital of Switzerland is Bern. Switzerland is considered one of the most beautiful places to visit.

The land is mountainous, with 60 percent of the land being mountains. The rest of the land is hills and plateaus. The Alps run through the middle of Switzerland.[4] The size of Switzerland is 15,941 square miles or 41,290 square kilometers.

Economy

Switzerland has always had one of the most stable economies in the world. It has managed to stay out of most major and minor wars in the world. The country's workforce is highly skilled, and there is very little unemployment. The country's Gross Domestic Product per capita is estimated to be $53,967 for 2007.[5] Switzerland is known as the safe haven for banking.[6]

Switzerland's import partners are Germany, at 31.6 percent; Italy, at 10.5 percent; France, at 10 percent; the United States, at 5.6 percent; the Netherlands, at 4.8 percent; Austria, at 4.6 percent; and the United Kingdom, at 4.4 percent. Switzerland's export partners are Germany, at 19.4 percent; the United States, at 10.9 percent; Italy, at 9.1 percent; France, at 8.7 percent; the United Kingdom, at 5.4 percent; and Spain, at 4.1 percent.[7]

The World Economic Forum's 2006 Global Competitiveness Report ranked Switzerland the most competitive world economy. The country has a very good infrastructure, efficient markets, high education standards, high levels of technological innovation, high levels of scientific research, good intellectual property protection, and an efficient judicial system. Consistent with the country's desire to remain neutral, Switzerland is not a member of the European Union (EU) or the North Atlantic Treaty Organization (NATO).[8] Switzerland did join the United Nations in 2002.

Population, Languages Spoken, Ethnic Groups, and Religions

Switzerland's population was estimated at 7.6 million in 2007.[9] The population growth rate is 0.38 percent.[10] Resident immigrants and working immigrants make up 20 percent of the population.[11]

Switzerland has four national languages. The three official languages are German (63.7 percent of the population), French (20.4 percent), and Italian (6.5 percent). *Romansch*, also called *Ladin*, is spoken in the southern part of the country by 0.5 percent of the population. Other languages that are spoken include Serbo-Croatian, Albanian, Portuguese, Spanish, and English.[12] Many businesspeople speak English.[13]

The four main ethnic groups are Germans (65 percent), French (18 percent), Italians (10 percent), Romansch (1 percent), and other ethnic groups (6 percent). All the people are called Swiss.

The religions practiced by people of Switzerland are Roman Catholic (41.8 percent), Protestant (35.3 percent), Islam (4.3 percent), Orthodox (1.8 percent), and other Christian sects (0.4 percent); 11.1 percent of the population do not profess a religious belief.[14]

Country Codes, Time Zones, and Currency

The country code for Switzerland is 41. City codes include 31 for Bern, 22 for Geneva, and 44 for Zurich. When calling from the United States to

Switzerland, for example, dial the International Access Code (011), followed by the country code (41), the city code, and the local telephone number.[15]

Switzerland's time is six hours ahead of U.S. Eastern Standard Time. Thus, when it is 8 AM in New York City, it is 2 PM in Switzerland. In Universal Time the times would be written according to the 24-hour clock as 0800 and 1400, respectively. Daylight Saving Time is observed in Switzerland.[16]

The Swiss *franc* (CHF) is Switzerland's currency; it continues to remain very stable.[17] While *euros* will be accepted in major cities, your change will be given in Swiss *francs*.[18] A currency converter is available at http://coinmill.com/AED_calculator.html that will convert any currency in the world into any other currency.

BUSINESS AND SOCIAL CUSTOMS

Greetings, Introductions, and Business Cards

As Switzerland is very formal and polite, greetings are also formal and polite. Greetings involve a firm handshake and good eye contact. Women may also include kisses on the cheek in the German-speaking areas of the country; both men and women in French or Italian areas will embrace.

Introductions are generally done by a third party. A form of "hello" or "good day" is said when shaking hands. Since this is a multiple-language country, you may hear many different languages being spoken during greetings. One will always stand when being introduced.[19] Introductions are important for doing business in Switzerland. Since Switzerland is a small country, people within a given industry know each other. If you do not know the people in the industry, then it is assumed you are not important. The title of Mr., Mrs., or Miss is used with first names, followed by surnames, during introductions.[20] In German-speaking Switzerland, you could use the courtesy title of *Herr* for a man and *Frau* for a woman. In French-speaking Switzerland, the title *Monsieur* is used for a man and *Madame* for a woman. In Italian-speaking Switzerland, *Signore* is the title used for a man and *Signora* is used for a woman. Using titles of *Frau*, *Madame*, or *Signora* for women professionals indicates a respect for their profession and social standing.[21]

Business cards are important; the business card should be translated into the language of the person with whom you are conducting business. If you are not sure of the language, German is generally a safe choice. Since many businesspeople speak English, you may not need to have your card translated.[22] Be sure to give business cards to the secretary as well as to the person with whom you are meeting.[23]

Business Entertaining and Seating Customs

Lunches and dinners are popular for business entertaining. While lunches will be quite informal and quick, dinners will be used to impress the client and should always be at a nice restaurant. Swiss restaurants are usually open for dinner from 6:30 PM to 11:00 PM. The Swiss do not tend to invite businesspeople to their homes. If invited to a Swiss home, the evening will end early.[24]

You should allow your host to indicate where you are to sit. The guest of honor is typically seated in the middle of table facing the door when dining in someone's home; however, when eating at a restaurant, seating is open.[25]

Dining, Toasting, and Tipping Customs

The Continental style of eating is used by the Swiss; the fork remains in the left hand and the knife in the right. Foods that are typically eaten with the fingers in many countries, such as sandwiches, fruit, or cheese, are usually eaten with utensils. Follow your host's lead when deciding whether to eat certain foods with your utensils or with your hands. While dining, be sure to keep both hands above the table. You may rest your wrists lightly on the table's edge, but you should not place your elbows on the table. Wait until everyone at the table has been served before you begin eating.[26] Do not request salt or pepper, as this would imply that the food has not been seasoned properly and would be viewed as an insult. Dinner may start with a pre-dinner drink, such as an aperitif, wine, or Campari. Mixed drinks and beer are not served before dinner. With dinner you will be offered red or white wine or beer. Coffee is served at the end of the meal with a fruit-flavored liqueur. In Switzerland you are expected to clean your plate; therefore, if you are served from a series of platters, be sure to take only as much as you are sure you can eat. You are also expected to try every dish that is served. When you have finished eating, place the knife and fork parallel to each other on the right side of the plate. To indicate that you have not finished eating, cross the fork and knife in the middle of your plate. Some of the authentic Swiss dishes include *fondue*, *raclette*, and *Rösti*. Swiss chocolate is excellent and is used in a number of dishes.[27]

The toast is very formal. The host will propose a toast and look directly into everyone's eyes. You are expected to clink glasses with those close to you before drinking. When you are proposing a toast, make eye contact with everyone at the table before taking a drink.[28] In German-speaking Switzerland the toast is *Prost* (cheers); in French-speaking Switzerland the toast is *Votre Santé* or *Santé* (to your health); and in Italian-speaking Switzerland the toast is *Salute* (to your health).[29]

Tipping is expected in Switzerland. You may tip interpreters and guides with personalized gifts rather than money.[30] Hotels, cafés, restaurants, and bars will add 15 percent to your bill automatically. If you have extraordinary service, leave an extra amount.[31]

Gift-Giving Customs

Although gifts are appreciated, they are not considered necessary to doing business in Switzerland.[32] Your Swiss colleague should initiate the giving of gifts; you would then present your gift. The exchanging of gifts will take place only after a contract has been signed. Gifts of cognac, whiskey, or a photographic book of your part of the country would be appreciated. Gifts should be modest; expensive gifts may be viewed as bribes. Avoid gifts with sharp points, such as scissors or cutlery, as they signify a desire to sever the relationship. Company logos on gifts should be small.[33]

If invited to someone's home for a meal, bring a gift of wine, flowers, or Swiss chocolates. You should not give red roses, however, as they are reserved for lovers; also avoid gifts of chrysanthemums and white asters as these flowers are used for funerals.[34] A small gift of candy or toys for the children is appreciated when invited to a Swiss home.

Business Meetings

Meetings are by appointment only, and you should arrive early for the meeting. The Swiss are good negotiators without being demanding or aggressive. Swiss products are excellent and expensive; the Swiss make purchasers feel that they are getting a superior product. The Swiss are direct in their negotiations and are not known to do a lot of bargaining. They are known, however, for their confidentiality.[35]

When negotiating with the Swiss, be sure to use objective facts when speaking to the German or French portion of the population and subjective feelings when negotiating with the Italian segment of the population. When conducting business with all groups, faith, nationalism, and utopian ideals will influence the truth.[36]

Contacts are important in Switzerland, as are age and seniority. If a young executive is sent alone to a major business meeting, he or she will probably not be taken seriously. Since the age of a company is important, be sure the year your company was established is on your business card and letterhead.[37]

Dress and Appearance

Conservative business dress is important. Men wear tailored wool suits in dark colors, white cotton shirts, and plain silk ties. Women wear skirted suits with the length below the knee or pantsuits that are classic in design. All clothing should be clean and pressed.[38] Jewelry should be simple except for your watch; it should be expensive and preferably Swiss.[39] After your initial visit, you may wear business-casual attire if the people at the firm with which you are dealing wear casual dress. A Swiss businessperson meeting you for the first time would dress formally and conservatively, and you should do the same. If you do not dress appropriately, including shoes that are well shined and well maintained, the Swiss will not trust you.[40]

Holidays

Festivals and holidays are very important to the Swiss; they tend to get very involved in the activities of the holiday. Following are the major holidays in Switzerland.[41]

- New Year's Day (January 1)
- Baerzelistag Day (January 2)
- Easter holidays (March/April)
- Whit Monday (varies)
- Labor Day (May 1)
- Corpus Christi (in Roman Catholic cantons or provinces) (May)
- Ascension (June 5)
- Fete-Dieu (in some cantons) (June 18)
- Swiss National Day (August 1)
- Assumption Day (in some cantons) (August 15)
- Toussaint (in some cantons) (November 1)
- St. Nicholas' Day (in some cantons) (December 6)
- Christmas Day (December 25)
- St. Stephen's Day/Boxing Day (December 26)

Conversational Customs

The Swiss are cautious, modest communicators; they will appear to be very pragmatic and detached in their discourse. The Swiss are good listeners and remember what they have been told. Good topics of conversation include sports, positive aspects of Switzerland, travel, food, international politics, and work.

Some taboos in conversations with the Swiss include boasting, being overly curious, and invading someone's privacy.[42] Asking personal questions, such as age, income, or religious beliefs, is impolite.[43] Other topics to avoid include discussing with your Swiss host the 2004 Olympic Winter Games and the Swiss role in World War II. Discussing dieting during meals is inappropriate.

Humor

Switzerland is not known for its humor. The Swiss are known for being overly serious, polite, proper, and cautious.[44] Swiss humor is understated wit that is quick and intelligent. Reparteé is very common; however, it is not loud; it is done to elicit smiles and laughter. If you cannot understand the joke, do not ask for a translation.[45] You will find more humor among people in the French and Italian areas of Switzerland than in the German areas. As is true throughout the world, humor is difficult to translate. What is humorous in one part of the world is not in another.

Attitude toward Women in Business

On the Human Development Index (HDI), Switzerland ranks 9 out of 177 nations.[46] The HDI is a measure of empowerment; it is based on life expectancy, literacy, infant mortality, and real GDP. The assumption is that societies that provide an opportunity for education, access to healthcare, and adequate wages are inclined to be more democratic and exhibit a respect for human rights.[47]

Switzerland continually ranks high on many different quality-of-life indices: highest per capita income, one of the highest computer and Internet usages per capita, highest insurance coverage per capita, and high healthcare costs.[48]

While equal rights for men are guaranteed by the Swiss constitution, the same is not true for women. The role of Swiss women in society is somewhat traditional. Women have to worker harder than men to be successful; they hold few high-level positions. Businesswomen from other countries who wish to be successful in their business dealings with the Swiss should be very professional in their dress and behavior.[49]

Public Behavior

Public behavior is very proper. The Swiss believe in obeying the rules and in doing things correctly.[50] Men usually raise their hats when passing acquaintances on the street. Some rules you will be expected to follow include not walking against a red light or washing a car or mowing your lawn on Sunday mornings; these activities are illegal. You can expect some pushing and shoving in queues; you may find it necessary to do the same.[51] Show respect to the elderly by giving them your seat on public transportation and by helping them in other ways, such as by carrying parcels for them or holding doors open for them.[52]

NONVERBAL COMMUNICATION

Gestures and Posture

The Swiss use few gestures while communicating. The Swiss do not talk with their hands, nor do they put their hands in their pockets, especially during conversations. Chewing gum in public is improper; crossing an ankle over the other knee is disrespectful; and backslapping is simply not done.[53] Use your full hand to point to something as the index finger when used alone could be seen as an obscene gesture.[54] When entering or leaving a building, holding the door open for the next person is a considerate gesture.[55]

The Swiss consider straight, erect posture important. While it is common to cross the legs, stretching them out is inappropriate. Slouching in your chair is also inappropriate, as is placing your feet on chairs or tables. Leaning forward indicates agreement, and leaning back indicates suspicion of what the other person is doing or saying.[56]

Eye Contact and Facial Expressions

Eye contact is expected when you are introduced to someone and during greetings. The Swiss are conservative and do not believe emotions should be displayed.[57] Therefore, facial expressions will be minimal.

Space and Touch

Because most of Switzerland is mountainous, space is cherished in this society. Strong territorialism exists on the part of the individual concerning personal, communal, and cantonal space.[58] Touching and backslapping are not appreciated.

Punctuality and Attitude toward Time

The Swiss are very punctual; only the Germans are more controlled by the clock. The Swiss will not rush a business meeting; however, they do not want to waste your time or theirs. If you want to make a good impression on your Swiss colleagues, arrive about 15 minutes before the announced beginning of the meeting. The message you will be conveying is that you place great importance on meeting with them. To emphasize their attitude toward punctuality, the Swiss have this saying: "People who are late are either not wearing Swiss watches or are not riding Swiss trains."[59] Deadlines are important to the Swiss; you are expected to meet your agreed-upon deadlines.

TRAVEL TIPS

- A passport is required for entry into Switzerland.
- The police may ask to see your passport at any time; thus, you will need to carry your passport with you at all times. Be sure to have copies of your passport that you can leave in your hotel room and with your company at home.
- Workers in Switzerland have a generous amount of vacation time; many take their vacations during July and August, so these are not particularly good months to conduct business.
- Hotels may vary from small hotels where you will share a bath to luxurious Western-style hotels. Be sure you ask about the accommodations when making reservations.
- Public toilets, typically identified by W.C., are found in restaurants and trains and are usually very clean. Have some change with you as you will need to pay before entering a stall.[60]
- Public transportation includes buses, streetcars, and trains. Taxis are available at taxi stands located at airports and railroad and bus stations; taxis are luxurious by U.S. standards. If you drive in Switzerland, remember that seat belts are mandatory. Never drink and drive as punishments are severe, including incarceration.[61]
- The emergency number to call when you need the police is 117 or 112; for an ambulance call 144 or 112; and for the fire department call 118 or 112.
- Do not be surprised if strangers join you at your table in restaurants when there are no free tables. You are not expected to converse with them.
- Littering is not tolerated and is enforced by the population in general. You may be verbally chastised by the locals or taken to the local police department for littering.
- Violent crimes are rare in Switzerland.
- Switzerland does not have a minimum age for drinking alcoholic beverages; teenagers are often seen drinking wine and beer.
- Phrases such as "We must get together again soon" are interpreted literally; the Swiss will expect you to follow up.

- Jaywalking is improper; the Swiss are law-abiding citizens and will expect you to be also.[62]
- Greet everyone, including other customers, when you go into shops. Do not, however, try to bargain with the shopkeepers.
- For additional information on Switzerland, contact one of the following: The Embassy of Switzerland, 2900 Cathedral Avenue NW, Washington, D.C. 20008 (202-745-7900) or Switzerland Tourism, Swiss Center, 608 Fifth Avenue, New York, NY 10020 (877-794-8037).

NOTES

1. U.S. Census Bureau, "Foreign Trade Statistics," http://www.census.gov/foreign-trade/statistics/highlights/top/top0612.html (accessed March 4, 2008).
2. Ibid.
3. CIA the World Factbook, "Switzerland," as of June 19, 2007, https://www.cia.gov/library/publications/the-world-factbook/geos/my.html (accessed June 25, 2007).
4. Ibid.
5. List of countries by GDP (nominal) per capita, http://en.wikipedia.org/wiki/List_of_countries_by_GDP_(nominal)_per_capita (accessed March 5, 2008). Figures (in U.S. dollars) are estimates for 2007 from *The World Factbook* provided by the Central Intelligence Agency (updated February 12, 2008). These figures do not take into account cost-of-living differences; using additional economic data is advisable when making country comparisons.
6. Ibid.
7. U.S. Department of State, "Background Note: Switzerland," as of March 2007, http://www.state.gov/r/pa/ei/bgn/3204.htm (accessed May 9, 2007).
8. U.S. Department of State, "Background Note: Switzerland."
9. U.S. Census Bureau, "*IDB: Countries and Areas Ranked by Population*," as of 2007, http://www.census.gov/cgi-bin/ipc/idbrank.pl (accessed January 16, 2008).
10. CIA the World Factbook, "Switzerland."
11. U.S. Department of State, "Background Note: Switzerland."
12. CIA the World Factbook, "Switzerland."
13. U.S. Department of State, "Background Note: Switzerland."
14. CIA the World Factbook, "Switzerland."
15. Country Calling Codes, http://www.countrycallingcodes.com (accessed June 15, 2007).
16. U.S. Naval Observatory, "What is Universal Time," as of October 30, 2003, http://aa.usno.navy.mil/faq/docs/UT (accessed May 9, 2007).
17. Foreign Exchange, *The Commercial Appeal*, June 13, 2007, C4.
18. Paul Dray, *Switzerland: Public Behaviour* (Executive Planet). http://www.executiveplanet.com/index.php?title=switzerland
19. Michael Powell, *Behave Yourself! The Essential Guide to International Etiquette* (Guilford, CT: The Globe Pequot Press, 2005), 122; Terri Morrison and Wayne A. Conaway, *Kiss, Bow, or Shake Hands*, 2nd ed. (Avon, MA: Adams Media, 2006), 493.
20. Morrison and Conaway, *Kiss, Bow, or Shake Hands*, 493–494.

21. Paul Dray, *Switzerland: First Name or Title* (Executive Planet), http://www.executiveplanet.com/index.php?title=Switzerland:_First_Name_or _Titlte%3F (accessed August 18, 2007).
22. Morrison and Conaway, *Kiss, Bow, or Shake Hands*, 492.
23. Carol Turkington, *The Complete Idiot's Guide to Cultural Etiquette* (Indianapolis, IN: Alpha Books, 1999), 146.
24. Morrison and Conaway, *Kiss, Bow, or Shake Hands*, 493.
25. Dray, *Switzerland: Prosperous Entertaining-Part1* (Executive Planet). http://www.executiveplanet.com/index.php?title=switzerland.
26. Morrison and Conaway, *Kiss, Bow, or Shake Hands*, 493.
27. Dray, *Switzerland: Cuisine, Wine and Toasts* (Executive Planet). http://www.executiveplanet.com/index.php?title=switzerland.
28. Morrison and Conaway, *Kiss, Bow, or Shake Hands*, 493.
29. Dray, *Switzerland: Cuisine, Wine and Toasts.*
30. Morrison and Conaway, *Kiss, Bow, or Shake Hands*, 494.
31. Turkington, *The Complete Idiot's Guide to Cultural Etiquette*, 150.
32. Richard D. Lewis, *When Cultures Collide: Leading Across Cultures* (Boston: Nicholas Brealey International, 2006), 219.
33. Morrison and Conaway, *Kiss, Bow, or Shake Hands*, 494; Turkington, *The Complete Idiot's Guide to Cultural Etiquette*, 149.
34. Ann Marie Sabath, *International Business Etiquette: Europe* (Franklin Lakes, NJ: Career Press, 1999), 290.
35. Lewis, *When Cultures Collide: Leading Across Cultures*, 242.
36. Morrison and Conaway, *Kiss, Bow, or Shake Hands*, 490.
37. Ibid., 485.
38. Dray, *Switzerland: Guidelines for Business Dress* (Executive Planet). http://www.executiveplanet.com/index.php?title=switzerland.
39. Morrison and Conaway, *Kiss, Bow, or Shake Hands*, 494.
40. Ibid., 487.
41. Turkington, *The Complete Idiot's Guide to Cultural Etiquette*, 144.
42. Lewis, *When Cultures Collide: Leading Across Cultures*, 242.
43. Powell, *Behave Yourself: The Essential Guide to International Etiquette*, 123.
44. Ibid.
45. Morrison and Conaway, *Kiss, Bow, or Shake Hands*, 493.
46. *CultureGrams, Europe, Switzerland* (Ann Arbor, MI: ProQuest CSA, 2008), 696.
47. *CultureGrams, Concepts and Terminology* (Ann Arbor, MI: ProQuest CSA, 2008), A-14.
48. U.S. Department of State, "Background Note: Switzerland."
49. Sabath, *International Business Etiquette: Europe*, 293.
50. Powell, *Behave Yourself! The Essential Guide to International Etiquette*, 123.
51. Dray, *Switzerland: Public Behaviour* (Executive Planet).
52. Nancy L. Braganti and Elizabeth Devine , *European Customs and Manners* (New York: Meadowbrook Press, 1992), 245.
53. Morrison and Conaway, *Kiss, Bow, or Shake Hands*, 494.
54. Dray, *Switzerland: Public Behaviour* (Executive Planet).
55. *CultureGrams, Europe, Switzerland*, 694.
56. Roger E. Axtell, *Gestures: The Do's and Taboos of Body Language around the World* (New York: John Wiley & Sons, 1998), 157–158.
57. *CultureGrams, Europe, Switzerland*, 694.

58. Lewis, *When Cultures Collide: Leading Across Cultures*, 240.
59. *CultureGrams, Europe, Switzerland*, 694.
60. Braganti and Devine, *European Customs and Manners*, 246–247.
61. Ibid., 252.
62. Ibid.

CHAPTER 21

Taiwan

Taiwan, officially the Republic of China, is the tenth largest export market of the United States. When both exports and imports are considered, Taiwan is the ninth largest trading partner of the United States.[1]

The United States exports the following product categories to Taiwan: agricultural products, petroleum products, steelmaking materials, metals, finished metal shapes, wood products, plastics, chemicals, industrial supplies, mineral suppliers, generators, electrical apparatus, metalworking machine tools, instruments, industrial machines, photo machinery, electronics, laboratory instruments, medical equipment, aircraft, vehicles and parts, pharmaceuticals, and military items.[2]

COUNTRY SPECIFICS

Location, Topography, and Land Mass

Taiwan is located in Eastern Asia and is an island bordering the East China Sea, the Philippine Sea, the South China Sea, and the Taiwan Strait. The country is north of the Philippines and is on the southeastern coast of China. The eastern two-thirds of the country is mountainous, with gently rolling plains in the west. Taiwan experiences frequent earthquakes. In addition to air and water pollution, low levels of radiation from radioactive waste disposal are problems that visitors to the country will encounter.[3] The capital of Taiwan is Taipei. The area of Taiwan is 13,892 square miles or 35,980 square kilometers.

Economy

Taiwan is one of the Asian Tigers. Taiwan has a capitalistic economy, with decreasing guidance from the government on investments and foreign trade. Industrialization has made Taiwan an export country with trade surpluses; the country has the world's third-largest foreign reserve. China is Taiwan's largest export market; Hong Kong is second, and the United States third. After Japan, China is the second-largest importer from Taiwan. China is also Taiwan's destination for foreign direct investment.

Unemployment in Taiwan is below 4 percent. The Gross Domestic Product (GDP) per capita is $16,243.[4] Services make up 73.3 percent of the GDP, industry accounts for 25.2 percent, and agriculture comprises 1.5 percent. The economic infrastructure is very good in Taiwan.[5]

Population, Languages Spoken, Ethnic Groups, and Religions

The population of Taiwan was estimated at 22.9 million in 2007.[6] Mandarin Chinese is the official language; in addition, Taiwanese (Min) and the Hakka languages are spoken. The Taiwanese, including the *Hakka*, make up 84 percent of the population; mainland Chinese make up 14 percent of the population; and other indigenous peoples account for 2 percent.

Although Taiwan does not have an official religion, most of the people, 93 percent, practice a mixture of Buddhism, Confucianism, and Taoism; 4.5 percent are Christian; and 2.5 percent belong to other religions.[7] Buddhism and Confucianism are actually ways of life and are not technically religions because they have no deity. Religious freedom is guaranteed in Taiwan.

Country Codes, Time Zones, and Currency

The country code for Taiwan is 886. City codes include 7 for Kaohsiung, 6 for Tainan, and 2 for Taipei. When calling from the United States to Taipei, for example, dial the International Access Code (011), followed by the country code (886), the city code (2), and the local telephone number. [8]

Taiwan is 13 hours ahead of U.S. Eastern Standard Time. This means that when it is 8 AM in New York, it is 9 PM in Taiwan. In Universal Time the times would be written according to the 24-hour clock as 0800 and 2100, respectively. Daylight Saving Time is not observed in Taiwan.[9]

The Taiwan dollar is pegged to the U.S. dollar. The symbol for the Taiwan dollar is the U.S. NT$ (NT$12.55, for example). A currency converter is available at http://coinmill.com/AED_calculator.html that will convert any currency in the world into any other currency.

BUSINESS AND SOCIAL CUSTOMS

Greetings, Introductions, and Business Cards

A common greeting is to ask you if you have eaten (*Chyr bau le meiyou?*). The greeting comes from a tradition of never allowing anyone to go hungry. The polite response is to say that you have eaten even if you have not. "How are you?" (*Ni hau ma?*) is a common greeting and is more formal. Other greetings include "Hello" (*Ni hau*), "Morning" (*Zao*), or "Please sit" (*Ching tzuo*) when greeting visitors to your home. After these greetings, polite everyday questions will follow—inquiries about health and family.[10]

Taiwanese names are listed with the family name first, followed by the given name. When you do not know them, address the Taiwanese by their entire name: surname first, followed by their title, such as Kim Young Sheng (Mr. Kim) or *chie* for females. If the individual has an official title, such as General, Governor, President, or Committee Member, his or her title would be used instead of Mr., Mrs., or Miss. Many times a Taiwanese person will adopt a Western name for Western colleagues. Women maintain their maiden name when they marry.

During introductions the Taiwanese nod their heads and smile. Shaking hands is also common in business and for formal occasions. Bowing slightly shows respect. Friends will grasp each other's hands as a sign of warmth and hospitality.[11]

Business cards should be exchanged with everyone you meet, so bring a large supply. The card should be presented with both hands and turned so that the receiver can read the print. The card should have English on one side and the Mandarin Chinese translation on the other side. Use a translator who knows Taiwan Mandarin, as the characters are not the same as mainland China's characters.[12] Not exchanging a business card would be seen as rude. Receiving a business card is an honor; therefore, you should refrain from casually putting the card in your pocket.[13] Use a nice business card holder for the cards you receive. If you are in a meeting, put the cards in front of you on the table so that you can refer to them.

Business Entertaining and Seating Customs

Whoever issues the invitation to dine at a restaurant is expected to pay. While a guest may offer to pay, the guest should not insist.[14] Business entertaining can go on into the night, so you may not want to start your appointments until late in the morning. Leaving an evening of entertainment early because you have an early appointment the next day is rude.

Business is not discussed during meals unless the host starts the discussion. Chitchat about families, food, and culture are polite during meals. If hosting a business dinner, it is polite to invite the wives of the businessmen you are entertaining. When hosting a large banquet, you would pay for it before it is held or before the meal ends. As business entertaining tends to run late, you can become very tired after a few days. Since business entertaining and dining are very important for building relationships, you should accept all invitations that are extended to you. If you must decline an invitation, give a good reason so that the person issuing the invitation does not lose face.[15]

In a Taiwanese group the highest-ranking person sits in the middle, with the second-ranking person at his right and the third-ranking person at his left. People of equal rank will be seated across from each other.[16]

Dining, Toasting, and Tipping Customs

If you are entertained in a Taiwanese home, expect dinner conversation related to the meal. Common foods include rice, soup, seafood, pork, chicken, vegetables, fruits, and noodles. Dessert is usually fresh fruit.[17] Chopsticks and a spoon for soup are the eating utensils you will be provided. Remember that chopsticks should never be placed across the rice bowl as this is viewed as bad luck.

The host will indicate when everyone is to begin serving themselves. Many courses will be served, so it is best to take only a small amount of each item. If you are hosting the meal, you may want your Taiwanese associate to order the food to be sure the correct amount of food and the proper numbers of courses are ordered. The food will typically be placed on a revolving Lazy Susan in the middle of the table. Be sure you do not pick up any food with the ends of the chopsticks you are using for eating; it is permissible to use the other ends of your chopsticks to place food from the serving dishes onto your plate.[18]

Cocktails are not usually served before meals. Toasting is generally done with *Shao-Hsing* wine and can be served warm or cold. You should hold the glass with both hands when toasting. Some of the toasts are *Gahn bay* (dry cup), *Sway byen* (as you wish), or *Sway yi* (drink whatever you wish). If you are toasted, nod your head to indicate that you accept the toast. The host generally begins the toasting; however, there is no set order as to who may toast when.[19]

Tipping is optional in many situations in Taiwan. Taxi drivers receive the change from your fare and NT$30 per each bag that they help with. Porters receive NT$80 per bag, hotel maid receives NT$100; the concierge also receives NT$100. Generally a 10 percent service charge will be added to your restaurant charges; however, if it is not added, you should leave 10 percent or more if the service is good.

Gift-Giving Customs

Gifts are exchanged using both hands and are not opened in the presence of the giver. You should not admire objects too much or the owner will feel he/she needs to give it to you as a gift.[20] Be prepared to give a gift if you receive one. Expect gifts to be refused, but continue to offer the gift until it is accepted.[21]

If invited to someone's home, give the person fruit, cookies, candy, or specialty tea. Flowers, clocks, watches, and handkerchiefs are not given as gifts. Gifts should not be expensive, as the receiver will feel it is necessary to reciprocate with a gift of like value.[22] Popular business gifts include scotch, subscriptions to *National Geographic* or *Reader's Digest*, a signed baseball, or nice pen sets. In Taiwan the business gifts are given to the individual rather than to the firm.[23]

Use red, gold, pink, or yellow wrapping paper for your gifts and avoid black and white gift wrap. Since there are lots of superstitions around numbers, the number of gifts you give could be important. Gifts of four or 13 are considered unlucky; gifts that are in sixes or eights are considered lucky.[24]

If you are an employer in Taiwan, it is important to know that red envelopes with bonuses are mandated by law to be given to employees prior to the Chinese New Year, the Dragon Boat Festival, and the Moon Festival.[25]

Business Meetings

A letter of introduction is advantageous to getting an appointment. Several trips are necessary because you have to build a relationship before the Taiwanese will want to do business with you. It is also best if there is a group with at least one senior executive from your firm. Send your presentation or proposal ahead of time if possible so that it can be translated before the meeting. Be prepared for very detailed questions to be asked. When the Taiwanese say "yes," they probably mean that they are listening rather than that they understand or that they agree with you. Further, the word "no" is considered rude and is never used.[26] Seating at a business meeting is generally done so that the guest of honor faces the door.[27]

Business meetings will begin with the formal greetings, followed by coffee or tea and chitchat. The Taiwanese will indicate when it is time to start the business discussion. Money issues should not be discussed first. Because the Taiwanese believe in the good of the whole, it will not be unusual for contracts to be renegotiated when changes occur. In other words, a contract is never final. Since your seal, or chop, is considered the official signature, it would be a good idea to get your own chop with which to seal agreements.[28]

Many times before beginning a construction project, a *feng-shui* man has to be consulted. He makes sure that the design, entrances, and the like are placed in harmony with the environment. Senior executives may wait for one of the lucky days of astrology or geomancy to make a decision.[29] In Taiwan business decisions tend to be made by one individual rather than the group.[30]

The Taiwanese are very business oriented and will expect you to work 12 to 15 hours per day while you are there as they will do the same. The Taiwanese believe that the professional life comes first and the personal life second.

Dress and Appearance

Ethnic clothing is reserved for special occasions. Western-style business clothing is worn in Taiwan. The business clothing styles will be conservative in cut and colors. Your personal appearance should be neat and clean. Men tend to wear suits and ties, and women wear skirts or pantsuits.[31] As red and gold are worn during festivals, these colors should not be worn for business. Women should wear comfortable shoes; high-heeled shoes are not recommended as there are many potholes and cracks in the sidewalks. Women should not wear revealing clothing.[32] Shoes are typically removed when entering someone's home.

Holidays

The Chinese New Year is celebrated with fireworks, feasts, worship, and ancestor remembrance. Businesses tend to close during this time period, so it is not a good time to try to conduct business in Taiwan. However, it would be a good time to build a relationship by participating in the celebration. The Chinese New Year varies from year to year because it is based on the lunar calendar; however, it is generally slated in early spring. The other major holidays include the following.[33]

- Republic of China's Founding Day (January 1)
- Chinese Lunar New Year (January/February)
- Lantern Festival (February 6)

- Memorial Day (February 28)
- Youth Day (March 29)
- Tomb Sweeping Day (April 5); anniversary of Chiang Kai-shek's death
- Dragon Boat Festival (late May/mid-June; the fifth day of the fifth lunar month)
- Confucius' Birthday and Teacher's Day (September 28)
- Mid-Autumn Moon Festival (September/October)
- Double Ten National Day (October 10)
- Taiwan Restoration Day (October 25)
- Chiang Kai-shek's Birthday (October 31)
- Dr. Sun Yat-sen's Birthday (November 12)
- Constitution Day (December 25)

Conversational Customs

Visiting with others is very much a part of the Taiwanese culture. Before making a visit to someone's home, you are expected to give advance notice.[34] Good conversational topics include information about your family, hobbies, the area you are from, or food. It is acceptable to talk about the People's Republic of China and Taiwan's independence. You may be asked personal questions.[35] If you are complimented, you should refuse the compliment modestly.[36]

Humor

Chinese proverbs and parables are used to convey humor. Because humor does not cross cultural boundaries easily, avoid humor when making business presentations. If you feel a humorous story is needed, choose one about husband-wife relationships or youth and old age. Restaurant jokes or stories about golfers are also appropriate. Humor related to sex, government leaders, or politics should not be used. Most humor in one culture is incomprehensible in another culture.[37]

Attitude toward Women in Business

Taiwan is not listed in the Human Development Index (HDI), which is a measure of empowerment; it is based on life expectancy, literacy, infant mortality, and real GDP. The assumption is that societies that provide an opportunity for education, access to healthcare, and adequate wages are inclined to be more democratic and exhibit a respect for human rights. There have been problems in Taiwan with women and children, mainly from Vietnam, being trafficked for forced labor and sexual exploitation. Most of the foreign workers from Vietnam, Thailand, and the Philippines are legally recruited for low-skill jobs. Sexual exploitation trafficking of Taiwanese women to Japan has also been reported. Taiwan is on the Tier 2 Watch list for human trafficking of forced labor and sexual servitude.[38]

The Taiwanese should be informed ahead of time if one of your team members is a woman as Taiwanese women are still not represented in a number of professional positions in that country.[39] However, there are more professional businesswomen in Taiwan than in China. If a businesswoman invites a Taiwanese businessman to dinner, she should pay for the meal even though the businessman will offer to pay.[40]

Public Behavior

The Taiwanese are reserved, quiet, generous, and friendly. The concept of saving face is very important to them. You should never make a scene in public nor cause another person to be embarrassed. The Taiwanese also do not acknowledge others, smile, or engage in conversation in public with those they do not know.[41] A person's actions reflect on the entire family. Good social and family relationships are important in this society.

Other public behaviors considered inappropriate in Taiwan include showing affection to members of the opposite gender and eating while walking down the street.[42] In addition, when offering criticism, do so without being abrupt or excessively frank. Offer criticism subtly and with humor.[43]

NONVERBAL COMMUNICATION

Gestures and Posture

Understanding the meanings of gestures in Taiwan will make communicating with the Taiwanese easier. When pointing, use the open hand, rather than the index finger. To beckon someone, extend and contract your fingers, palm down. Never put an arm around someone's shoulders nor touch someone on the head. If a person is shaking a hand from side to side with the palm forward, the person is saying "no." While seated, place your hands in your lap. When giving an object to another person, use both hands. Touching your nose during conversation indicates that you are speaking about yourself. Treat the elderly with great respect, including standing when they enter a room and opening doors for them.[44] A gesture that is somewhat unusual is the writing of a character in the air while explaining the meaning of the character.

Good posture when seated is important. Men should sit straight with both feet on the floor. Women should also sit straight, but they may cross their legs at the ankles or knees.[45]

Eye Contact and Facial Expressions

Minimum eye contact is important, particularly with those who are your senior. Eye contact is minimized by looking away.[46] Emotions should be controlled; do not let your facial expressions reveal your true feelings.[47] Winking at others is impolite.[48] The Taiwanese smile readily; however, the smile could have many meanings, including happiness, embarrassment, attentiveness, or something else.

Space and Touch

People stand within touching distance while conversing and often touch each other on the arm or shoulder while talking.[49] Young girls often hold hands while walking down the street. The head is sacred and should not be touched. Do not use your feet to move an object, as it is considered rude to touch items with your feet, which are considered the dirtiest part of the body. While they generally do not like to be touched by strangers, the Taiwanese will often push and shove when in a crowd.[50]

Punctuality and Attitude toward Time

While you are expected to be on time for meetings, the Taiwanese are flexible about meeting and appointment times. Thus, you should not be offended when they are late. If you know you are going to be delayed, call your Taiwanese hosts to let them know why you will be late.[51]

TRAVEL TIPS

- Passports are required and must be valid for six months from the date of entry. Visas are required for more than a 30-day stay.
- October is a busy month for hotels, and it can be difficult to get a room during this time unless you book your reservation well in advance. When making hotel reservations, check to confirm that the hotel provides Western-style bathroom facilities. Otherwise, you may find that the facilities consist of a flat commode in the floor over which you must squat.
- Luggage may be opened for inspection after clearing security. If you do not agree to such inspections, your luggage may not be put on the plane.[52]
- Visitors may be interested in certain facts about Taiwan. Taiwan was ceded to Japan in 1895 and then returned to Chinese control after World War II.

In 1949, two million Nationalists fled to Taiwan and established their own government separately from China. China has never recognized Taiwan as a separate country and continues to work for reunification.[53] Another important fact is that the Taiwanese refer to the People's Republic of China as Mainland China, and you should also.

- Use public transportation or a taxi for city travel and chauffeured limousines or rental cars for longer trips.
- Pedestrians should be aware that the numerous scooters can be dangerous as their drivers often drive on the wrong side of the street; it is not unusual for as many as five people to crowd onto the same scooter.[54]
- Visitors to Taiwan during the Chinese New Year will observe that the holiday is celebrated with visits and gifts. Money is given to children in red envelopes, and adults receive gifts of smoked ham, dried duck, fruit, or nuts. The Dragon Boat Festival is in honor of Chu-Yuan's death; the expatriate community participates in the Dragon Boat races.[55]
- Be prepared for the loud noises associated with fireworks; the Taiwanese enjoy shooting off fireworks. Also be prepared for the frequent earthquakes.[56]
- Babies are considered one year of age at birth.[57]
- Drink bottled water while in Taiwan because of water pollution.
- Numbers to call in case of emergencies include 110 for police and 119 for an ambulance or for the fire department.
- Food sold on the streets may not be safe for foreigners to eat due to a lack of sanitary handling of the food during preparation.
- Diplomatic representation for Taiwan, such as Embassies, does not exist in the United States. You may contact the following agencies for additional information about Taiwan; they unofficially maintain commercial and cultural relations with the United States: The Taipei Economic and Cultural Representative Office, 4201 Wisconsin Avenue, NW, Washington, D.C. 20016-2137 (202-895-1800) and the American Institute in Taiwan, Washington Headquarters, Suite 1700, 1700 North Moore Street, Arlington, VA 22209 (703-525-8474).[58]

NOTES

1. U.S. Census Bureau, "Foreign Trade Statistics," http://www.census.gov/foreign-trade/statistics/highlights/top/top0612.html (accessed March 4, 2008).
2. Ibid.
3. CIA the World Factbook, "Taiwan," as of June 19, 2007, https://www.cia.gov/library/publications/the-world-factbook/geos/my.html (accessed June 25, 2007).
4. List of countries by GDP (nominal) per capita, http://en.wikipedia.org/wiki/List_of_countries_by_GDP_(nominal)_per_capita (accessed March 5, 2008). Figures (in U.S. dollars) are estimates for 2007 from *The World Factbook* provided by the Central Intelligence Agency (updated February 12, 2008). These figures do not take into

account cost-of-living differences; using additional economic data is advisable when making country comparisons.

5. Ibid.

6. U.S. Census Bureau, "*IDB: Countries and Areas Ranked by Population*," as of 2007, http://www.census.gov/cgi-bin/ipc/idbrank.pl (accessed January 16, 2008).

7. Ibid.

8. Country Calling Codes, http://www.countrycallingcodes.com (accessed June 15, 2007).

9. U.S. Naval Observatory, "What is Universal Time," as of October 30, 2003, http://aa.usno.navy.mil/faq/docs/UT (accessed May 9, 2007).

10. *CultureGrams, Asia, Taiwan* (Ann Arbor, MI: ProQuest CSA, 2008), 702.

11. Ibid.; Carol Turkington, *The Complete Idiot's Guide to Cultural Etiquette* (Indianapolis, IN: Alpha Books, 1999), 217; Mary Murray Bosrock, *Put Your Best Foot Forward: Asia* (St. Paul, MN: International Education Systems, 1997), 468–469.

12. Terri Morrison and Wayne A. Conaway, *Kiss, Bow, or Shake Hands*, 2nd ed. (Avon, MA: Adams Media, 2006), 502.

13. Lillian H. Chaney and Jeanette S. Martin, *Intercultural Business Communication*, 4th ed. (Upper Saddle River, NJ: Pearson/Prentice Hall, 2007), 178; Ann Marie Sabath, *International Business Etiquette: Asia & The Pacific Rim* (New York: ASJA Press, 2002), 173.

14. *CultureGrams, Asia, Taiwan*, 703.

15. Elizabeth Devine and Nancy L. Braganti, *The Travelers' Guide to Asian Customs and Manners* (New York: St. Martin's Griffin, 1998), 273; Sabath, *International Business Etiquette: Asia & The Pacific Rim*, 173.

16. Devine and Braganti, *The Travelers' Guide to Asian Customs and Manners*, 272; Sabath, *International Business Etiquette: Asia & The Pacific Rim*, 174, 179.

17. *CultureGrams, Asia, Taiwan*, 703.

18. Sabath, *International Business Etiquette: Asia & The Pacific Rim*, 174.

19. Devine and Braganti, *The Travelers' Guide to Asian Customs and Manners*, 264.

20. *CultureGrams, Asia, Taiwan*, 703.

21. Sabath, *International Business Etiquette: Asia & The Pacific Rim*, 176.

22. Devine and Braganti, *The Travelers' Guide to Asian Customs and Manners*, 270.

23. Ibid., 273; Sabath, *International Business Etiquette: Asia & The Pacific Rim*, 177.

24. Sabath, *International Business Etiquette: Asia & The Pacific Rim*, 177.

25. Ibid.

26. Devine and Braganti, *The Travelers' Guide to Asian Customs and Manners*, 271.

27. Ibid., 265.

28. Sabath, *International Business Etiquette: Asia & The Pacific Rim*, 178.

29. Devine and Braganti, *The Travelers' Guide to Asian Customs and Manners*, 272; Turkington, *The Complete Idiot's Guide to Cultural Etiquette*, 215.

30. Sabath, *International Business Etiquette: Asia & The Pacific Rim*, 181.

31. *CultureGrams, Asia, Taiwan*, 702.

32. Devine and Braganti, *The Travelers' Guide to Asian Customs and Manners*, 263.

33. *CultureGrams, Asia, Taiwan*, 704; Devine and Braganti, *TheTravelers' Guide to Asian Customs and Manners*, 265; Sabath, *International Business Etiquette: Asia & The Pacific Rim*, 171.

34. *CultureGrams, Asia, Taiwan* , 703.

35. Devine and Braganti, *The Travelers' Guide to Asian Customs and Manners*, 260.

36. Ibid., 261.
37. Roger E. Axtell, *Do's and Taboos of Humor Around the World* (New York: John Wiley & Sons, 1999), 77–78; Richard D. Lewis, *When Cultures Collide: Leading Across Cultures*, 3rd ed. (Boston: Nicholas Brealey International, 2006), 12–13.
38. CIA the World Factbook, "Taiwan."
39. Sabath, *International Business Etiquette: Asia & The Pacific Rim*, 180.
40. Bosrock, *Put Your Best Foot Forward: Asia*, 488.
41. Sabath, *International Business Etiquette: Asia & The Pacific Rim*, 175.
42. *CultureGrams, Asia, Taiwan*, 702.
43. Devine and Braganti, *The Travelers' Guide to Asian Customs and Manners*, 261.
44. *CultureGrams, Asia, Taiwan*, 703; Turkington, *The Complete Idiot's Guide to Cultural Etiquette*, 217; Bosrock, *Put Your Best Foot Forward: Asia*, 471.
45. Chaney and Martin, *Intercultural Business Communication*, 135.
46. Ibid.
47. Sabath, *International Business Etiquette: Asia & The Pacific Rim*, 176.
48. *CultureGrams, Asia, Taiwan*, 703.
49. Ibid.
50. Devine and Braganti, *The Travelers' Guide to Asian Customs and Manners*, 261–262.
51. Chaney and Martin, *Intercultural Business Communication*, 135.
52. Devine and Braganti, *The Travelers' Guide to Asian Customs and Manners*, 276.
53. CIA the World Factbook, "Taiwan."
54. Michael Powell, *Behave Yourself! The Essential Guide to International Etiquette* (Guilford, CT: The Globe Pequot Press, 2005), 126.
55. Devine and Braganti, *The Travelers' Guide to Asian Customs and Manners*, 274.
56. Powell, *Behave Yourself! The Essential Guide to International Etiquette*, 126.
57. Ibid.
58. U.S. Department of State, "Background Note: Taiwan," as of April 2007, http://www.state.gov/r/pa/ei/bgn/35855.htm (accessed May 9, 2007).

CHAPTER 22

United Kingdom

The United Kingdom (UK) is the fifth largest export market of the United States. When both exports and imports are considered, the UK is the sixth largest trading partner of the United States.[1]

The United States exports goods to the United Kingdom in the following categories: agricultural products, fuel oil, petroleum products, nuclear fuel materials, steelmaking machinery, metals, precious metals, wood products, plastics, mineral supplies, tapes (audio and video), industrial supplies, generators, electrical apparatus, oilfield equipment, excavating machinery, industrial engines, metalworking machine tools, material handling equipment, industrial machines, photo machinery, electronics, laboratory instruments, medical equipment, aircraft, marine engines, vehicles and parts, apparel, pharmaceuticals, books, toiletries, art supplies, furniture, appliances, toys, jewelry, gem diamonds, and military items.[2]

COUNTRY SPECIFICS

A country's location, topography, economy, and population provide insight into understanding its culture. In addition, knowledge of ethnic groups, religions, time zones, and currency is helpful.

Location, Topography, and Land Mass

The United Kingdom is located in Western Europe and occupies the northern one-sixth of the island of Ireland plus the main island of Great Britain (which includes England, Scotland, and Wales). The country is located northwest of France with the North Atlantic Ocean to the west, the North Sea to the east, Scotland to the north, and the English Channel to the south. The capital of the United Kingdom is London.

In terms of topography, 50 percent of the land is meadows and pastures; the remainder is rolling hills and cliffs. The climate is temperate; however, the weather changes very quickly from rain to sun, but the islands have few extreme temperature days.[3]

The country is slightly smaller than Oregon at 94,247 square miles or 244,820 square kilometers.

Economy

In Western Europe the United Kingdom is a leading financial center and trading partner. The per capita Gross Domestic Product (GDP) is $40,674.[4] Major markets for UK exports are the United States and the European Union (EU); the UK's major imports are from the United States, the EU, and Japan.[5]

During the last 20 years, the government has decreased public ownership and social welfare programs. Agriculture is very efficient, producing 60 percent of the country's food using less than 2 percent of the labor force. Energy production accounts for 10 percent of the GDP. Services account for the largest share of the GDP: banking, insurance, and business services. Thus, industry is decreasing in importance as a percentage of GDP. Inflation, interest rates, and unemployment remain low in the United Kingdom.[6]

Population, Languages Spoken, Ethnic Groups, and Religions

The population of the United Kingdom is approximately 60.8 million people, with a growth rate of .275 percent. The population is the third largest in the EU and the twenty-first largest in the world. The capital of London is the largest city in Europe, with a very dense population. People of the UK are called Britons or British.

English is the official language. Welsh is the language spoken in Wales; Gaelic is spoken in Northern Ireland; and a Scottish form of Gaelic is spoken in Scotland.[7] The United Kingdom is made up of Wales, Scotland, England, and Northern Ireland. While all of the people of the UK are known as British, the people of Wales are also known as Welsh, in Scotland as Scottish, in England as English, and in Northern Ireland as Irish.

The white population comprises 92.1 percent of the population. The remaining 7.9 percent is made up of blacks (2 percent), Indians (1.8 percent), Pakistanis (1.3 percent), and people whose background is mixed or who are members of other ethnic groups (2.8 percent).[8] In addition, Arabs from many countries live in, work in, or visit London.

While the Church of England and the Church of Scotland are the official churches in the UK, most world religions are represented in this country. Christians make up 71.6 percent of the population, Muslims 2.7 percent, Hindus 1 percent, and other religions 1.6 percent. Almost one-quarter, or 23 percent, of the population professes no religious affiliation.[9]

Country Codes, Time Zones, and Currency

The country code for the United Kingdom is 44. City codes include 121 for calls to Birmingham, 151 for Liverpool, 171 for inner London, 181 for outer London, and 161 for Manchester. When calling from the United States to Manchester, for example, dial the International Access Code (011), followed by the country code (44), the city code (161), and the local telephone number. [10]

Time in the United Kingdom is five hours ahead of U.S. Eastern Standard Time. Thus, when it is 4 PM in New York, it is 9 PM in the United Kingdom. In Universal Time the times would be written according to the 24-hour clock as 1600 and 2100, respectively. Daylight Saving Time is observed in the UK.[11]

The national currency of the United Kingdom is the British *pound* (£), commonly called "quid." People of the United Kingdom have not been interested in changing their currency from the *pound* to the *euro*. A currency converter is available at http://coinmill.com/AED_calculator.html that will convert any currency in the world into any other currency.

BUSINESS AND SOCIAL CUSTOMS

Greetings, Introductions, and Business Cards

When planning a meeting for the first time, the meeting should be arranged through a third party.[12] This first meeting should be between the top members of both companies.

When you are first introduced, last names will be used. After you meet with the British a few times, first names will be common. But wait for them to give you permission to use their first names. When writing UK names, do not use the middle initial. Also do not use periods after Mr, Mrs, Ms, or Dr. Also, when you first meet, jackets and ties will be worn, but the jackets will be removed and sleeves rolled up after they get to know you.[13]

The common greeting in the United Kingdom is, "How do you do?" The British will then shake hands. The handshake is not a firm grip; eye contact is maintained during the handshake. When the handshake stops, the eye contact is broken. Women may or may not shake your hand. "Sir" will precede the name of someone who has been knighted by the Queen. The person would then be addressed using "Sir" and the first name, such as "Sir Harry." The title "Doctor" is only used to refer to medical doctors in Scotland; however, in the rest of the United Kingdom the title "Doctor" is used to refer to either an M.D. or to someone with a doctorate.

Business cards are written in English and are normally exchanged at the end of a meeting.[14] Business cards should include titles; however, there is no specific ritual for business card exchange.[15]

Business Entertaining and Seating Customs

Business entertaining in England is more likely to be done in restaurants, while in Scotland entertaining is done at the host's home. While it is appropriate for a woman to invite a businessman to dinner, the spouse should also be invited. Lunch meetings are a more acceptable practice, and a woman may invite a businessman to lunch without his wife. You are expected to keep your hands on the table at all times during the meal.[16] Business associates do not invite each other out for breakfast, lunch, or dinner until they know each other fairly well.[17]

The host and hostess will be seated at opposite ends of the table. The most important male guest will be seated to the right of the hostess, and the most important female guest will be seated at the right of the host.

Dining, Toasting, and Tipping Customs

The British use the Continental style of eating, with the fork in the left hand and the knife in the right. To indicate you have finished eating, you would place the fork and knife together on the plate.[18]

British food includes lots of meat and potatoes served with cooked vegetables. Tea and beer are popular drinks; however, mixed drinks or water will usually be served with only one ice cube or with no ice. Some specialties that you may want to sample include crumpets, steak and kidney pie, and Scotch eggs.

Toasting in Scotland is generally done with the national drink, which is Scotch whisky; it will be served either straight or with limestone water. The toast is generally made at the beginning of the meal. The host will say *Shlante*, which means "to your health." In England, a toast is given by the host before the meal begins; at the end of the meal a toast is offered "to the Queen."[19] Proposing a toast to those who are older than you or who are your senior is inappropriate.[20]

Tipping is similar to other European countries; restaurant servers and taxi drivers are given a gratuity that is equal to 10 percent to 15 percent of the bill. Some restaurants automatically add a service charge to the bill; you would then leave an additional tip only for exceptional service.[21] Porters receive one pound per day; hotel maids receive five pounds for a stay of a few days or 10 pounds when you stay a week.[22]

Gift-Giving Customs

Gifts between business associates are not usually exchanged in the United Kingdom.[23] Christmas is the appropriate time to give a British colleague a gift. The gift could be a nice desk accessory, book, or other inexpensive item.[24] If invited for a dinner, it would be appropriate to bring a bottle of wine, chocolates, or flowers (no white lilies).[25]

Business Meetings

Scheduling business meetings in the summer is difficult because most British take their vacation during this time period.[26] Moderate behavior and emotional restraint are valued by the British. The British are self-deprecating and cynical about the world. Exaggerations and strong statements are viewed suspiciously by the British. Social status is changing from the class system to one defined by a person's education and profession.[27]

When meeting with the British, be prepared and have all necessary information with you. The British are very serious when conducting business. Telling a business associate what to do is rude; associates are more likely to take a suggestion.[28]

British negotiators will not usually make decisions at the first meeting. They will agree when possible but tend to qualify their statements. While the British may be smiling during negotiations, their smiles may be deceiving. They are tough negotiators and use charm, vagueness, humor, and understatement to disarm their adversaries. The British have many unwritten rules about what is fair when negotiating with others. While it is acceptable to be competitive, do not direct your criticism at one individual.[29]

Developing a friendship is not important for doing business in the United Kingdom.

Dress and Appearance

Business attire in the United Kingdom tends to be made of heavier fabrics and in darker colors than is typical of business dress in many countries. Formal suits are expected to be worn by both men and women in the workplace. Women tend to wear more skirted suits than trouser suits. In the United Kingdom the word "pants" refers to underwear; the term "slacks" or "trousers" is used for the outer garment. Thus, the term "pantsuit" does not convey the same image as it does in the United States. The Scottish men may wear kilts. Since striped ties reference military units in the United Kingdom, it would be best not to wear a striped tie for conducting business in that country.[30] Dress for dining out is more casual, and dress away from the office is also casual. Follow the example of your British host.[31]

Holidays

The United Kingdom celebrates fewer holidays than any of the other European countries. Those holidays include the following

- New Year's Day (January 1)
- Good Friday
- Easter Sunday and Monday
- May Day (May 1)
- Spring Bank Holiday
- Queen's Birthday (second Saturday in June)
- Late Summer Holiday
- Guy Fawkes Day (November 5)
- Remembrance Day (closest Sunday to November 11)
- Christmas (December 25)
- Boxing Day (December 26)

Northern Ireland also celebrates:

- St. Patrick's Day (March 17)
- Battle of the Boyne (July 12)

Wales also celebrates:

- Patron Saints Day
- St. David's Day (March 1)

Scotland also celebrates:

- Robert Burns Birthday (January 25)
- Remembrance Day (closest Sunday to November 11)

Conversational Customs

The British reserve is sometimes mistakenly interpreted as aloofness or unfriendliness. Respect their need for privacy; keep your distance until they indicate a desire for a personal or professional relationship. During conversations the British are not quite as straightforward as are people from the United States. They avoid being direct because they do not want to offend anyone.[32]

Topics that are appropriate for general conversation include travel, weather, outdoor activities, history, architecture, and sports. Avoid asking personal questions; this includes asking about someone's profession. In addition, do not provide personal information about yourself. Discussions about race or class should likewise be avoided. Politics or the struggles between the ethnic groups (Welsh, Irish, Scottish, and English) are also inappropriate subjects of conversation.[33] While the British will be rather formal at first, after a few encounters they will discuss children, vacations, and reminisce about themselves.[34] The British will sometimes avoid direct eye contact with the person to whom they are conversing.[35]

When meeting after work, it is considered improper to discuss business.[36] Conversation should be polite; you are expected to show interest in what the other person is saying. Try to keep the conversation moving; it is preferable to avoid lapses in the conversation.[37]

Humor

Humor is a common part of life in the United Kingdom. The British appreciate humor that is sarcastic, sexist, and self-deprecating. Humor is considered an effective weapon in British business. The British will use humor to break tension, to speed up discussions, to direct criticism, to introduce something new or out of the ordinary, or to provide a break in a very rigid conversation or negotiation. When meetings get lengthy, for example, the British will use different types of humor to keep things interesting.[38] Being able to match the British in their use of humor may result in your being able to gain their confidence. The wry sense of humor of the British is sometimes difficult to understand, but being able to laugh at yourself is very important in this country.

While the Royal Family is respected, jokes are made about them by the British; however, it would be improper for a visitor to make such jokes.[39]

Attitude toward Women in Business

On the Human Development Index (HDI), the United Kingdom ranks 18 out of 177 nations. The HDI is a measure of empowerment; it is based on life expectancy, literacy, infant mortality, and real GDP. The assumption is that societies that provide an opportunity for education, access to healthcare, and adequate wages are inclined to be more democratic and exhibit a respect for human rights. [40]

The Gender-Empowerment Measure of the HDI lists the United Kingdom as 16 out of 75 countries for the share of seats held in government by women, the number of professional women in the country, the earned income disparity between the genders, and economic independence.[41]

Women in business, like men, are expected to act professionally and to display knowledge of the business under discussion. As long as women work hard and are professional, they are respected in England.[42] While the number of women professionals still lags behind the number in the United States, the United Kingdom has had women in high-ranking positions. Prime Minister Margaret Thatcher is a good example.

Public Behavior

Since the British do not like to call attention to themselves, they converse in public using a low voice; the British do not appreciate yelling or speaking loudly. They comport themselves with dignity. The enthusiasm and effusiveness often displayed in public by Americans stand out in sharp contrast to the calm, composed demeanor of the British. Talking in public is intended to share opinions rather than to display passion about a topic. Displays of emotion, sentimentality, or criticism in public should be avoided.[43] "Please" and "thank you" should be used generously to avoid being perceived as rude. Even though your behavior in public may be offensive to the British, they are too polite to tell you or to convey their unfavorable opinion of you with a disapproving stare.

NONVERBAL COMMUNICATION

Gestures and Posture

The British do not depend on such nonverbal communication as gestures to convey their message. They tend to keep their hands at their sides rather than using them for gestures to augment the verbal message. Hands should not be placed in your pockets when carrying on a conversation.[44] Expansive gestures with your arms would be considered rude because gesturing attracts attention, which the British consider embarrassing. If you want a waiter's attention, simply lift your hand and move it like you are signing a check.[45] The "V" for victory sign is done with the palm facing outward; when used with the palm inward, it is rude and offensive. Do not point using a single finger. Tapping the nose means that what is being said is confidential.[46]

The British have very good posture. They believe they have the correct degree of formality, which is neither too formal nor too familiar.[47] The accepted posture for men when sitting is crossing their legs at the knees rather than placing one ankle across the other knee; women cross their legs at the ankles.

Eye Contact and Facial Expressions

While speaking to someone in the United Kingdom, you will have broken eye contact. Eye contact is maintained only for short periods of time; staring is considered impolite.[48]

The British are known for their stoic facial expressions because it is improper to show emotions in public. In smaller cities people will greet each other and make eye contact; however, in the large cities they generally do not make eye contact.

Space and Touch

People in the United Kingdom generally expect an arm's length of space between speakers in a conversation. They do not hug each other or slap each other on the back. The British appreciate their space and respect the space of others.[49] Closeness while talking is very uncomfortable for the British.[50] While talking with strangers is more common in the north, in big cities people do not speak to strangers. The exception is when waiting in line; strangers will often initiate conversations with people around them.[51] Although touching is uncommon, it is acceptable for a male or female friend to kiss a woman on the cheek.[52]

Punctuality and Attitude toward Time

The British are very punctual people when conducting business and believe in arriving at the meeting location at the correct time. Being a few minutes late, however, is acceptable as long as you are well prepared for the meeting. Being early is not expected. When making business appointments, it is preferable to make them months in advance.[53]

TRAVEL TIPS

- Passports are required for entry into the United Kingdom.
- Early-morning tea may be delivered to your hotel room. A Continental breakfast is included in the room price at many larger hotels.

- Plug adapters and electrical converters are needed to use small U.S. appliances.
- Always remember to walk on the left side of the sidewalks or stairs and to look to the left as well as to the right when crossing streets.
- Public transportation is very good and includes subways, trains, and buses. Taxis can be hailed on the street or summoned by telephone. Driving in the United Kingdom does not require an International Driver's License. Drivers from other countries, however, should keep in mind that the steering wheel of vehicles is on the right side and driving is on the left side of the road. Strict fines are levied for drinking and driving. Signs indicating distance will be in miles rather than in kilometers.
- The emergency number to call should you need an ambulance, the fire department, or the police is 999. British police are especially helpful and friendly and happy to help travelers with directions or other problem situations.
- Always stand when "God Save the Queen," the national anthem, is played.
- The legal age for drinking alcoholic beverages is 18.
- Get in line and await your turn; never "jump the queue" or break in line as it is considered rude.[54]
- When you are shopping in markets, do not handle vegetables or fruits; this makes store personnel unhappy as they prefer to make selections for you.
- Public toilets (also known as WCs and lavatories) are widely available and are usually clean. Have change available in case there is a small charge.
- Become acquainted with differences in terms used by Americans and the British. For example, an elevator is called a lift, an apartment is called a flat, and the subway is called the tube or the underground.
- Women should not take offense when they are called "Love" or "Dearie" by conductors and other service personnel.
- For additional information, you may contact the following: the British Embassy, 3100 Massachusetts Avenue NW, Washington, D.C. 20008 (202-588-6500), the British Tourist Authority, 551 Fifth Avenue, 7th Floor, Suite 701, New York, NY 10176 (800-462-2748), the U.S. Embassy in the UK, 24 Grosvenor Square, W1A 1AE, London (44-207-499-9000).

NOTES

1. U.S. Census Bureau, "Foreign Trade Statistics," http://www.census.gov/foreign-trade/statistics/highlights/top/top0612.html (accessed March 4, 2008).
2. U.S. Census Bureau, "Foreign Trade Statistics."
3. U.S. Department of State, "Background Note: The United Kingdom," as of February 2007, http://www.state.gov/r/pa/ei/bgn/3846.htm (accessed May 9, 2007).
4. List of countries by GDP (nominal) per capita, http://en.wikipedia.org/wiki/List_of_countries_by_GDP_(nominal)_per_capita (accessed March 5, 2008). Figures

(in U.S. dollars) are estimates for 2007 from *The World Factbook* provided by the Central Intelligence Agency (updated February 12, 2008). These figures do not take into account cost-of-living differences; using additional economic data is advisable when making country comparisons.

5. Ibid.
6. CIA the World Factbook, "United Kingdom," as of June 19, 2007, https://www.cia.gov/library/publications/the-world-factbook/geos/uk.html (accessed June 25, 2007).
7. U.S. Department of State, "Background Note: The United Kingdom."
8. CIA the World Factbook, "United Kingdom."
9. Ibid.; U.S. Department of State, "Background Note: The United Kingdom."
10. Country Calling Codes, http://www.countrycallingcodes.com (accessed June 15, 2007).
11. U.S. Naval Observatory, "What is Universal Time," as of October 30, 2003, http://aa.usno.navy.mil/faq/docs/UT (accessed May 9, 2007).
12. Carol Turkington, *The Complete Idiot's Guide to Cultural Etiquette* (Indianapolis, IN: Alpha Books, 1999), 161.
13. Richard D. Lewis, *When Cultures Collide: Leading Across Cultures*, 3rd ed. (Boston: Nicholas Brealey International, 2006), 197; James C. Scott, "Dear???: Understanding British Forms of Address," *Business Communication Quarterly*, 61 (1998): 53.
14. Ann Marie Sabath. *International Business Etiquette: Europe* (Franklin Lakes, NJ: Career Press, 1999), 85, 257.
15. Jeanette S. Martin and Lillian H. Chaney, *Global Business Etiquette* (Westport, CT: Praeger, 2006), 32.
16. Sabath, *International Business Etiquette: Europe*, 82, 87, 89, 255.
17. Terri Morrison and Wayne A. Conaway, *Kiss, Bow, or Shake Hands*, 2nd ed. (Avon, MA: Adams Media, 2006), 541.
18. *CultureGram, Europe, United Kingdom* (Ann Arbor, MI: ProQuest CSA, 2008), 759.
19. Sabath, *International Business Etiquette: Europe*, 88–89.
20. Morrison and Conaway, *Kiss, Bow, or Shake Hands*, 541.
21. *CultureGram, Europe, United Kingdom*, 759; Michael Powell, *Behave Yourself! The Essential Guide to International Etiquette* (Guilford, CT: The Globe Pequot Press, 2005), 136.
22. Sabath, *International Business Etiquette: Europe*, 87–88.
23. Turkington, *The Complete Idiot's Guide to Cultural Etiquette*, 158.
24. Sabath, *International Business Etiquette: Europe*, 85, 257.
25. *CultureGram, Europe, United Kingdom*, 758.
26. Sabath, *International Business Etiquette: Europe*, 89.
27. *CultureGram, Europe, United Kingdom*, 758.
28. Sabath, *International Business Etiquette: Europe*, 86, 258.
29. Lewis, *When Cultures Collide: Leading Across Cultures*, 198–199.
30. Sabath, *International Business Etiquette: Europe*, 81, 255.
31. *CultureGram, Europe, United Kingdom*, 758.
32. Nancy L. Braganti and Elizabeth Devine, *European Customs and Manners* (New York: Meadowbrook Press, 1992), 100.
33. Sabath, *International Business Etiquette: Europe*, 83, 256.
34. Lewis, *When Cultures Collide: Leading Across Cultures*, 197.

35. Morrison and Conaway, *Kiss, Bow, or Shake Hands*, 542.
36. Turkington, *The Complete Idiot's Guide to Cultural Etiquette*, 159.
37. Powell, *Behave Yourself! The Essential Guide to International Etiquette*, 135.
38. Lewis, *When Cultures Collide: Leading Across Cultures*, 14, 195, 197.
39. Mary M. Bosrock, *Put Your Best Foot Forward: Europe* (St. Paul, MN: International Education Systems, 1995), 461; Sabath, *International Business Etiquette: Europe*, 89.
40. *CultureGrams, Concepts and Terminology* (Ann Arbor, MI: ProQuest CSA, 2008), A-14.
41. Human Development Report 2006, http://hdr.undp.org/hdr2006/statistics/countries/ (accessed June 16, 2007).
42. Sabath, *International Business Etiquette: Europe*, 89, 259.
43. Ibid., 83–84, 256; Lewis, *When Cultures Collide: Leading Across Cultures*, 200.
44. Sabath, *International Business Etiquette: Europe*, 83–84.
45. Ibid., 260.
46. Morrison and Conaway, *Kiss, Bow, or Shake Hands*, 543.
47. Lewis, *When Cultures Collide: Leading Across Cultures*, 197.
48. Sabath, *International Business Etiquette: Europe*, 257.
49. Ibid.
50. *CultureGram, Europe, United Kingdom*, 758.
51. Powell, *Behave Yourself! The Essential Guide to International Etiquette*, 136.
52. Martin and Chaney, *Global Business Etiquette*, 67.
53. Sabath, *International Business Etiquette: Europe*, 86, 258; Lewis, *When Cultures Collide: Leading Across Cultures*, 199.
54. Lewis, *When Cultures Collide: Leading Across Cultures*, 195.

CHAPTER 23

Future U.S. Trading Partners

The United States exports over $904 billion. Total U.S. imports are about $1,670 billion, and total goods traded are almost $2,600 billion.

As U.S. companies continue to expand their international markets, it is important to examine countries that promise to be major markets for U.S. goods in the future. Four countries that are growing markets for U.S. goods include Ireland, The Republic of South Africa, the Kingdom of Thailand, and the United Arab Emirates. Information covered for each of the four countries includes country specifics, such as location, economy, population, languages, and ethnic groups; business and social customs, including greetings, dining customs, gift-giving customs, attire, and negotiating tips; and public behavior and nonverbal communication, including gestures, eye contact, and touch.

IRELAND

U.S. exports to Ireland include the following: electrical apparatus; measuring, testing, and control instruments; computers and accessories; semiconductors; medicinal equipment; civilian aircraft and engines; pharmaceutical preparations; telecommunications equipment; industrial machines; corn; animal feeds; wine; agricultural products; coals and fuels; iron and steel products; precious metals; finished metal shapes; newsprint; plastic materials; chemicals; finished textile supplies; synthetic rubber; nonmetallic minerals; mineral supplies; tapes, audio and visual; logs and lumber; generators; and metalworking machine tools.[1]

Country Specifics

Ireland shares an island with Northern Ireland. The country is bordered by the North Atlantic Ocean, Celtic Sea, Irish Sea, and North Channel.[2] The size of Ireland is 27,135 square miles or 70,280 square kilometers.[3] The capital of Ireland is Dublin.

Ireland's Gross Domestic Product (GDP) per capita is $53,467.[4] The country's economy has been growing rapidly mainly due to high-tech corporations. Tourism, textiles, chemicals, machinery, and services are all growing areas of the economy. The *euro* is the currency of the country.[5]

The population of Ireland was approximately 4.1 million in 2007.[6] The majority of the population is Celtic, with a strong Norman influence and small English minority. The main language is Irish-Gaelic, and the second language is English. The vast majority of the population, 88 percent, is Roman Catholic; 3 percent belong to the Anglican Church of Ireland; and 9 percent are of other faiths or have no religious affiliation.[7]

Business and Social Customs

The Irish greet each other with "Hello" and "How are you?" While they address friends, relatives, and acquaintances by their first names, they address others using titles and last names. A man will generally wait for a woman to extend her hand for a handshake. Handshakes are used for greetings and goodbyes. Business cards are exchanged and may be printed in English.[8]

Business lunches are more popular than dinners. Irish meals are usually informal, and the Continental style of eating is used. Generally, the host will indicate where you should sit. As Ireland is a clean-your-plate society, you should eat everything on your plate. Since beer is a favorite drink of the Irish, they may take offense if you decline without an explanation. Women are not expected to drink beer as are the men; they will usually drink juice or soda. Toasting is common, but the host should initiate the first toast. The common toast is *Slainte* ("To your health"). Tips are generally added to the bill; however, if no tip has been included, add 10 percent to 15 percent. Tipping is expected at restaurants only, not at pubs.[9]

Gift giving is not common. Extravagant gifts in particular are not advisable. If you want to give a gift, take your Irish colleagues to dinner or to the pub or give them tickets to a sporting event. If invited to someone's home, bring wine or chocolates as well as gifts for the children.[10]

Punctuality is expected for business meetings. However, this expectation of promptness does not carry over to meeting a deadline. As July and August are vacation months, these are not good months for business visits. The Irish celebrate many holidays, so be sure to check the country's holiday calendar before making a business visit.[11]

Business dress is casual in Ireland; however, as a visitor you would be expected to be more formally attired. Female executives should not wear low-cut attire for business meetings. Conservative dress and colors are recommended. The Irish will take away an impression of you based on your dress.[12]

Public Behavior and Nonverbal Communication

The Irish have a good sense of humor and enjoy laughing, telling jokes, and teasing. The Irish are people-oriented and will want to learn more about you. Thus, you can expect to be asked personal questions. During conversations with the Irish, avoid discussing religion and Irish politics. [13] Pushing other people is rude; grooming in public and eating while walking on the street are also inappropriate.

Hand gestures are not used very much during conversations.[14] The "V" for victory or peace sign is an obscene gesture and should be avoided. Since the Irish are low-contact people, they value their personal space.[15] Eye contact is maintained during conversations. The Irish find silence uncomfortable and impolite. While they expect punctuality for business, they are much more flexible when it comes to being on time for social events.

THE REPUBLIC OF SOUTH AFRICA

U.S. exports to South Africa include the following: agricultural grains; alcoholic beverages; petroleum products; agricultural equipment; iron and steel; aluminum; nonferrous metals; finished metal shapes; pulpwood; newsprint; plastic materials; chemicals; cloth; minerals; logs and lumber; glass; generators; electric apparatus; drilling and oilfield equipment; mining equipment; excavating machinery; industrial engines; metalworking machine tools; pulp and paper machinery; measuring, testing and control instruments; materials handling equipment; industrial machines; agricultural equipment; computers and accessories; semiconductors; telecommunications equipment; medicinal equipment; civilian aircraft and parts; marine engines; passenger cars; trucks and buses; pharmaceutical preparations; books; toiletries; writing and art supplies; household appliances; boats and motors; toys, games, and sporting goods; records, tapes, and disks; gem diamonds; and aircraft and engines.[16]

Country Specifics

South Africa is bordered by the Indian Ocean to the south and east, the South Atlantic Ocean to the west, and the countries of Namibia,

Botswana, Zimbabwe, and Mozambique to the north. The countries of Lesotho and Swaziland are inside of South Africa.[17] South Africa is approximately 471,445 square miles or 1,221,043 square kilometers. The capital of South Africa is Pretoria.

Health issues are a major concern in South Africa. The country lacks adequate supplies of potable water and is experiencing an HIV/AIDS epidemic that has infected approximately one-fifth of the adult population.[18]

South Africa's Gross Domestic Product per capita is $4,921. The country is the richest on the continent of Africa. The *rand* (ZAR) is the unit of currency. A wide gap exists between the income of the white and black population. Most of the country's exports are minerals, metals, platinum, gold, diamonds, chrome, and coal.[19]

The population of South Africa is 79 percent black, 9.6 percent white, 8.9 percent of mixed race, and 2.5 percent Indian. English is the language of business. While South Africans are taught in their native language through grade 7, they are taught in English during grades 8 through 12. Many languages are spoken in South Africa; there are 11 official languages. Over half of Africans (primarily whites and mixed-race persons) are Christians. Most Indians are Hindus; however, some are Muslim and others are Christians. About 20 percent of the population adheres to indigenous beliefs.[20]

Business and Social Customs

Just as there are many languages in South Africa, there are also many greetings. The greetings used in business are usually "Hello" and "Good morning." Parting phrases imply a future meeting, such as "See you." The people of South Africa shake hands upon meeting; however, the handshake differs depending upon where you are. Some people use a firm handshake, while others use a light handshake. Some people shake with only one hand; others shake with two hands. Professional titles and last names are used until you know each other well.[21] Maintaining eye contact during the handshake is important. Business cards are exchanged at the beginning of a meeting.[22]

Meetings are generally conducted during lunch or dinner. While business may be discussed at a restaurant, it is not discussed when you are invited to a person's home.[23] Generally, the Continental style of eating is used. Allow the host to indicate where you should sit.

Entertaining is an important part of doing business in South Africa. The cuisine includes a large selection of dishes from around the world as well as local delicacies. Toasts are common and vary according to the makeup of the group dining together. Tipping is not required but is generally given for excellent service.

If invited to someone's home, bring flowers, chocolates, or a bottle of wine. Gifts should not be lavish. In business it is improper to give someone a gift until you have developed a relationship with that person; otherwise, the gift may appear to be a bribe. Some of the ethnic groups will decline a gift three times before accepting it, so you need to continue to insist that they accept the gift.[24] After a relationship has been developed, a personalized gift, such as a high-quality pen or a dozen personalized golf balls, is appreciated.[25]

Letters of introduction carry a great deal of weight in setting up meetings and are instrumental in starting to do business quickly. Appointments should be scheduled one to two months in advance. When you schedule meetings, avoid the summer (from mid-December through mid-January), the week before Easter, and during Jewish holidays.[26]

Business dress is on the conservative side, with tropical-weight materials being worn most of the year. Western-style clothing is often worn for business. Men wear suits, while women wear dresses or pants. Women should avoid sleeveless or low-cut garments and should not wear expensive accessories because of problems with crime. Casual wear is very similar to what is worn in the United States.[27]

South Africans are very friendly and talkative. The term "ethnic group" should be used in place of "tribe" or "native." A lot of handshaking, handholding, and backslapping goes on with black Africans. Interrupting others when they are talking is rude.[28] Humor can be very ethnic or gender based as South Africa is a very macho-based society.

Few women hold high positions in either industry or government. Women are treated as second-class citizens. Sexual harassment is not unusual in the workplace. Women make up 41 percent of the workforce; however, they typically receive half of what their male counterparts do for the same positions. A number of laws have been passed in an attempt to bring about gender equality in the workplace.[29]

Public Behavior and Nonverbal Communication

While a brief hug or kiss may be done between friends in public, contact between the genders is not common. The feet are considered unclean by many South Africans; moving anything with your feet or touching something with your feet is rude. Since there are many Muslims and Hindus in South Africa, do not show the soles of the feet.[30] When going through a doorway, it is customary for African men to precede the women.

Hand gestures are common when South Africans are engaged in a conversation. Certain gestures, however, are rude and should be avoided. For example, pointing at someone or using the peace sign is rude. Talking with your hands in your pockets is also rude. Eye contact is very important because business is often based on trust, and giving eye contact is associated with building trust. Black businessmen will give a handshake and put an arm around your shoulder to indicate a successful meeting.[31] Punctuality is important for business; for social engagements you should be less than a half hour late. Time is viewed differently by the white and black cultures in South Africa. Blacks are more casual toward time than the whites. Overall, however, the concept of time is very Western. When arriving for an appointment, it is normal to wait up to 10 minutes, during which time you will be served coffee or tea. When it comes to deadlines, though, South Africans have a *mañana* attitude toward them.[32]

THE KINGDOM OF THAILAND

U.S. exports to Thailand include the following: agricultural grains; animal feeds; dairy products and eggs; fruits and frozen juices; vegetables; nuts; bakery products; fish and shellfish; nonagricultural foods; raw cotton; tobacco; hides and skins; petroleum products; steelmaking materials; aluminum; copper; pulpwood; newsprint; plastic material; chemicals; cloth; finished textile supplies; leather and furs; synthetic rubber; nonmetallic minerals; manufactured mineral supplies; tapes, audio and visual; logs and lumber; glass; generators; electric apparatus; drilling and oilfield equipment; excavating machinery; industrial engines; food and tobacco machinery; metalworking machine tools; sewing machines; wood; glass; plastic; pulp and paper machinery; measuring, testing, and control instruments; materials handling equipment; industrial machines; computers and accessories; semiconductors; telecommunications equipment; laboratory testing instruments; medicinal equipment; civilian aircraft and parts; passenger cars and parts; pharmaceutical preparations; toiletries and cosmetics; writing and art supplies; household appliances; toys, games, and sporting goods; jewelry and gem diamonds; and military aircraft and parts.[33]

Country Specifics

Thailand is located in Southeast Asia in the South China Sea with Malaysia to the south, Burma to the west and north, Laos to the north and east, and Cambodia to the south. The size of Thailand is 198,455 square miles or 514,000 square kilometers. The capital of Thailand is

Bangkok. Tropical diseases are common in rural areas. HIV/AIDS is a problem, with approximately 1.4 percent of the adult population infected.[34]

Thailand's Gross Domestic Product (GDP) per capita is $3,244.[35] Thailand is very export dependent, with goods and services accounting for 68.6 percent of the GDP. The Thai currency is the *baht*. Approximately 40 percent of the labor force is employed in agriculture. Thailand is the largest exporter of rice in the world. Other agricultural products that are exported include fish, tapioca, rubber, corn, sugar, pineapple, and frozen shrimp. The manufacturing area of the economy produces computers, electronics, furniture, wood products, canned food, toys, plastic products, gems, and jewelry. The United States, Japan, and China are Thailand's largest export markets. Thailand imports machinery and parts, vehicles, electronic integrated circuits, chemicals, crude oil and fuels, iron, and steel. Tourism is important to the economy.[36]

The people of Thailand are called Thai, and approximately 89 percent of the population is of that ethnic group; 11 percent are members of other ethnic groups. Thai is the official language; English is the second language and the language of business in Thailand. Buddhism is the major religion, with 94 percent of the population being Buddhist. Four percent of the people are Muslims, and 1 percent is made up of other religions, such as Christian, Hindu, and Brahmin.[37]

Business and Social Customs

The Thai greeting begins with the *wai:* two people place their palms together at chest level with the fingers upward; men bow slightly and women curtsy. The younger person initiates the greeting. More respect is shown by a higher placement of the hands and a deeper bow or curtsy. Monks do not participate in the *wai* greeting. First names are used; surnames are reserved for very formal occasions. In an English-speaking situation, "Mr.," "Mrs.," or "Miss" will precede the first or last name. Close friends do not use the *wai;* they address each other using nicknames. Foreigners should not initiate a *wai.*[38] Take an ample supply of business cards as they are exchanged often.

When you entertain business colleagues, take your guests to a prestigious hotel's best restaurant for a small group. For a larger group, arrange a buffet supper at a good restaurant. When you entertain a group, always invite the Thai wives as well. You will be provided a fork and spoon. Knives are unnecessary as all food is served in small pieces. The fork is used to push food onto the spoon; only the spoon goes into the mouth.

Tea or beer is served with meals; when drinking water, use only bottled water. Do not finish the last bit of food in a serving bowl. Tipping is not done by Thais. However, foreigners are expected to tip 5 percent to 10 percent in restaurants and one dollar per bag for porters. Taxi drivers are not tipped.[39]

Schedule a meeting in Thailand between November and March, as April and May are vacation months. Also, avoid the weeks before and after Christmas. A meeting should be arranged with an intermediary via a letter of introduction. Appointments are expected to begin on time. Since negotiations can be lengthy, allow sufficient time. Do not be in a hurry. In addition, avoid excessive assertiveness and losing control of your emotions, as these behaviors are perceived as unprofessional. Always allow people to save face. Remember that Thais have difficulty saying "no" or accepting a direct negative answer.[40]

When invited to a meal at a Thai home, bring flowers, cakes, or fruit. Avoid marigolds and carnations, as these varieties are considered funeral flowers. Other gift items that are appropriate include technology items, handicrafts from your country, nice pens and stationery, liquors, and coffee table books from your home city, state, or country.[41]

Since this is a tropical climate, men should wear lightweight suits or slacks, white shirts, and ties. Women would wear lightweight dresses or skirts and blouses. Sleeveless tops are inappropriate. Both genders wear jeans for casual wear; shorts may be worn but not in the temples. Shoes should be of good quality; rubber thong shoes should not be worn as they are considered low class.[42]

Public Behavior and Nonverbal Communication

Public displays of affection, except for holding hands, are not tolerated. Never touch Thais on the head, hug them, or kiss them in public. Although Thais are a no-touch culture, they tend to stand rather close to one another. When Thais are embarrassed, angry, or when they disapprove of something, they will often smile to disguise their feelings. A smile can mean many things, ranging from embarrassment, a greeting, an expression of thanks, or an apology. Thus, you will want to exercise caution in trying to interpret the meaning of a smile in this country.

Women should remember that it is inappropriate for them to touch a monk or to hand anything directly to a monk; monks are not allowed to have contact with women. Another behavior related to monks is that you are expected to give your seat on a bus or train to a monk if he is standing. People from other cultures should keep in mind that Buddhists hold all life sacred, so deliberately killing anything, even an insect, is offensive to them.[43]

Some gestures and other nonverbal behaviors are rude and should be avoided. For example, the soles of your feet or shoes should never face someone. You should tuck your feet under you when sitting on the floor. Other gestures to avoid include patting a person on the back or shoulders, putting your hands in your pockets while talking, or placing your arm over the back of a chair in which someone is sitting. When you wish to beckon someone, face the palm down and wave the fingers toward the body.[44]

UNITED ARAB EMIRATES

U.S. exports to the United Arab Emirates (UAE) include the following: agricultural products, metals, precious metals, chemicals, generators, electrical apparatus, oilfield equipment, excavating machinery, instruments, industrial machines, photo machinery, electronics, aircraft, vehicles and parts, toiletries, gem diamonds, and military items.[45]

Country Specifics

The United Arab Emirates, consisting of seven emirates, is located on the Saudi Arabia peninsula. The UAE is bordered to the north by the Arabian Gulf, to the east by the Gulf of Oman and the Sultanate of Oman, and to the west by Saudi Arabia and Qatar; the country is located on the Persian Gulf. [46] The size of the UAE is about 32,400 square miles or 83,900 square kilometers. Abu Dhabi is the capital, and Dubai is one of the major cities.

The economy of the UAE is based on oil and natural gas sales. The oil production is in the two emirates of Abu Dhabi and Dubai; therefore, these two emirates dominate the political and economic scene in the UAE. The country imports 9.4 percent of its needs from the United States; other major suppliers of goods are the United Kingdom, Germany, France, Japan, China, Singapore, and India. The Gross Domestic Product (GDP) per capita is $27,408. Oil and gas account for 30 percent of the GDP. However, the economy has a high per capita income and an annual trade surplus. The oil income has allowed the area to be transformed into a modern state with a high standard of living. In early 2004, the UAE signed the Trade and Investment Framework Agreement with the United States; later that year the country undertook negotiations toward a Free Trade Agreement with the United States. The UAE is very dependent upon a large expatriate workforce.[47] The currency is the UAE *dirham* (AED).[48]

The population estimate of the United Arab Emirates was 4.4 million in 2007;[49] only 15 percent to 20 percent are UAE citizens. The official language of the country is Arabic; however, English, Hindi, Urdu, and Persian are also widely spoken. With more immigrant workers than UAE citizens, English is becoming the *lingua franca* of the country, particularly in the private sector, board meetings, and semi-governmental organizations. Expatriates make up almost 85 percent of the population. Of this group, 45 percent are primarily Indian, with smaller percentages from Iran, other Arab nations, and Western countries. The local population is made up of people who were originally from Persian and Gulf countries or who are descendants of Arab tribal confederations.[50] The religion practiced by a majority of the UAE citizens, 80 percent, is *Sunni* Muslims, with a small *Shi'a* minority of 16 percent. While most foreigners are Muslims and Hindus, Christians make up a portion of the foreign population.[51]

Business and Social Customs

The greeting depends upon the relationship between two people. Men who are acquainted shake hands and touch noses. Men who are not acquainted simply shake hands. Women greet by kissing on the right and left cheeks multiple times. Women who are not well acquainted only shake hands. Only verbal greetings are used between men and women unless the woman extends her hand first to shake hands. The common greeting is *Assalaam alikum*, which means "may peace be upon you;" the correct response is *Wa alikum assalaam*, which means "and peace be upon you." First names are used between friends and relatives; otherwise, the professional title and name are used between those who do not know each other well. The greeting time can be lengthy as it is used to get to know you better; cutting this time short would be considered rude. Bring business cards to distribute to everyone. A nice touch is to have the cards translated into Arabic on the reverse side of the card that is printed in English. [52]

Business entertaining may be done during the lunch hour or in the evening, usually at restaurants or hotel restaurants. Other business entertainment includes a Bedouin feast in the desert or hospitality boxes at a horse race. If you are entertaining UAE nationals and they decline an offer of more food, be sure to make the offer more than once. You are expected to accept all invitations; the term *In shallah* ("God willing") is used when you cannot accept. Visitors should remember that during Ramadan there will be no business lunches, no coffee or tea breaks, and no smoking.[53]

Family dining customs include sitting in a circle on the floor and eating from a common platter using the fingers of the right hand. Everyone is careful to cover their legs and feet with their dresses or robes. You are expected to leave a little on your plate to indicate that you have had sufficient food. Coffee will be served after a meal; guests are expected to leave after the coffee is consumed.[54] Toasting is not as common as in many other countries; this may be because of rules regulating alcohol consumption. Some Emirates do not allow alcohol. In places where alcoholic drinks are served, such as at bars in Dubai, you will probably hear people say "cheers." Tipping is not necessary. However, most restaurants and hotels will add a 10- to 15-percent service charge to the bill. If a service charge was not added, just add 10 percent for a tip. While taxi drivers are not usually tipped, you may wish to tip hotel personnel if they were particularly helpful.[55]

Gift giving is not a common practice in the UAE. Upon your first visit to the country, however, bringing a gift is appreciated. Symbolic items of your home country are appropriate gifts. Corporate gift giving includes items with your company logo, such as pens and diaries. Be careful about admiring possessions of Emirates; they may feel obliged to give them to you. Opening gifts in the presence of the giver is not customary.[56]

When you schedule business meetings in the United Arab Emirates, keep in mind that many UAE residents take vacations to Europe or to the Americas during July, August, and September to escape the high temperatures. Therefore, it may be difficult to get appointments during this time period. Successful business interactions with your UAE business partners include supporting the international market in the UAE. Be flexible, loyal, and supportive by making a special effort to understand the psychology of this culture. Sending letters of appreciation following your visit is very important. Generally, if you are successful with one firm, you will have opportunities to expand business in the Emirates as family members and friends will speak positively about you and your company to others.[57]

Adult males in the United Arab Emirates will wear the traditional white robe (*dishdasha* or *kandurah*) with the white scarf (*kitra*) tied by a black headband (*agal*). When women appear in public, they wear a black robe to cover their dress (*ab'a*) and a scarf covering the head (*shailah*). It is not unusual for women to wear Western clothing under the ab'a. Very conservative Muslim women may also wear the *burqa* or *ghishwa* that covers the face. Men and women wear sandals, which are removed before entering a home. Consistent with the requirement of modesty in public, loud colors are not worn by men or women. Foreign women should wear loose-fitting, long-sleeved garments, scarves to cover their heads, and should generally dress modestly.[58]

During conversations, honesty is important; promises or agreements should be kept. Appropriate topics for conversation include geography, traditions, history, and archeological discoveries as well as business. Humor should be conservative and should not include jokes or stories with sexual undertones, especially in mixed-gender settings. Humor should be consistent with Islam and its social values. Therefore, an understanding of Islamic social values would be helpful.[59]

Public Behavior and Nonverbal Communication

Touching in public between the genders is inappropriate, even if the two people are married. Other inappropriate public behavior includes walking in front of people who are praying, whistling, or arguing or raising your voice. Privacy for people in the UAE is important. Criticism is always done in private. Elders are shown respect by having doors opened for them, by having younger people give up their seats on public transportation for them, and by seating them in the front seat of private vehicles. Women should not smile in public.[60]

Certain gestures are considered rude in the UAE and should be avoided. For example, using the left hand to give something to someone or to shake hands is rude. The right hand is used for shaking hands, eating, and gesturing. When passing an item, use both hands. Pointing with a single finger is impolite; use the entire hand. Turning your back to someone is also rude; it is respectful to face people. Do not point the bottom of the foot or sole at another person as the bottom of the foot is considered the most unclean part of the body.[61] Emiratis are expressive and have very direct eye contact; do not break eye contact with them during conversations. People of the UAE stand closer to one another than do Westerners when they talk and are very exuberant in their conversation. Men or women who are friends will hold hands; if your UAE business associate holds your hand while conversing, the gesture shows that you are considered a close friend. Visitors will need to remember that UAE nationals and Westerners look at time differently. People of the UAE are polychronic in their view of time; they will do several things while meeting with you, such as taking telephone calls or signing documents. In addition, they view appointment times as approximations of the actual meeting time. However, they expect Westerners to be on time.[62]

THE FUTURE

As the world works toward total industrialization at the lowest possible cost, yesterday's third-world nation will become tomorrow's industrialized nation. Therefore, in the future new nations will take the position of the cheapest place to produce goods in the world. Then, as the new nation's costs increase and its GDP increases, industry will move to the next third-world country that is ready. Today, this is also happening with the services industry. Eventually, all currencies will have an equal value; there will be no cheaper place to produce. Nations and workers will then play on a more level playing field. Until then, industries will chase the cost of production to wherever it takes them in the world. Today's workers compete with everyone else in the world to do a job for a cheaper price.

NOTES

1. U.S. Census Bureau, "Foreign Trade Statistics," http://www.census.gov/foreign.trade/statistics/highlights/top/top0612.html (accessed March 4, 2008).
2. U.S. Department of State, "Background Note: Ireland," as of October 2007, http://www.state.gov/r/pa/ei/bgn/3180.htm (accessed December 3, 2007).
3. *CultureGrams, Europe, Ireland* (Ann Arbor, MI: ProQuest CSA, 2008), 333.
4. List of countries by GDP (nominal) per capita, http://en.wikipedia.org/widi/List_of_countries_by_GDP_(nominal)_per_capita (accessed March 5, 2008). Figures (in U.S. dollars) are estimates for 2007 from *The World Factbook* provided by the Central Intelligence Agency (updated February 12, 2008). These figures do not take into account cost-of-living differences; using additional economic data is advisable when making country comparisons.
5. *CultureGrams, Europe, Ireland,* 336.
6. U.S. Census Bureau, "*IDB: Countries and Areas Ranked by Population,*" as of 2007, http://www.census.gov/cgi-bin/ipc/idbrank.pl (accessed January 16, 2008).
7. *CultureGrams, Europe, Ireland,* 334.
8. Ibid., 334; Ann Marie Sabath, *International Business Etiquette: What You Need to Know to Conduct Business Abroad with Charm and Savvy* (The Career Press, 1999), 154, 156.
9. Sabath, *International Business Etiquette: What You Need to Know to Conduct Business Abroad with Charm and Savvy,* 154, 158.
10. Morrison and Conaway, *Kiss, Bow, or Shake Hands,* 255.
11. Ibid., 252.
12. Ibid., 255.
13. Sabath, *International Business Etiquette: What You Need to Know to Conduct Business Abroad with Charm and Savvy,* 155.
14. *CultureGrams, Europe, Ireland,* 334.
15. Sabath, *International Business Etiquette: What You Need to Know to Conduct Business Abroad with Charm and Savvy,* 155.
16. U.S. Census Bureau, "Foreign Trade Statistics."
17. *CultureGrams, Africa, South Africa* (Ann Arbor, MI: ProQuest CSA, 2008), 661; U.S. Department of State, "Background Note: South Africa," as of October 2007, http://www.state.gov/r/pa/ei/bgn/2898.htm (accessed December 3, 2007).
18. *CultureGrams, Africa, South Africa,* 664; U.S. Department of State, "Background Note: South Africa."
19. *CultureGrams, Africa, South Africa,* 664.
20. U.S. Department of State, "Background Note: South Africa."
21. *CultureGrams, Africa, South Africa,* 662.

22. Powell, *Behave Yourself! The Essential Guide to International Etiquette*, 112–113.
23. Morrison and Conaway, *Kiss, Bow, or Shake Hands*, 454.
24. Ibid., 456.
25. Charles Mitchell, *Passport South Africa* (San Rafael, CA: World Trade Press, 1998), 50.
26. Ibid., 46.
27. Ibid., 78–79.
28. Ibid., 70, 73.
29. Ibid., 41–42.
30. Morrison and Conaway, *Kiss, Bow, or Shake Hands*, 456.
31. Mitchell, *Passport South Africa*, 81–82.
32. Ibid., 51, 53.
33. U.S. Census Bureau, "Foreign Trade Statistics."
34. U.S. Department of State, "Background Note: Thailand," as of October 2007, http://www.state.gov/r/pa/ei/bgn/2814.htm (accessed December 3, 2007).
35. List of countries by GDP (nominal) per capita, http://en.wikipedia.org/widi/List_of_countries_by_GDP_(nominal)_per_capita (accessed March 5, 2008). Figures (in U.S. dollars) are estimates for 2007 from *The World Factbook* provided by the Central Intelligence Agency (updated February 12, 2008). These figures do not take into account cost-of-living differences; using additional economic data is advisable when making country comparisons.
36. Ibid.
37. Ibid.
38. *CultureGrams, Asia, Thailand* (Ann Arbor, MI: ProQuest CSA, 2008), 714–715.
39. Morrison and Conaway, *Kiss, Bow, or Shake Hands*, 511.
40. Ibid., 510–511.
41. Ibid., 513.
42. Ibid.
43. Powell, *Behave Yourself! The Essential Guide to International Etiquette*, 130.
44. Ibid.; Morrison and Conaway, *Kiss, Bow, or Shake Hands*, 512.
45. U.S. Census Bureau, "Foreign Trade Statistics."
46. CIA, *The World Factbook*, "United Arab Emirates," https://www.cia.gov/library/publications/the-world-factbook/geos/my.html (accessed June 25, 2007); Harvey Tripp and Margaret Tripp, *Culture Shock! Success Secrets to Maximize Business in the United Arab Emirates* (Portland, OR: Graphic Arts Center Publishing Company, 2002), 15.
47. CIA, *The World Factbook*, "United Arab Emirates."
48. *CultureGrams, Middle East, United Arab Emirates* (Ann Arbor, MI: ProQuest CSA, 2008), 756.
49. U.S. Census Bureau, "IDB: Countries and Areas Ranked by Population," as of 2007, http://www.census.gov/cgi-bin/ipc/idbrank.pl (accessed January 16, 2008).
50. *CultureGrams, Middle East, United Arab Emirates*, 753.
51. Ibid., 755.
52. Mohammad Al-Sabt, *Arabian Business and Cultural Guide* (TraderCity.com, 2006), 26.
53. Tripp and Tripp, *Culture Shock! Success Secrets to Maximize Business in the United Arab Emirates*, 133.
54. *CultureGrams, Middle East, United Arab Emirates*, 754.

55. Elizabeth Devine and Nancy L. Braganti, *The Travelers' Guide to Middle Eastern and North African Customs and Manners* (New York: St. Martin's Press, 1991), 84.
56. Ibid., 153.
57. Al-Sabt, *Arabian Business and Cultural Guide*, 98–100.
58. Ibid., 40.
59. Ibid., 20, 24, 53.
60. Ibid., 25, 60; *CultureGrams, Middle East, United Arab Emirates*, 754; Trip and Tripp, *Culture Shock! Success Secrets to Maximize Business in the United Arab Emirates*, 136.
61. *CultureGrams, Middle East, United Arab Emirates*, 754.
62. Ibid.; Al-Sabt, *Arabian Business and Cultural Guide*, 31–33.

Resources

BOOKS

Axtell, Roger E. *Gestures: The Do's and Taboos of Body Language Around the World.* New York: John Wiley & Sons, Inc., 1998.

———. *Do's and Taboos of Humor Around the World.* New York: John Wiley & Sons, 1990.

Bosrock, Mary Murray. *Put Your Best Foot Forward: Asia.* St. Paul, MN: International Education Systems, 1997.

———. *Put Your Best Foot Forward: Canada/Mexico.* St. Paul, MN: International Education Systems, 1995.

Braganti, Nancy L., and Elizabeth Devine. *European Customs and Manners.* New York: Meadowbrook Press, 1992.

———. *Put Your Best Foot Forward: Europe.* St. Paul, MN: International Education Systems, 1995.

———. *Put Your Best Foot Forward: South America.* St. Paul, MN: International Education Systems, 1997.

Chaney, Lillian H., and Jeanette S. Martin. *The Essential Guide to Business Etiquette.* Westport, CT: Praeger, 2007.

CultureGrams. Ann Arbor, MI: ProQuest CSA, 2008.

Devine, Elizabeth, and Nancy L. Braganti. *The Traveler's Guide to Asian Customs and Manners.* New York: St. Martin's Griffin, 1998.

———. *The Traveler's Guide to Latin American Customs and Manners.* New York: St. Martin's Griffin, 2000.

———. *The Traveler's Guide to Middle Eastern and North African Customs and Manners.* New York: St. Martin's Press, 1991.

Harris, Philip R., Robert T. Moran, and Sarah V. Moran. *Managing Cultural Differences,* 6th ed. Burlington, MA: Elsevier Butterworth-Heinemann, 2004.

Jandt, Fred E. *An Introduction to Intercultural Communication,* 4th ed. Thousand Oaks, CA: Sage Publications, 2004.

Klopf, Donald W. *Intercultural Encounters: The Fundamentals of Intercultural Communication,* 5th ed. Englewood, CO: Morton Publishing Company, 2001.

Lewis, Richard D. *When Cultures Collide: Leading Across Cultures*, 3rd ed. Boston: Nicholas Brealey International, 2006.

Martin, Jeanette S., and Lillian H. Chaney. *Global Business Etiquette: A Guide to International Communication and Customs*. Westport, CT: Praeger, 2006.

Morrison, Terri, and Wayne A. Conaway. *Kiss, Bow, or Shake Hands*, 2nd ed. Avon, MA: Adams Media, 2006.

———. *Kiss, Bow, or Shake Hands*: Latin America. Avon, MA: Adams Media, 2007.

Powell, Michael. *Behave Yourself! The Essential Guide to International Etiquette*. Guilford, CT: The Globe Pequot Press, 2005.

Sabath, Ann Marie. *International Business Etiquette: Asia and the Pacific Rim*. New York: ASJA Press, 2002.

———. *International Business Etiquette: Europe*. Franklin Lakes, NJ: Career Press, 1999.

———. *International Business Etiquette: Latin America*. Franklin Lakes, NJ: Career Press, 2000.

Samovar, Larry A., and Richard E. Porter. *Communication Between Cultures*, 5th ed. Belmont, CA: Wadsworth/Thomson Learning, 2004.

ONLINE SOURCES (ACTIVE AT THE TIME THIS BOOK WAS WRITTEN)

Rankings of largest export partners of the United States and major U.S. exports:
www.census.gov/foreign-trade/statistics

Country-specific passport and visa requirements:
www.abriggs.com/high_level/foreign_entry_requirements.php

Country-specific travel information:
www.executiveplanet.com
www.worldtravelguide.net
www.eupedia.com
www.en.wikipedia.org/wiki
www.worldatlas.com

Business gift-giving customs in different countries:
www.netique.com/giftsearch/international.html

Worldwide daylight saving time:
www.webexhibits.org/daylightsaving/g.html

Toasts used in different countries:
www.awa.dk/glossary/slainte.htm

ELECTRONIC MEDIA

Beijing or Bust (2005). 978-1-4213-2846-1. This film presents firsthand accounts of businesses in China. http://ffh.films.com.

Case Studies from the Multinational Marketplace (2005). 978-1-4213-1981-0. How do major multinationals deal with intensified competition, a failed product launch, corporate fraud, and the scrutiny that comes with rapid growth? This five-part series analyzes some of the situations that multinational companies face as they conduct their business in the global marketplace. A BBCW Production. Five-part series, 29–39 minutes each. http://ffh.films.com/id/12048/.

China on the Rise: Paul Solman Reports (2007). 978-1-4213-5121-6. This MacNeil/Lehrer Production includes four episodes on China's growing economy, the Chinese consumers, the cult of Mao Zedong, and misinvestments in China. http://ffh.films.com/id/12772/

Doing Business in Asia (1990). The four videocassettes each contain a case study on Japan, Hong Kong, Taiwan, and South Korea. Originally prepared by Northwest Airlines, these videos are now available from Big World Media.

Doing Business in Latin America (1997). Videos cover Argentina, Brazil, Chile, and Mexico. They are available from Big World Media.

Doing Business in Southeast Asia (1998). Videos cover the countries of Malaysia, Singapore, and Indonesia. They are available from Big World Media. (Additional videos on other countries are available from Big World Media at www.bigworldmedia.com.)

Explaining Globalization (2006). 978-1-4213-8956-1. This MacNeil/Lehrer Production explains globalization through interviews and psuedo-debates about globalization.

Face and Place: Business Beyond the Bonds of Culture (2001). 978-1-4213-6904-4. This program profiles three executives who typify the changing style of business in Asia: James C. Louey, senior executive of the world's largest bus company, KMB in Hong Kong; Dr. Jannie Tay, CEO of The Hour Glass, a retail chain based in Singapore that sells watches throughout Asia; and Brijesh Wahi, managing director of Cellstream Technologies, a software services and engineering company based in Bangalore. http://www.srpublications.com/.

The First Red Multinational (2005). 978-1-4213-5845-1. This program presents a case study of TCL—China's first multinational corporation and the parent company of Thomson Color TV and other major manufacturers—giving viewers an unprecedented look inside Chinese business practices. http://ffh.films.com.

Global Corporate Citizenship (2005). 978-1-3213-6580-0. Can global corporations remain profitable and foster social consciousness, environment stewardship, and respect? http://ffh.films.com/id/13756/.

Management in Chinese Cultures (2001). This program describes key elements of modern Chinese entrepreneurship, such as teamwork, harmony, deference to authority, and *guanxi*. www.films.com.

Microeconomics in the Global Marketplace (2006). 978-1-4213-8958-5.

1-800-INDIA: Importing a White-Collar Economy (2006). 978-1-4213-5673-0. This program explains the lives and experiences of the Indian professionals who work white-collar jobs for U.S. corporations. http://www.fmgondemand.com/id/13046/.

Outsourcing: White Collar Exodus (2005). 978-1-4213-2678-8. This program examines the pros and cons of white-collar outsourcing, highlighting emotional and ideological divisions on the topic. It also studies real-life examples of outsourcing in action. An in-depth look at India's booming call center industry—which provides systematic training for Mumbai workers in American standards of speech and culture—illustrates the extent to which American business relies on overseas labor. http://ffh.films.com.

Redefining Success (2005). 978-1-4213-6578-7. This program explores alternative ways to define national success. http://ffh.films.com.

The Transformation of Work (2005). 978-1-4213-6641-8. This program inquires into twenty-first-century work paradigms, presenting commentary from scholars and business leaders about what it means to be an employee today—and what it will mean in the future. http://ffh.films.com.

Working with Japan (1992). This six-part series on doing business in Japan includes topics on preparation, negotiation, business entertaining, and women in business. It is available from Big World Media.

Yen for a Dollar: Doing Business in Asia (2001). This series makes an excellent introduction for foreigners to the subtleties and challenges of successfully conducting business in Asia by profiling leaders of some of the biggest companies in the region who are examples of the new trends sweeping the continent. It is a four-part series, 27 minutes each. http://www.srpublications.com.FFMBVL31123V.

Your Cultural Passport to International Business (1995). 978-1-4213-4674-8. People who have worked in different cultures offer insights into international business. http://ffh.films.com.

WEB SITES FOR INTERNATIONAL ASSOCIATIONS AND CONSULTANTS

SIETAR–Society for Intercultural Education, Training, and Research (www.sietarhouston.org).

The Interchange Institute (www.interchangeinstitute.org), a research organization to facilitate understanding between people moving to a country and their new environment; the monthly e-mail newsletter is specifically for people who are newcomers to the United States.

George Simons International (www.diversophy.com), an intercultural research, consulting, and training company.

IPR–International Professional Relations Inc. (www.iprconsulting.com), a U.S. consulting firm specializing in cross-cultural training.

Trompenaars Hampden-Turner (www.7d-culture.com), a consulting firm providing training for international clients.

Index

About the Authors

Jeanette S. Martin is Professor at the University of Mississippi School of Business. She has served as associate editor of the *Journal of Business Communication* and is the recipient of several national awards. The author of dozens of articles, book chapters, and conference presentations on intercultural business communication, emotional and cultural intelligence, and management information systems, she is co-author of *Global Business Etiquette* (Praeger, 2006) and *The Essential Guide to Business Etiquette* (Praeger, 2007).

Lillian H. Chaney is Professor of Management Emeritus at The University of Memphis. She is the author of over 100 articles and presentations, with a specialty in intercultural business communication, and she has received many teaching and research awards in the field. An active consultant, she has conducted training programs on communication and international and U.S. business etiquette for corporations, educational institutions, and government agencies. She is co-author of *Global Business Etiquette* (Praeger, 2006) and *The Essential Guide to Business Etiquette* (Praeger, 2007).